LIFE JOURNEY

Dear Dot
Blessings on your
Journey!
Pastor Gary.

First published as a Life Pathways paperback 2000

The text of this book is composed in FB Californian-Roman

Composition by TBA+D
Manufacturing by Crest Impressions
Book design by Jenn Roberts

Library of Canadian Cataloguing in Publication Data
Buzza, Barry J. (Barry James), 1947 -
1. Spiritual life. 2. Self-realization --Religious aspects.
I. Van Herwaarden, Vicky.
II. Title.
BL624.B89 2000
291.4'4 C00-911065-8

ISBN 0-9687652-0-3

Life Pathways
1477 Lougheed Hwy., Port Çoquitlam, BC, Canada V3B 7M6

1 2 3 4 5 6 7 8 9 10

LIFE JOURNEY

UNVEILING THE MYSTERY OF YOUR LIFE'S DESTINY

BARRY JAMES BUZZA

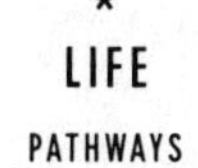

WITH DEEP GRATITUDE

Over the past four years that *Life Journey* has been in process, I have been awed by the love and participation of my family and friends. Above us all has been the Lord our shepherd, who has been faithfully guiding me over the hills and through the valleys of life for the past fifty years. Secondly thank you to my darling wife Susan, who has been so patient in letting me spend hundreds of hours of our personal time fulfilling my dream. Thirdly, thank you to Vicky Van Hewaarden for her partnership in this book. Vicky has been much more than an insightful editor, who has sacrificed her own schedule to bring my many words to life; she is also a highly valued friend.

Many others worked diligently to make my scrawlings look good. Thank you to Linda Kennedy, Tracey Krahn (this project might never have begun without my friend Tracey's encouragement,) my daughter Kristy Low, Julia Miller, Carol Rogers, Maria Santosa. Others graciously critiqued and sharpened my writing; my dad Allan, my brother Dave, Laura Briscoe, Wes Classen, Rochelle Grant, Bev Huston, Dr. Ron Mehl, Diane Neumann and Bette Thomson. My son-in-law Tom Brown created both the cover and book design; Jennifer Roberts skillfully prepared the artwork and Koos Dykstra provided the cover photo.

I owe a great debt of gratitude to Bruce and Marjorie Jackson, and Vern and Diane Neumann, who have supported me during this long project. (Diane along with Ingrid Janzen and Bev Miller have also been my inexhaustible cheerleaders!) Heidi Rossignol has gently guided me through the publishing maze. Reinhold Krahn and Warren Lauwers have given me wise counsel.

Thank you friends and family for your grace and encouragement. This is our work!

These thirteen letters are dedicated to my eldest daughter,
Kelly Alynn Brown,
as a small expression of my deep love and respect for her.

CONTENTS

INTRODUCTION

AS BOTH HIS PASTOR and his best friend, I stood over John's open casket and wondered out loud to the grieving congregation: What if it is true that when I die my soul lives on? What if it is true that the real me is the person inside, rather than the body which others see? What if it is true that my entire life journey was planned before I was born and that I really do have a purpose and a destiny? How would I live my daily life if I believed that the answers to these questions were, "Yes, it is true!" Would it make a difference?

Even though I loved him as a friend, I was always a little bit envious of John. He seemed to have everything that we guys secretly wished we had. He was six-foot-four, had dark, well groomed hair and deep brown eyes. His white teeth sparkled when he smiled. And he smiled a lot. Why wouldn't he? John was not only handsome, he was also generously gifted. I think much of his confidence flowed from the fact that people tended to be attracted to him right from his childhood. Wherever its source, John exuded charisma.

It didn't surprise me at all when he landed that prized job with the stock exchange, right out of university. He seemed to attract money like a magnet. And women—John had the pick of the crop. He appeared to have it all—success, applause, romance, athletic prowess, personality—at least until that fateful Thursday, only days before his thirty-ninth birthday. While taking a shower, he found a lump the size of a golf ball in his groin.

It all happened faster than any of us expected. The malignant tumour spread aggressively, ultimately hitting his liver. John only lived eighty days after the day of his diagnosis. I remember so vividly one afternoon, sitting beside him in his small hospital room. He was a sallow, yellowy, frightened shadow of his former self. He was scared that he would not see the next day. I'll never forget the words that John spoke to me just before he drifted off to sleep that day, "Barry, I'm so empty on the inside...I didn't know it would be over so quickly." His voice was just a whisper and his last lament still echoes in my memory. "I didn't plan for this day!" I held my friend's hands and prayed for him as he closed his eyes and fell into a restless sleep. Three days later, John was dead.

There I was, his friend as well as his pastor, officiating at his funeral. As I reflected on the questions that I had asked the congregation and the deeper meaning of life, I knew the answers. Yes, it is true that when we die, our souls live on. It is true that the person inside is who we really are; our bodies merely house the real us. It is true that our entire life journey was planned before our parents conceived us. We really do have a personal destiny and there is a larger purpose to our lives. Life is more than looking good, making money and having a beautiful family and home. The health of our souls has a great deal to do with the way we cross the finish line.

A poem with a purpose

THREE THOUSAND YEARS ago, a young shepherd named David, was inspired to write a poem about our life journey. We simply call it the Twenty-third Psalm. This psalm is likely the best known passage, in the most widely read book, ever written in history. It holds the keys to living with inner health and ultimate purpose. Psalm Twenty-three provides for every reader a map for our life journey. It clearly marks the hills, valleys, pathways, stopping points and destination of life. It also introduces us to the shepherd, who is always with us, to show us how to walk securely and purposefully throughout our journey. It reads:

The Lord is my shepherd, I shall not want.
He makes me lie down in green pastures;
He leads me beside quiet waters.
He restores my soul;
He guides me in the paths of righteousness
For His name's sake.
Even though I walk through the valley of the shadow of death,
I fear no evil; for You are with me;
Your rod and Your staff, they comfort me.
You prepare a table before me in the presence of my enemies;
You have anointed my head with oil;
My cup overflows.

Surely goodness and lovingkindness will follow me
All the days of my life,
And I will dwell in the house of the Lord forever.

My highest priority

IN MY LIFE, just as in yours, there are many responsibilities that I carry. As the senior pastor of a large church, I feel the daily weight of teaching, counselling and practicing what I preach. I feel a deep sense of commitment to my church family, as well as to my larger circle of influence in the community in which I live. I am convinced, however, that of all my responsibilities and obligations, my highest priority is to pass on a legacy to my children and grandchildren. Not a legacy of material things, but one of values, virtues and purpose.

The answers to my questions at John's funeral motivated me to write my thoughts on the subject. *Life Journey*, written to my first born daughter Kelly, is the first of three series of letters that I am writing. The second series of letters, called *Life Purpose*, is written to my youngest daughter, Kristy. The third series, *Life Pillars*, is written to my grandchildren.

Life Journey is part of the legacy that I am leaving to my family. It will explain, from my perspective, how to live life in a healthy, happy and successful way. As you read it, you are invited to peek in on my relationship with my daughter, Kelly. Learn along with us how the Lord, our shepherd, has planned a unique and wonderful life journey for each of us. In Psalm Twenty-three, David gives us invaluable guidelines to show us how to live our lives with meaning and ultimate purpose.

I'd like you to meet my daughter

MANY YEARS AGO, as I was emerging from my teenage years, my life took a different turn than that of my friend John. After high school, I began a five year stint at Bible College, attending mostly night classes, while working at a lumber yard during the day. At the age of twenty-two, I married Susan, my seventeen year old sweetheart. Shortly before Susan turned twenty, our first daughter, Kelly Alynn, was born. I had just graduated with my ministerial diploma three months before her arrival. Now there were three of us; young, energetic, zealous visionaries, ready to save the world!

When children enter your life, everything seems to change. Susan quit her job at the grocery store to be with our beautiful daughter full time. I continued to drive a truck at the lumber yard, while serving as a volunteer youth pastor during the evenings and weekends. Life was tough because we seemed to always be strapped for cash, Kelly was often sick and I was working long hours. Within a few months, Susan was expecting again. Our youngest daughter, Kristy Leigh, came along months before Kelly was even sleeping through the night.

Susan was very weary by the time our second daughter was born, so we made an agreement that I would continue to get up with Kelly, and Susan would handle Kristy's night feedings. Little did we know that over the next six months, Kelly would continue to be sickly and need constant support, while Kristy would peacefully sleep through the nights. Susan was delighted with the choice she had made.

During those preschool years, Kelly and I grew close. She became my little buddy. Whenever we went out as a family for a day or on summer vacations, my daughter would never leave my side. I loved being the father and protector of my timid, fragile, blonde haired girl. As she grew through her childhood and teenage years, Kelly, like all of us, had many experiences and life lessons which shaped her. Parents have this wonderful privilege of witnessing their children being transformed from caterpillars into beautiful butterflies. Today, twenty-nine years later, Kelly is a very confident, capable and beautiful woman. She is a loving wife and mother, who is highly educated and serves successfully in the medical field. I count it as a great honor to be her family's pastor, but it's as her dad that I've written these thirteen letters to my daughter.

My friend John's death bed confession, "I didn't plan for this day", shook me to the core of my being. I made a silent vow at that point that I would not only live my life with a plan and a purpose, but that I would also teach my children to do the same. As you read these letters, I hope you will find answers to your own questions about life.

PART I

He's Got The Whole World In His Hands

CHAPTER ONE

The Game Of Life

He's got the whole world in his hands.

EACH OF OUR LIVES has been preplanned with a purpose, direction, defining rules, many choices and a final destination. To help us find our way in life, each of us has been given a map, road signs and a guide.

Dear Kelly,

This series of letters which I have written to you, called *Life Journey*, is among the most important works that I have ever done. I am in the process of writing another series to your sister, called *Life Purpose*. The letters which I am writing to Kristy are about the reasons why we exist and how to find our own personal destiny. I've also written another series of letters to my grandchildren, called *Life Pillars*. When my grandchildren are old enough to understand, my hope is that they will read the letters which underscore lessons that I've learned from my own experiences, and build their lives on what I believe are twelve foundational principles for a healthy life.

You will understand my heart more fully Kelly as you read these letters, but I would like you to know a couple of things before you read them. Above all else, I want to tell you how much I love you and Kristy.

You girls are by far the most important blessings of your mom's and my lives. Neither of us have desired anything as much as seeing you mature into the beautiful and successful women that you have become. We are very proud of you both!

These letters in *Life Journey* have been written at the right time. Not only have I moved into my sixth decade and am ready to pass on some of my learned life experiences, but you are just now reaching your thirtieth year, where I believe adulthood really begins. Even though you have been married for a decade and have two children, there is a wide unexplored horizon which lies before you. I pray not only that you will thoroughly enjoy the discoveries of the life ahead of you, but also that your mom and I will have the privilege of cheering you on for many years to come.

I've felt for a few years now that, although my primary privilege is to father you girls, my secondary responsibility is to pass on what I've learned to a wider circle. Thank you for allowing me to open the pages of our family album to the world. I believe we will all be better for having shared our lives with others.

The game of life

I'M SURE YOU remember the family evenings that your mom and I used to spend with you and Kristy as you were growing up at home. Some of the happiest memories of my life are of the four of us playing games, snacking on chips and pop, and talking in the living room. One of the games which we loved to play was called *The Game of Life*. I've still got it somewhere in our garage, but you'll remember it as a twenty-four inch board game with hills and valleys, and a winding road running from one corner to another, throughout the plastic terrain. That was supposed to be the road of life. It wound from birth to college, marriage, family, and career. The roadway included a wide array of experiences, both good and bad. Each player had a different colored plastic car, with little pink or blue pins representing our spouse and children. At the end of the game, one of us would win by finishing first, with the most money in our bank account.

Playing the game together gave us a good opportunity to talk about life choices; such as what paths you and Kristy would choose to take in university, what careers each of you would pursue, and what you thought about marriage and having children. Not that we were anxious for you to move on, but it was important for all of us to be planning our futures.

I hope we told you, as we played *The Game of Life* together, that it was not based on a healthy view of life. Neither how quickly we maneuver the road of life, nor how much money we earn along the way, is an accurate marker of our success. There was however, a good lesson on perspective that the game taught us, which has helped me over the last twenty years. It is this: Life is more than a random series of lucky breaks. Life has a purpose, direction, defining rules, parameters, many choices and a final destination.

As we played *The Game of Life* several times, I got to know the journey better. Although you've picked up most of the same lessons as I have during your journey, I'll share with you a few more things that I have learned along the way. One of them is that life really does have a beginning and an end, with countless choices in between. Each choice that we make has a corresponding consequence. In the game, if I were to choose to take the slower and more costly path and become a doctor, later on I would reap the rewards of a higher salary and a more comfortable lifestyle. Or if I were to choose one of the more risky roads along the way, which promised quick financial rewards; in the long run it usually wouldn't pay off and I might even be left penniless at the end of the game.

Honey, this relates to our own lives. Our daily choices carry huge cumulative consequences. The degree of our success, as we reach life's final destiny, is determined by a harmony between the creator of the game, who made the rules, and also by each player's moment by moment decisions. Just as in the game, you have discovered that the wise educational choices which you and Tom made early in your lives, have affected your income levels today. We learn as we go, how to maneuver tight corners; how chance corresponds to each risk we take; and how failure, or at least mediocracy, usually follows not taking any risks at all.

Playing that game twenty years ago became a pivotal point in shaping my perspective of life. Looking at the game board on our table, it was easy to see that each of our lives has a starting and finishing point, as well as a defined pathway, purpose and destiny. It was in playing *The Game of Life* with you and Kristy, that I began to understand the concept of a life journey.

Lessons in Disneyland

OUR FAMILY MADE at least a dozen trips to California over the twenty years that you lived at home. From the time when Kristy was six months old, we would pack up our Toyota and head down south for warmer weather and a trip to Disneyland. I can still remember many of our experiences as if they happened yesterday. In order to save a few bucks, we would sleep overnight in rest areas along the way. Kristy was on the floor in her little bassinet and you slept on the back seat, while your mom and I tried to catch a couple of winks up front. One time during one of those long dark nights, we were terribly frightened by the rap of a beggar on our window. You cried so hard afterwards that we gave up on sleep and drove through the rest of the night. In the end though, it was worth the journey when we finally arrived and got to spend a day at Disneyland together.

A map, road signs and a guide

WE WOULD OFTEN TRY to start our day and get to Disneyland early so we could beat the crowds, but we were never successful. It seemed like a million other families had the same idea as we had. When we purchased our tickets on that first visit, at the park's entrance, the cashier gave us an instruction booklet and a map to help us find our way around. I remember how excited we all were about our day at Disneyland. Once inside the gate we were anxious to get on with the adventure, but first we had to study the map. It was my job as dad to decide on our route and to guide our family from sight to sight. We sat down on the grass, in front of Mickey Mouse's flower drawn face and learned the layout of the land. Your mom and I decided that we'd make better time if we went against the traffic flow and so we began with Tomorrowland. We ultimately realized over the years that there really is no hurry–the joy of Disneyland is in the journey itself. Without the map though, we'd never have made it through the day.

The next thing that we needed to do before we ventured out was to take note of the signs. If we hadn't seen a turn along the way, we could have missed out on an entire village within the huge amusement park. We watched very carefully for each road sign and when we saw one that matched the map, we followed it because we knew it would lead us to the next adventure.

One of the many reasons that our family kept returning to Disneyland was because of the gracious and well trained staff. They were cheerful, friendly and helpful to the frazzled parents, who had children that had eaten too much junk food, were exhausted or were lost. Visitors could even hire a tour guide or join a group, if they wanted to have someone explain the history of each land or show them where to go and what to do next.

Disneyland provided three things for all their guests; a map, road signs and a guide. They were given to help each traveller through the huge maze of attractions. Kelly, in our own life journey, we too have been issued a map, road signs and a guide.

Over the years that you have been in Sunday School, you have learned about King David and the little poem which he wrote called Psalm Twenty-three. You even memorized it at an early age. Although this short poem was written over three thousand years ago, its message is still current. Psalm Twenty-three will be the map that I'll use to describe the life journey we are on. In one of the letters which I have written to you, I've explained what the road signs are along the way and where you'll find them. You'll discover that your friends, your Bible, the quiet inner voice inside you, life circumstances, and even nature itself are all signs. They will become easier to read and understand as you proceed throughout your journey.

Most importantly, you have a guide to show you the way. Someone once said that life can only be understood backwards, but must be lived forwards, and that is the reason that we need a guide. We need someone who has already been down the road a few times to show us where to step and where to avoid stepping. In my next letter Kelly, I'll introduce you to the good shepherd, who will be our guide throughout our entire life journey.

A quick look at the road ahead

A PROFESSOR ONCE told me when I was learning how to preach, that every sermon should have three parts to it. He said, "Tell them what you're going to tell them; tell them what you want to tell them; and tell them what you have just told them!" I've taken his advice to heart and so to begin, I've written what I'm going to tell you.

In your Bible, Psalm Twenty-three is divided into six verses, but David didn't write it that way originally. Verse numbers in the Bible were inserted hundreds of years after it was written to help us find certain sections for public readings, but this psalm falls more naturally into four parts.

The first part introduces our shepherd to us. He is the only adequate guide who exists for our life journey. Here David presents his main thesis:

The Lord is our shepherd.

Part two describes the hills, which are the up times in our life. I love these refreshing and exhilarating seasons. From on top of the hills we can clearly see the pathway before us and we are ready to run ahead with enthusiasm. The hills of life are the green pastures, the quiet waters, restored souls and the path of righteousness.

The third part of the psalm brings our journey down into the dark valley, where life becomes more difficult and at times, painful. But even there, in the shadows, we can find healing and growth. This section winds to the climax of our life journey and introduces us to our destiny. The trek becomes slower, but the life lessons learned in the valley are worth the struggle. The valley experiences include the shadow of death, encounters with evil, the rod of discipline and the staff of comfort, a feast while surrounded by our enemies, an anointing for our destiny and an overflowing cup.

And finally, part four encourages the traveller again. The poet reminds us that there is a purpose and a plan to our life. The designer of our unique journey has our best interests at heart. The psalm has a delightfully happy ending, promising that goodness and lovingkindness will follow us all the days of our life, and that we will live in the house of the Lord forever.

Kelly, we have been on many journeys together, from walks through the neighbourhood to vacations far away; but nothing that we have ever done as father and daughter or as a family, compares to the adventure that your shepherd has ahead for you on your life journey. My prayer for you and for your family is that you will stay on the right path; pay close attention to your map; watch out for road signs; and listen attentively to the loving wisdom of your shepherd, as he shows you where to go and how to live each new day to the fullest. I love you, Honey!

Love Dad

CHAPTER TWO

Someone Bigger Than Me

The Lord is my shepherd. I shall not want.

THIS LETTER INTRODUCES the reader to the Lord, our shepherd. It explains how our shepherd not only knows what is best for his sheep, but lovingly and firmly leads those who choose to follow him on a predetermined pathway to their ultimate destiny.

Dear Kelly,

What I'm writing to you in this letter is one of the most important things that I have ever told you, because it holds the secret to success for the rest of your life journey. It begins with the first line of Psalm Twenty-three; *The Lord is my shepherd. I shall not want*. You, as well as your family, were born for a purpose. There is destiny in your genes; and the only way that you can fulfill that destiny is by making the Lord your shepherd.

Recently I was in Saskatoon on a business trip. During the afternoon, there was a break in my schedule, so I thought I would take a walk down a scenic trail along the Saskatchewan River. I had never been in Saskatoon before, but a couple of people had told me that the walk would be worth taking. My first stop was at the front desk of the hotel. I asked the desk clerk how I would get to the walkway that runs beside the river. He told me exactly how to get to the path, "Just go out the front doors, turn right and walk a couple of blocks toward the north. When you see the sign, Saskatchewan River, follow the arrow another block until you get there. That will get you on the right path. You can walk about three miles down the path until you arrive at the citadel look-out. Enjoy your walk!"

I followed his directions precisely, found the walkway just where he had told me it would be and I walked all the way to the citadel. The walk was every bit as beautiful as people had described it. If I had received wrong directions from the hotel clerk, had not followed his directions correctly or had gone my own way, I would not have reached my intended destination. The clerk gave me good directions and because I followed them exactly, my afternoon was a great success.

That little walk helped me to again realize the simple importance of following our shepherd. When we follow our shepherd's lead, we will journey down the right pathway, which has been specifically designed for us. Keeping to this pathway is the only way that we can fulfill our destiny and arrive successfully at our chosen destination. The reason we follow him, instead of choosing our own way, is because he knows the best way and he has our best interests at heart. Kelly, understanding that the Lord is your shepherd is the key which will open the door of success for the rest of your life journey. Follow his lead and you will succeed; veer too far from the path and you will miss out on what he has for you. That's what this letter is about.

A story of a bug who lived in a rug

IN THE ENTRY hall of Tom's and your home, you have a beautifully woven Persian rug. Of course we don't like the thought of it, but we're told that even the cleanest of our rugs has tiny dust mites in it. These microscopic creatures live their entire lives in that small, six foot long, world. Let's imagine for a moment that the mites could speak to each other. You might hear something like this:

After an exhausting day of hiking up and down the rug fibres which loom high above him, one little bug comments to his friend, "You know, this world we live in doesn't make sense. It seems like it's just a purposeless maze of hills and valleys with no design whatsoever!"

The other bug stops chewing long enough to respond to his friend, "I know what you mean buddy. Our world does seem meaningless and ex-hausting at times."

The bugs' imaginary conversation reminds me of a quote which I heard from Bertrand Russell, the unofficial high priest of our sixties' generation, just before you were born. He said, "The life of man is a long march through the night, surrounded by invisible foes, tortured by weariness and pain, toward a goal that few can hope to reach and where none can tarry long. One by one, as they march, our comrades vanish from our sight, seized by the silent orders of omnipotent death. Brief and powerless is man's life. On him and all his race the slow, sure doom falls, pitiless and dark. Blind to good and evil, reckless of destruction, omnipotent matter rolls on its relentless way. For man condemned today to lose his dearest, tomorrow himself to pass through the gates of darkness, it remains only to cherish, ere yet the blow falls, the lofty thoughts that ennoble his little day."

The two little senseless mites lacked the same thing that Bertrand Russell did when he made that statement. They did not have the perspective of someone up above. Their view of life was narrowly restricted from where they stood. If those tiny bugs, Kelly, could stand where you stand every day and look over the entire Persian carpet, they would realize the value of their world. Your rug is a masterpiece of color, texture and design, all of which are clearly evident from a human perspective. The dust mites simply cannot see it from where they are confined in their little world between the giant fibres. Mr. Russell would have also been surprised and delighted with life if he could have seen it from the shepherd's perspective.

I understand his view though, because sometimes life for me, and likely for you too, doesn't seem to make much sense from where we sit. I have many "Why?" and "How come?" questions to ask my shepherd one day. Why did my mom, as pure and sweet as she was, die of cancer when she was only forty-one? Why did that earthquake devastate Turkey last month? Why was that pitbull allowed to rip apart my friend's child's flesh? You could add your own questions to my long list, but for now, knowing that someone bigger than I knows the answers and has a higher and broader perspective than I do, helps me to trust in him with my life circumstances.

Looking at life from the front

KELLY, DO YOU remember your mom learning to do needlepoint when you and Kristy were young? Auntie Carol taught her how to do those stitch by number pictures and she did pretty well. I framed some of her creations and hung them on our bedroom wall for a few years. If you were to have looked at her two embroidered pictures which hung on our wall back then, you would have seen well crafted, beautiful, brightly colored baskets of flowers. However, if you had taken the frames apart and turned the pictures over, you would have seen them from an entirely different perspective. They simply looked like a disorderly maze of short and long colored threads going in every direction. From the back view, you could never have guessed what picture was on the front.

It was interesting to me that one side of the embroidery made perfect sense, while the opposite side seemed entirely senseless, because that's the way it is with our lives at times. It all depends on which side of the picture that we are looking at.

Over the years, there have been many seasons when my life appeared to me like the backside of your mom's needlepoint—a senseless array of unassociated events, conversations and experiences. But just as her needlework was orderly, sensible and beautiful on the front side, so there has been another side to the story of my life, and yours too, Kelly. Our shepherd does have a design and plan for each of our lives and it makes perfect sense from his higher and broader perspective. Let me further illustrate what I mean with a story from my journal.

Remember when our church family began the long and challenging process of purchasing land to build our new sanctuary? It was one of the most difficult three years of my life. We finally found the perfect piece of property on a major intersection of our city. The price for the lot back then in 1985, was six hundred and fifty thousand dollars, down considerably from the one point two million dollars that it had been listed for a couple of years earlier. Even though you were in your early teens, you'll remember that our denominational authorities, whom I work under, would not approve the purchase. After all, they reasoned, our church was a relatively young congregation with perhaps a little more zeal than wisdom and we did not have the financial resources to pull the whole building program together.

I don't know if I hid it well from you and Kristy, but your mom knew how disappointed I was with their decision. I had felt strongly that this was the right place and that it was the right time to build. I had prayed fervently and felt like we had a green light from the shepherd. Everything was coming together except for the approval of those eight men. "Who did they think they were anyway!?" I questioned to myself.

Our hopes and plans seemed to be unravelling before our eyes. Nothing was making sense from our limited perspective. As always, the Lord, our shepherd had a better plan all along. We could only see the back of the picture, but he could see it from the front. The whole story did not begin to unfold until about a year later. By that time, the property had sold to another purchaser and we thought that it was all over. Our window of opportunity to buy the property seemed to have been slammed shut in our faces.

Then just as we were coming to grips with the sad reality that we would fail in our venture, news came that the new deal had fallen through and that maybe the vendor would be open to an even lower offer. After some prayer and discussion, we went back and offered him four hundred and fifty thousand for the five and a half acres. That was down two hundred thousand dollars from our previous proposal. After thinking about the offer for awhile, the exhausted owner looked up from the contract into our eyes and said, "I've had this piece of property on the market for a couple of years now. The price has dropped from one point two million and I need to sell it. I'll tell you what I'll do, if you wrap this deal up quickly, I'll let it go for four hundred thousand dollars!"

We looked at him with stunned faces to see if he was serious—and he was! He was telling us that he would accept a quarter of a million dollars less than we had offered him last year and fifty thousand dollars less than what we were offering him at that moment. We signed the deal and within a year we were worshipping in our beautiful new church building.

Throughout that year Kelly, while I was thinking that everything was unravelling before us and nothing made sense, our shepherd had it all under control. He knew exactly where the whole process would lead us to a year earlier and why our authorities had refused to allow us to close the first deal. He knew the lessons that I had to learn along the way of trust, submission and patience. He had already seen the front of the completed picture. He knew where our life journeys were headed, and when we were supposed to take our next steps.

You see Honey, there is someone who is bigger than you and I. He has a thoroughly mapped out pathway for each of our journeys. Our personal stories and their ultimate meanings may never be understood in this lifetime, but one day in eternity, we will see that all along there was an intricate, well designed plan. After all, the Lord is our shepherd and he knows exactly what he's doing!

The shepherd and his sheep

TO GIVE MORE clarity to this first statement which King David wrote in Psalm Twenty-three Kelly, let us go back in time about three thousand years. We'll take a closer look at the author of this poem, where he lived and the setting in which he wrote it. This psalm was likely written by David long before he became the king of Israel. Can you picture him? This young shepherd on a warm starry evening in distant Israel, sitting at rest under a tamarisk tree, strumming his small homemade harp. While his sheep are lazily lying all around him, inspiration comes and David begins to sing a new song.

The Lord is my shepherd. I shall not want...

We don't use the word Lord very much anymore. I'll define it for you so that you can fully grasp what the young shepherd had in mind. First of all, David understood the word Lord to mean owner. In those days, if a shepherd was called Lord, it clearly meant that he was more than just a hired hand or even the child of the owner. He was the man who had paid good money for every one of his sheep. He had the full rights that go with ownership. They were his sheep - an investment worth serious care. Because the shepherd's best interests were at stake, he devoted himself to his flocks. In the metaphor that David used in his psalm of the shepherd and his sheep, his meaning is clear that the Lord is our shepherd. Like any good shepherd, the Lord owns us, has devoted himself to our care and always has our best interests at heart.

We then are his sheep, and unlike horses, cows or dogs, we are totally dependant on our shepherd. Sheep do not simply take care of themselves. Both sheep and owner belong to each other and need each other. Without their shepherd's watchful and loving care, sheep would inevitably die. They are not smart enough to find their own food and water; they cannot care for themselves when injured; and they have no natural protection from predators. Sheep need to have good shepherds.

It is not by coincidence that God compares human beings to sheep. Besides our needing constant care like sheep do, we also are stubborn. Our sheep-like stubbornness becomes evident even as young children. It's humorous to watch your son Alexander, Kelly, who is almost two years old. He already wants to do his own thing. The other evening when your mom and I were babysitting, Alex wanted desperately to play with our computer. I said, "No, Alex. Don't touch the computer." Although he knew exactly what I was saying, he continued to press the keys. I then went to him, carried him a few feet away and diverted his attention with his favorite toy. However, he still wanted to do what he wanted, so back to the computer he walked, turned to look me straight in the eyes and then began to play with the buttons again. He's less than two years old and already his inherited stubbornness and desire for independence are showing.

We all seem to be like Alexander in one way or another. Thankfully you were very compliant growing up Kelly, but I remember well when I was sixteen. I thought I knew better than my mom and dad how late I should stay out at night, how fast I should drive my dad's car, what kind of friends I should hang out with and generally what life was all about. Of course, when I became a parent myself and began to see life from a higher and wider perspective, I soon came to realize how dependant I had been on my own parents' loving and protective care. Even by the time I got to be thirty or forty years of age and had gained wisdom in some areas of life, I still found myself tempted to think that I was old enough and smart enough to run my own world and plan my own future. The fact is though, that not one of us was ever intended to live independently from our creator.

All of us are dependant on the goodness, wisdom and ability of our owner. I love knowing that the Lord is my shepherd; and even though your mom and I are your parents and love you very much, I feel very secure knowing that ultimately the Lord is your shepherd too. Throughout your life Kelly, especially when I haven't had the right answers for you or have felt inadequate as a dad, I've always been aware that our good shepherd has been standing with both of us pointing the right way for us to walk.

I'm not sure that sheep are smart enough to know this (sometimes I wonder if I really understand it myself), but the truth is that the one who has a good master has a priceless treasure. I'll write in my next letter to you Kelly how a wise shepherd leads his sheep to healthy pastures and watering holes, protects them from enemies and plans their futures in advance, long before the sheep even realize where they are going.

* * *

Who is the Lord, our shepherd?

IF WE ARE going to follow someone Kelly, we had better know who he is. Is he trustworthy? Does he know where he is going? Does he have our best interests at heart? Who is the Lord our shepherd? Why should we follow him? The two little words, *the Lord* are made up of only seven letters between them, but deserve a book just on themselves. If we understand their meaning now, it will help us to understand the rest of this psalm.

In order for us to do this, let's go way back into history, about thirty-five hundred years ago and observe a day in the life of a man named Moses. You'll remember him from your Sunday School lessons. He led his people, the Israelites, out of the captivity of Pharaoh in Egypt, into their promised destiny. (Actually, the Disney film *Prince of Egypt* beautifully illustrates the story.) Shortly before the dramatic crossing of the Red Sea, God revealed himself to Moses in a very profound way.

There he was, alone in the desert tending his father's-in-law sheep, when he saw a burning bush. The strange thing about it was that the bush was not being consumed by the fire. After staring at it in awe, Moses heard an audible voice coming from the bush. I can imagine his surprise and fear when he heard the voice. There was nobody else around and so he knew that this was God himself speaking to him. The conversation that this shepherd had with the great shepherd at that moment became a pivotal point in Moses' life. It was not only a pivotal point in Moses' life, but it was a pivotal point in world history. His entire life up to that point had been for the purpose of preparing him for a special assignment. His eighty year education as a prince of Egypt and as a shepherd of sheep was complete. It was graduation day for Moses and his life destiny was being unveiled before his widely opened eyes.

Moses began to realize his destiny that day. He had been chosen by the Lord to be the man who would free the Israeli people from captivity. This is one of the reasons why he had spent the last forty years being a shepherd. He had been learning some of the same life lessons that were later pictured in Psalm Twenty-three. But if he were going to be the chosen deliverer to free the Jews from slavery, he had better know who it was who was choosing him. The problem was that up to this point in his life, Moses did not really have much of a relationship with his shepherd. He had been brought up as a young boy with the stories of Adam and Eve, the great flood and Abraham, Isaac and Jacob; but he had never actually met or heard from the God of his history lessons. Up until this point in history, God had only been known to the Jewish people by a general term used for any god - Elohim. Even pagan gods were called by the same name, but now Moses would be the first person to know God's personal name. The great shepherd was going to reveal himself to Moses in a more intimate way than he had to anyone before him.

His name is I Am

FROM THE BURNING bush, the voice of God told the frightened shepherd Moses that his personal name is I AM. We tend to use God's name very flippantly these days. As a common expression we say, "Oh, my God!" without really considering what we are saying; but to Moses and the Jewish people, the name of God was too awesome to even whisper. This was the name of the creator and sustainer of the universe. This was the name of the God, who had not only made mankind, but has a plan for each of us every day of our lives. The Israelites revered him so highly that they figured it was more respectful to not even use his real name. That's why the writers of our Bible simply called him Lord, just as David did in Psalm Twenty-three. The original text was written; Jehovah (which means the I AM) is my shepherd, but out of reverence for the personal name of God, the translators of most of our Bibles, simply used the title, Lord. You've probably noticed in your Bible Kelly, that sometimes the word Lord is all capitalized. It's in those places that the word Lord is respectfully written in place of God's real name, Jehovah.

You'll see the word Lord two times in Psalm Twenty-three. At the beginning where David writes; The Lord is my shepherd and then again in the last line where he writes; I will dwell in the house of the Lord forever. This short psalm purposefully begins and ends with the Lord, Jehovah. To me, the fact this psalm begins with the Lord, is a picture of our utter reliance on his influence in our lives. Like the psalm, both you and I, Kelly, have the Lord holding us at our beginning point in our mothers' wombs and at the finish line, when others place our bodies in their graves.

The meaning of his name

THAT HISTORIC conversation between God and Moses at the burning bush unveils to the world a vital truth about our Lord, the good shepherd. God was revealing to Moses and to us in his name, I AM, that he sees all of history in the present tense. Kelly, this is such an important concept and so central to our understanding of this psalm that I want to explain it as thoroughly as I can.

The statement that I made about God seeing all of history in the present tense simply means that our Lord looks at all the past, present and future as happening right now. I'll use a couple of pictures which have helped me understand this abstract concept better.

Human Perspective Chronology

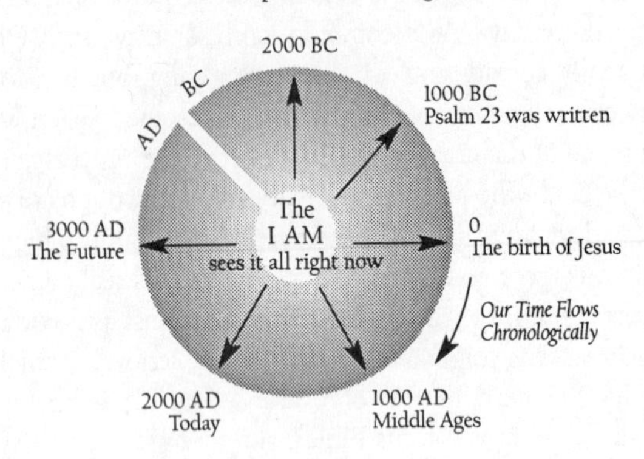

When you've already seen the game

KELLY, IMAGINE THAT Tom has invited me over to your house to watch a hockey game on television with him. The game on television is being played in eastern Canada, so it is delayed for broadcasting in our western province of British Columbia. In my car, while I am on my way to your home, I happen to listen to excerpts from the game on my radio. Tom, of course, is not aware when I arrive at your home, that I already know the final score, as well as who scored each goal. I, in effect, have already seen the game that we are about to watch together. I know what's going to happen and how it will all finish.

So to make our time together more interesting, I say to your husband, "Tom, why don't we put a few bucks on the outcome of the game. It will make it more exciting to watch!" Since Tom knows hockey better than I do and he knows the strengths and weaknesses of each of the two teams, he responds with a twinkle, "Sure, let's put ten bucks on the table." I secretly know not only which team will win, but also by how many points!

This illustration gives a better understanding of the Lord who sees our past, present and future as present tense. I don't predetermine the outcome, but I do know how the hockey game is going to be played and therefore I can adjust my behavior accordingly. If I were unscrupulous, I could make an easy ten bucks because I've already seen the entire game before it's even played on the television.

Think of the Lord, our shepherd, as the one who has already seen the game - your life. He has seen my life and your life from beginning to end. He sees the past and the future as present tense. He sees that wonderful day of October 13, 1971, when you were born; as well as you standing with Tom getting married, as happening at this very moment. Who better would there be than the Lord to guide me through each day? He has already seen the consequences of every choice that I make and can therefore show me the best path to take at every corner of my life.

Early Edition

KELLY, YOU'VE SEEN the Saturday evening program on television called *Early Edition*. The show is about a young man who has been given the rare privilege and weighty responsibility of knowing what's going to happen the next day. Each morning when Gary gets up and opens his apartment door, he finds tomorrow's paper on his doorstep. Reading the newspaper, he knows what accidents are going to happen, who is going to win every hockey game and what stocks are going to rise or fall. His daily assignment is to stop tragedy before it happens wherever he can. Although *Early Edition* is only an fictitious television show, it helps to illustrate the idea of a shepherd who has already seen our future and can therefore most adequately guide us through our present circumstances.

Both of the illustrations that I've used are inadequate to fully describe the meaning of the name of the Lord, but hopefully they will help you to understand why he is trustworthy as our life journey guide. Because of his perspective of seeing everything in the present tense, our shepherd already sees your entire life in process. He sees yesterday, today, tomorrow, next week and next year as happening right now! Do you see why I said to you earlier Kelly, that understanding this concept of the Lord is our shepherd, holds the key which will open the door of success for the rest of your life journey? We have a guide to lead us through life who has already seen the future. He's been this way before and so he knows exactly where the right path for every life journey should lead. We can trust him with our tomorrows.

The Lord is my shepherd

I REMEMBER A simple lesson that I learned in a marriage seminar on communication. The teacher taught us how important our tone of voice is when we are talking with our spouses. He said that our tone of voice carries more weight than the actual words we speak. To illustrate his point the teacher used the phrase, "I didn't say you were stupid," as an example. The exercise was for us to repeat the same sentence six times, each time emphasizing a different word. The first time we would say to our spouse, "*I* didn't say you were stupid."

The second time, we would say, "I *didn't* say you were stupid," and so on. We all laughed when we went through the exercise and heard the different emphases. It was quite revealing to see that each time we emphasized another word of the sentence the meaning changed dramatically! I tried the same exercise with the first line of this psalm the Lord is my shepherd. Take a minute Kelly, to do this and you'll be surprised how every time you read the sentence, with a different emphasis on each word, there is another valuable concept revealed.

The Lord is my shepherd. By emphasizing the article *the*, it underlines the uniqueness of the Lord. There is only one shepherd who is qualified to guide me through the hills and valleys of my life.

The *Lord* is my shepherd. When I emphasize the key word *Lord*, my attention is drawn to who he is. The Lord is the I AM - the ever present tense God, who sees my past, present and future. He knows me best.

The Lord *is* my shepherd. This small verb *is* reminds me that he is there for me now! Not, he may be there, or he should be there, or he could be there, but he is my shepherd now and always.

The Lord is *my* shepherd. This two letter pronoun *my* makes the concept of the Lord as shepherd very personal. He's my shepherd. Sometimes even though I have your mom, Kristy, you and friends around me, I feel lonely. To know that God really knows me and cares what happens to me personally is a great comfort. Even in the sheepfold, each sheep is given a unique mark to identify it as belonging to a certain shepherd. One ear of each sheep is cut in a distinct way to clearly show which sheep belongs to which shepherd. This is what it's like for you Kelly. You are intimately known by your shepherd; he loves you and has a wonderful plan for your life.

The Lord is my *shepherd*. Emphasizing the word *shepherd* underlines the metaphor of shepherd and sheep which graphically pictures our dependency, as well as his loving care and guidance.

It is significant to know that although sheep are very needy and dependant animals, many of them have a strong desire to be independent. Sheep have wills of their own and some set their wills to wander away from the watchful eye of their shepherd. Although this is foolish and dangerous and the shepherd does what he can to protect his sheep, many choose to reject their shepherd's care. I see this desire for independence, not only in little children like Alexander who don't know any better; but also in my own life. Although I find myself from time to time struggling to do it my way, I usually come to discover that his way is right and the best way for me. You and I both need a shepherd who knows the way we should walk throughout our entire life journeys..

Do we trust the shepherd?

LOOKING AGAIN AT this statement, the Lord is my shepherd, I'm pressed to re-examine my own life. Do I respect the wisdom of my shepherd enough to follow where he leads me? Today as I sit at my desk writing this letter to you, Honey, I am at one of those points on my life journey when I tend to feel a little abandoned. A team from our church had planned for several months to take a three week trip to Nigeria to do some work, at our own expense, for the Christian church there. Although the Nigerians were expecting our arrival three days ago and we have put thousands of dollars into the work there, we have been detained. Applications for our visas were made in plenty of time, but they remain on some Nigerian bureaucrat's desk, where they've sat for weeks, still unapproved. My human tendency is to be both frustrated and disappointed by the unnecessary delays, but through experience I have learned that God really does know what is going on in my life. He really does care about me as well as the Nigerian churches; and he has a better plan than I do.

I'm learning that the word disappointment actually is only one letter away from a healthier point of view. Change the "d" to "h", and the word disappointment becomes his appointment. Some puzzles, such as why our trip to Nigeria fell through, may never be solved on this side of heaven, but whether I can answer every question about life or not, I'm choosing to follow someone who knows the whole story. At times the wisest thing for me to do is to just trust him. As we adopt our shepherd's perspective, we begin to realize the truth of this statement; The Lord is my shepherd.

Understanding the idea that I have a shepherd who is there for me, as I wind my way through the hills and valleys of life, is a source of great comfort to me. No matter how isolated or alone we feel at times, he really does care what happens to us. He not only cares what is happening to us today, but he also has a plan for our entire life. Because he knows the end result of every circumstance, he is in a much better position to guide my day-to-day decisions. Thinking about my scheduled trip to Nigeria, I think that perhaps the Nigerians can do a more effective job with our money than we Canadians could have; perhaps the lessons that I am learning about patience and trust are more important than my going; or perhaps I'll never know the answer as to why our visas were denied. It doesn't really matter. After all, the Lord is my shepherd and he knows. That's what really matters. We are part of a bigger picture and the Lord is the artist and designer of every part of our life.

The Persian rug in your front hall Kelly and your mom's beautifully embroidered pictures are works of art, which have a grand overall design to them. The design in the rug was not apparent to the mites which crawled inside and the flowers on the front of your mom's tapestries were hidden from anyone who looked at the maze from the back side, but there was a plan in the mind of their creators.

Our lives too, may seem to just muddle along as a series of chance happenings with no purpose or design, but that's simply our view from a limited human perspective. The Lord, our shepherd, has in his mind a wonderful plan for each of us. We were planned by him long before we were even born and we are here on earth as people of destiny.

We are people of destiny

MY FUNK AND WAGNALL dictionary defines destiny as: The fate to which a person or thing is destined; the pre-ordained or pre-determined ordering of events; and the power that is thought to pre-determine the course of events.

Although I agree with the definition, I see destiny as something more. I see it as a tension between our shepherd's unique predetermined design for our life and our own free will choices. Consider the psalmist David's understanding of the Lord. He knew from what Moses taught that Jehovah sees all life as happening in the present tense. If we can accept it, the Lord saw us before we were even born; he sees us right now; and he sees where we will be one hundred years from now. He knows us before, during and after our human existence on earth.

The creator made each of us for a purpose, just as a shepherd buys each sheep for a reason. He already knows whether we will compliantly fulfill our purpose or if we will wander away from his plan. We, like sheep, have minds of our own. We have a choice to obey the shepherd and follow where he is leading us towards our destiny, or we can wander away from his directions and open ourselves up to danger or to becoming lost. He already knows both the good and the bad choices which we will make tomorrow, as well as the consequences of those choices. Based on those moment by moment choices, that he has already seen us make throughout the next several years of our life journey, the shepherd has designed a unique pathway, which we may or may not choose to take. Closely following his specially designed pathway will ultimately lead us to our destined purpose.

While my dictionary defines destiny as an unalterable fate, I see our destinies as within the sphere of our daily choices. How we will finish our life journey is actually determined by a tension between our shepherd's design and our own free will choices.

Let's say as an example, Kelly, that the shepherd has destined Alexander to be the Prime Minister of Canada in the year 2040. If that were the case, he would arrange hundreds of life experiences and tests over the next forty years to prepare Alex for the task ahead. The Lord would have endowed him at birth with certain gifts and abilities, place certain people in his pathway to help set his direction and plant a desire in the depth of Alexander's soul to become a national leader. All along his journey, Alex would still retain the freedom to move toward his assigned destiny or reject it. The shepherd's will and our own choices must ultimately connect.

One of the dictionary definitions of destiny; the power that predetermines the course of events, might be better defined as; the power that pre-determines who we are and what our personal purpose is. After our shepherd determines who we are and what our personal purpose is, even before we are born, he then creates a pathway for us to follow which will ultimately lead us to that purpose.

The healthy tension

IN THE PHILOSOPHICAL battle between fatalism, which eliminates personal choice; and self-determination, which negates the guiding shepherd concept, there is middle ground. There is a healthy and necessary tension which must stretch between the two extremes.

When you and Kristy were young, your mom and I took you on an outing to the Lynn Canyon Suspension Bridge in North Vancouver. It spans a ravine that extends downward at least two hundred feet. You were pretty timid as a little girl Kelly, and I remember how hesitant you were to cross over the wobbly foot bridge. Of course I always loved it when I could be the big brave Daddy, so I held tightly on to both of you girls as we walked carefully across the bridge.

To assure you of the safety of the suspension bridge, I showed you the large concrete pillars on each side. They support the four inch cables which run over the ravine and hold the bridge securely in its place. The secret of the bridge's strength are the four huge deeply rooted pillars and the strong, yet flexible suspended cables connected to them. If even one of the four pillars were to give way, the bridge would collapse.

I see our destinies illustrated by that bridge. The pillars on the east side are the secure belief that we have a loving shepherd, who has a unique plan for each of our lives. The pillars on the west side illustrate our free wills which give us freedom to make our own choices. Again, we must have the pillars on each side securely in place to ensure safe passage across the bridge. And this only happens when our moment to moment choices connect with our all knowing shepherd's uniquely designed purpose for our life.

We should also realize that the choices which we make all have corresponding consequences. For example, over thirty years ago your mom and I made a pivotal choice to get married. We were very young and because of that we had a couple of good friends advise us against marriage, at least for a couple of more years. We had to make a choice between getting married at that time or waiting a while longer. Either one of us could have changed our minds about getting married, which would have decided the issue for both of us, but we each chose to go ahead with our wedding vows. There have been over thirty years of wonderful consequences which have followed our decision, the best of which are you and Kristy and both of your families!

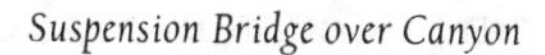

Suspension Bridge over Canyon

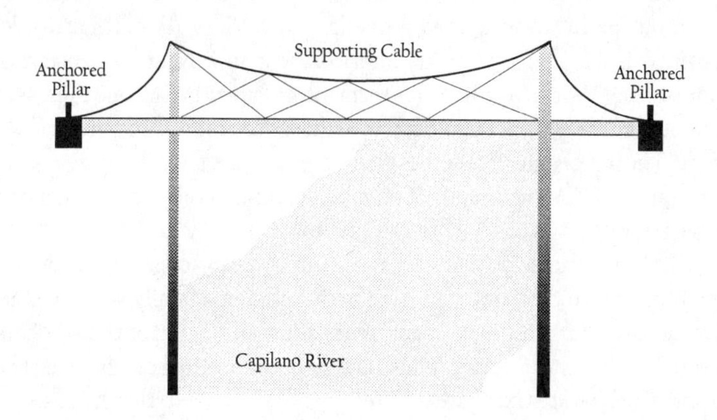

If we had chosen to marry other partners instead of each other, our shepherd would have rearranged our life pathways to match up with our choices of partners and the children we would have had together. It's hard to even imagine having gone a different way and I am certainly thankful that we made the choices that we did. The point is Kelly, that even though our shepherd has a destiny which he wants to see fulfilled in our lives, we still enjoy a free will to make our own life decisions. The facts that he has a destiny for us and that we each have a free will are both equally true and should work in tension with each other.

For the preceding diagram, the suspension bridge's cables strung between the four pillars illustrate my view of destiny. The foot bridge pictures my life pathway, which is supported mutually by the plans of the good shepherd and by the choices of my own free will. If either his plans or my ability to choose were not there, I would lose the security and freedom that I have with the Lord as my shepherd. I am secure because I have the shepherd who knows my past, present and future; who wants me to be successful and empowers me to fulfill the destiny he's prepared for me. And I am free because, rather than serving the Lord as his puppet, I can choose to go my own way or submit to his plans for my life.

The one thing nobody can take from me

ONE OF THE determining factors which will help us move successfully down our pathways is a good attitude. I love Victor Frankl's attitude, recorded in his memoirs of his imprisonment in a Nazi concentration camp during World War II. To his tormentors, he said, "The one thing you cannot take away from me is the way I choose to respond to what you do to me. The last of one's freedom is to choose one's attitude in any given circumstance." Life's success is not so much determined by what is handed to us, but by how we choose to respond to it.

The kind of attitude that we choose can have a profound effect on our life. I know two brothers who were both raised in a family with an abusive alcoholic father. I have spent hours counselling one of the brothers through his recent marriage failure and his own ongoing alcoholism. The problems of his attitude have affected every relationship that he has ever had over the last forty years. In one of our sessions together, I asked John why he kept on drinking when it was obvious how much havoc alcohol addiction had played in his life. He excused his behavior by telling me that, "It is because I had an alcoholic father." On another occasion, I was talking to John's brother who is a tea totaller and has been a successful husband and father for seventeen years. When I asked him why he abstained from alcohol, his surprising answer was the same as his brother's, "It is because I had an alcoholic father."

The fact is that both men were raised in the exact same environment and each man made his own life choices. One chose to drink and the other chose to abstain. The life journey that each of the two men is living out is directly related to their attitudes toward their father. One chose the high road and the other chose the low road. Life is not fatalistic. We are not doomed to either failure or success. Our daily choices determine whether each of us fails in our life assignment or fulfills our intended destiny.

I shall not want

THE LAST HALF of David's first sentence, *The Lord is my shepherd, I shall not want*, is a commentary on the consequence of following our shepherd -I shall not want. Remember the Thanksgiving meal that our family enjoyed together a while ago, Kelly? We all worked in the kitchen together preparing our own part of the feast. As I was carving the turkey, there were at least four of us snitching pieces of meat. We were very hungry and everything from the stuffing to the pumpkin pie smelled so good! After we gave thanks we devoured the meal; only thirty or forty minutes had passed since the turkey snitching and we were stuffed! When your mom asked, "Does anyone want some more turkey?" We all groaned. We had had enough! We did not want anymore! We were satisfied.

Satisfaction. It means to be filled up. It means that we don't need or want anything else. That's what the psalmist David was saying in this succinct sentence; I shall not want. I don't need or want anything else. All I want is to be under the loving guidance and care of my shepherd. He is confidently asserting that anyone who remains under the Lord's authority, care and love will be fully content within himself.

From David's perspective, he knew that sheep who were managed, guided and cared for by a loving shepherd were content with their lot in life. He knew that because he was a shepherd, and good shepherds were constantly looking out for the well being of their sheep. Even at night when their sheep were at rest, shepherds slept with one eye open. They were always ready to run to the aid of a sheep in need.

It's a mystery to me Kelly, why sheep would want to leave the capable and loving care of their shepherd, but I know that it does happen. I learned about recalcitrant sheep from my grandfather when I was ten years of age. Grandpa, in his retirement years, used to have several ewes and a ram on his small hobby farm. I vividly remember one of his sheep who was never content on the five acres of grass that grandpa had set aside for them. There was always plenty of food and water and a big red barn to protect them in the winter, but this one young ewe seemed to yearn for distant fields on the outside of grandpa's fence. She searched incessantly for spaces under the barbed wire where she could scratch her way to what she thought was freedom. Grandpa, teaching me one of the important lessons about life, told me that on at least three different occasions she had made her escape to the forest on the outside. Each time he had to hunt the sheep down and bring her back in order to save her life.

Finally, after one whole summer of her rebellion, grandpa was afraid she would upset the other sheep or lead them astray and so he had to take drastic measures. I still remember the bitter sweet taste of those lamb chops we had at grandma's dinner table. They were a sharp reminder that wandering away from the shepherd's care could prove to be disastrous.

Another memory which I have from when I was about the same age was of my sister, your Auntie Heather, and I having to stay with our uncle and aunt for two weeks while mom and dad went on a vacation by themselves. I loved my dear auntie and my cousins, but I was a little afraid of my uncle. My mom and dad never drank alcohol and so I had not been exposed to drunken behaviour. One day, my uncle had been drinking too much and he became overly aggressive with my sweet aunt. As he yelled at her and raised his hand to hit her, I remember being so scared that my little sister and I planned an escape.

We really had no idea where we were going, but we just knew that we had to get out of there. After breakfast the next day we made our break. Fortunately, my aunt found us about a half mile down the road and brought us safely home by lunch time. What my sister, Heather and I hadn't given much thought to was what we were going to do to survive outside of the loving care of my aunt. Although life wasn't perfect at their house, at least we were safe and well loved. I never ran away from their home or my own home after that day. However, there have been a few occasions when I have tried to run away from my shepherd. Thank God that he has always patiently led me back home again. Over the last half century of my life, I have experienced and have spoken with others who have also experienced the painful consequences of wandering away from our shepherd's care; and also the fulfillment which comes from living within the boundaries of his love. Kelly, the latter is much better. Staying inside the fence under the good shepherd's watchful eye is very satisfying. Like David said, when the Lord is my shepherd, I shall not want.

The life journey process

AFTER THE POET David states his thesis: The Lord is my shepherd. I shall not want, he reveals for us the lifelong process that each of us must go through. We all must learn the truth that the Lord really is our shepherd, he loves us, he knows what is best for us and he has a plan for our lives. In addition to the destiny which he has already set for us, he has prepared a right pathway which leads to the fulfillment of that destiny.

This process Kelly, is what I've called our life journey. It takes us up onto high mountains and down into deep valleys. In the next several letters, you and I, along with our shepherd, will continue our exhilarating journey up the winding mountain path to the flat tablelands. There we will be nourished by the lush green grasses and we will be refreshed in the cool mountain streams. We will be restored in our minds, imaginations and emotions as we lie down in the fragrant clover. Our shepherd will unfold his plans as he leads us along the path which he has distinctly chosen for each of us. From the mountain tops where the view is breathtaking, we will see for miles into the distant future. From up there everything is wonderful!

Then as the season turns, so will our journey. As surely as winter follows summer and night follows day, so will the valleys follow the mountains and the shadows follow the light. Hang on for the whole ride Kelly. The end is yet to come and it's well worth the difficult days. We'll discover together how every person who intersects with our lives and how every circumstance that we encounter, whether delightful or devastating, serves a distinct purpose in moving us closer to our unique destiny. Eternal goodness and lovingkindness are the promises to every one of us who hangs in there, under the shepherd's care, for the entire life journey! It's going to be fun!

Love Dad

PART II

The Hills Of Life

CHAPTER THREE

Green Pastures

He makes me lie down in green pastures.

GREEN PASTURES ARE a picture of the nourishment needed daily to feed our souls. Our shepherd leads us to these pastures and helps us remove the hindrances which keep us from lying down. Healthy nutrients are vital to the building of courageous wills, strong emotions and clear thinking minds.

Dear Kelly,

A couple of evenings ago, your mom and I watched the video called, *Meet Joe Black*. I was deeply touched by the movie; I even cried. Since then I've talked with a few friends who have seen the same movie, but they didn't react the same way at all. Let me explain to you why I was crying.

Without giving away the plot or the surprises, there were at least three story lines to the movie. One was a love story with Brad Pitt - your mom liked that one. Another was about power and control. Anthony Hopkins played a wealthy business owner named Bill. This second story was about his empire and the battle for control that he was engaged in. It was the third story though, the one which gave the movie its name, that gripped me emotionally. Death, named Joe Black, came to Bill and told him that he only had a few days to live. Immediately after his sixty-fifth birthday celebration, it would be the time for death to take him away to his eternal reward.

In those few days, during which Bill was not allowed by Death to tell anyone that he was dying, he began to analyze his entire life. As he thought about his accomplishments, and all the lives that he had influenced, he realized that his greatest possessions were not the millions of dollars in real estate that he owned, or the enviable power he wielded with hundreds of admirers. Rather, his most valued treasures were his two daughters. (Now, I was seeing the movie through the love that I have for you and Kristy, my two treasures.) Without being allowed to tell his adult daughters that he was dying, Bill had to somehow convey how much he loved them. He also wanted to express to them how deeply he felt that because of them, he had had everything he could ever have wanted from life.

I can hardly describe to you Kelly, the renewed sense of passion that I felt to pass on to you and Kristy (and your families) a legacy of lasting value. Your mom and I may not leave you a large amount of money when we die, but I aspire more than ever to pass on to you something worth more than anything money can buy. My highest goal is to leave behind lasting values for you and Kristy, to help you in your life journey.

That thought brings me to the subject of this letter - the health of your eternal soul. In contrast to your body, which will one day pass away, your soul will last forever. In this letter, I'm going to tell you how you can use the green pastures your shepherd leads you to, to nourish your soul and keep it healthy.

Before we take a look at the green pastures Kelly, it's important to know what your soul is. A soul is difficult to define. Webster refers to the soul as our immaterial essence; the actuating cause of an individual life. I'm not sure what that means, but when I refer to your soul, I am talking about who you are; the real you. Focusing primarily on our bodies gives us a distorted short term view of human worth. Although we Americans spend billions of dollars to look good on the outside; our skin colour, age, size, shape and the colour of our hair are all superficial packaging for the real us. Your soul is a combination of your will, mind, emotions, personality, temperament, imagination and attitudes. These intangible components of your soul are all temporarily packaged in your body, and altogether they determine who you are.

My 1952 black Hillman

A COUPLE OF YEARS before you were born Kelly, just after your mom and I were married, we were working at opposite ends of the city. Neither area was very accessible by transit so we needed a second car. Times were tough for us back then and my budget for a second car was only one hundred and fifty dollars. I was delighted, as well as surprised, when I came across a black 1952 Hillman for just that amount.

When I got it home, I invested in a couple of black spray bombs and repainted my purchase. I always figured if a car looked good, it would run better. Then I painted two white racing stripes from the front bumper to the rear bumper. Now, according to my theory, it not only looked good, but would no doubt go faster too! For a couple of months, my co-worker Calvin and I drove the Hillman every day without a problem, but then winter came and it got increasingly more difficult to start at six o'clock each morning. In order to get it going, I would have to get inside the car, put it into first gear and Cal would have to push me a few hundred feet. Finally, we would get her humming. By December, he was pushing me six blocks using my other car, just to get it to turn over every morning. The old engine had seen better days.

Spirit, soul and body

THAT 1952 HILLMAN serves to illustrate the parts of every person; their spirit, soul and body. To begin with, I owned the car. The papers and insurance were in my name and therefore it belonged to me. That right of ownership can be compared to my human spirit, which I'll be writing about in my next letter to you. My human spirit is owned either by me or by my shepherd. It's my way or his way. I can be the one in control of my destiny or I can give control to him. The choice is inevitably up to me, but my shepherd wants to own the title deed to my spirit. Then he, like I did with my Hillman, will have complete rights of ownership.

Secondly, my old Hillman looked good. It had the appearance of a fast race car, at least in my biased youthful thinking. In reality though, that ten dollar paint job and those fancy racing stripes were all show. It ran like a tank! The external appearance of my car compares to my physical body. I can look good and appear to have it all together, but at the same time be desperately trying to keep my soul from falling apart on the inside.

Many health fanatics spend hours a day pampering, primping and pumping their bodies, which will only last for seventy or eighty years, while often neglecting their souls, which will live eternally. When we are young, Kelly, we tend to think that our physical health will last forever, but the truth is that it won't. As I am discovering all too well in the second half of my life, eyesight fades, muscles weaken, joints stiffen and pains plague us. Of course it is wise to invest in the maintenance of our bodies with good nourishment, sleep and exercise, but ultimately, the better long term investment must be in the nurturing of our souls.

Thirdly, because of neglect, my car had many mechanical deficiencies. Even though it wasn't visible by its outside appearance, that old Hillman was dysfunctional in many ways. It is the same with our souls, which are the inner workings and intangible parts of our person. Our souls, like the engine of my car, while not externally visible, are far more important than our bodies.

In this new millennium Kelly, our bodies may be looking better than ever, but our souls are increasingly debilitated. The green pastures that David refers to in this psalm are places of necessary nutrition and rest which our souls must have in order to fulfill our destiny. We may look good on the outside, but without enjoying the benefits of green pastures throughout life where our souls are designed to be nourished, refreshed and repaired, we will end up as dysfunctional as my old car. Thank God that he makes me lie down in green pastures, because my tendency is to work hard at keeping the outside looking good, while neglecting the inside.

He makes me lie down

LIKE EVERY WORD in the first statement of Psalm Twenty-three has weighty meaning, so does every word in this second statement; He makes me lie down. Think about each of the following five words with a different emphasis.

He makes me lie down. The shepherd is ultimately in charge of my life.

He *makes me* lie down. The shepherd doesn't suggest that I lie down. He doesn't say, "lie down when you feel like it." He makes me lie down.

He makes me *lie down*. Lying down is a helpless, submissive position. We're not in control when we are lying down, but that's not such a bad place to be. It's actually a healthy, happy resting place. I wonder why we tend to resist our shepherd's encouragement to lie down? Do we feel like we are no longer in control of our life when we are prostrate in green pastures?

A few years ago Kelly, when you were a teenager and I was in my early forties, I came to a memorable green pasture in my life journey. Sometimes mid-life is a time when men tend to get off track. During that time, I had come to a plateau in my personal journey and from my perspective I wasn't quite sure where the road was taking me. Like many of my peers, I was feverishly running toward success in both our family and my vocation, but I wasn't sure where success was. Was it working long hours, having a big church, keeping your mom and you girls happy, making lots of money, dressing well, driving a new car? What was I pursuing so vigorously? My speed was fast and my intentions were good, but my wheels were spinning because I wasn't sure which of my many priorities to focus on.

Thinking back, I felt like the airplane pilot who was flying from Los Angeles to New York in the middle of the night. Two hours into the flight the pilot's voice calmly spoke over the intercom, "Ladies and gentlemen, this is your captain speaking. We're flying at an altitude of 36,000 feet at a speed of five hundred and fifty miles per hour. I have some good news and some bad news. The bad news is that we're lost. I have absolutely no idea where we are. But the good news is that we are making excellent time!"

That's where I was in my mid-life when my shepherd took action. Although I can't take credit for it, I have always enjoyed very good health. It certainly isn't because of my disciplined diet and exercise program. But one fine day, while in the midst of my hurried journey, I was struck by a piercing pain in my back and couldn't stand upright any longer. The only place where I could find relief for a few days was flat on my back on the floor. Lying down in my green pasture (our living room carpet) I found more than healing for my back - I was refreshed in the depth of my soul.

Before that green pasture experience, I had thought that I was indispensable. By my being forced to lie still for a long period of time, I learned some important lessons, the first being that I am not the center of the universe. I discovered the hard way that life goes on whether I am rushing in a frenzy, working twelve hours a day or whether I am just sleeping quietly on the sofa. During that several day period I slept often, watched television, read magazines and spent hours just thinking quietly. I even missed church on Sunday and discovered sadly that they could get along just fine without me! Lying quietly in green pastures, taking time out to reflect and rest our minds and emotions is a necessary part of our life journey. Without those seasons of rest to keep our souls healthy, we may never reach our destiny. Often times, if we don't voluntarily lie down in the green pastures of our life, our good shepherd will apply more pressure to ensure that we do.

Seasons of rest for our souls

ONE OF MY heroes is Dr. David Cho from Seoul, Korea. He pastors a church of almost one million people while still making time for a regular game of golf every week. Dr. Cho was speaking to a group that your mom and I were a part of a few years ago, and he shared some insights on rest that he had learned the hard way along his journey. When he was a young pastor in his late twenties, his church had already grown to about ten thousand members. He was working many hours in a week and felt the pressures of the world on his shoulders. He thought that he alone carried the weight of his church. Without his preaching, visiting, praying for and baptizing every person, he felt that almighty God would be severely handicapped. One day, while physically baptizing by immersion two hundred new members, Dr. Cho collapsed from exhaustion. His elders had tried to stop him earlier, but he was thinking to himself, "No one can baptize, but the pastor - the man of God, the Reverend Cho. Don't the elders realize how important I am?" After that embarrassing day, when he collapsed in front of his entire church, it happened again within a couple of weeks. Once more, this time while preaching in the fifth Sunday service, Dr. Cho fainted from exhaustion.

He told us that his physical and emotional exhaustion lasted for ten years. During that decade, he only had enough strength to preach each Sunday and then go back to bed for the rest of the week. The time that he spent flat on his back was the shepherd's way of making Dr. David Cho lie down in green pastures. He said that it was one of the most important periods of personal growth in his life. While lying down still, he learned valuable character lessons of humility and trust that prepared him to pastor the largest church in the world today. In those ten years, his church grew from ten thousand to fifty thousand members. We may never reach the heights or outward appearance of success that our heroes have Kelly, but the life principles that most of them have learned the hard way are the same for all of us. Without regular seasons of rest for our souls, we may never reach the destinies we were created to enjoy.

The psalmist David, while reflecting on his sheep's resting habits, found application from the pasture for all of us. Sheep are very fearful creatures, and they are therefore very unlikely to lie down in green pastures unless certain conditions are met. To feel secure enough to lie down and rest, they must be free from fear, free from friction, free from flies and free from the need to find food. Each of these requirements has significant application to our own personal rest.

Freedom from fear

FIRST, SHEEP MUST be free from fear. Besides being very timid animals, sheep are also one of the few creatures with little means of self defense. A stray dog or even a jack rabbit cannot only scare a single sheep, but can start a stampede of an entire flock. The shepherd must be constantly on the alert with his rifle and rod, to protect his sheep from either real or imagined predators. Usually the very presence of the shepherd in the field is enough to ensure their confident rest. With us, whether we are aware of our shepherd's presence or not, we are assured by God that he is constantly watching over us.

A friend of mine told me a story about his daughter that happened when she was only four. While she was sleeping, Sabrina had a nightmare. Her cry of terror immediately brought her mom and dad to her bedside. He told me of the tension in his daughter's little body as she sobbed in his arms, telling them what she had seen in her dream. They held her close for several minutes, assuring her that they loved her and that she was safe. When she finally fell asleep again, my friend's wife bent over to place the little girl in her bed and securely wrap her in her blankets. Sabrina whimpered softly again, so her mom placed her Holly Hobby doll very close and prayed that she would sleep peacefully. Thinking all was well, they quietly pulled away to go back to bed again. Little Sabrina cried softly, "Mommy, I need you to hold me some more." Her mom replied, "Honey, you're okay now. Everything is safe. Nothing will hurt you because God's angels are watching over you." The little girl smiled sweetly as she replied, "But Mommy, I need someone with skin on."

Sabrina was right. There is nothing like having someone nearby who loves you and makes you feel secure. Our shepherd, like any good shepherd in David's time, is constantly watching over his sheep. That doesn't mean that there will never be danger around Kelly, or that life's circumstances will not frighten you; but it does mean that no matter what you are going through, God is aware of it. He is there with you to take you through your difficult circumstances and to protect you from ultimate harm. Our shepherd is worthy of our trust. When we come to understand these truths that God loves us and that he watches over us, it helps us to enjoy freedom from fear and to lie down securely.

Freedom from friction

SECONDLY, SHEEP DO not lie down in green pastures unless they are free from friction. Animals have what is called in the world of chickens, a pecking order. With sheep, it's called a butting order. The most assertive ewe will battle any oncomers to gain her position as lord of the lot. Every sheep, from the boss down, knows her place in the order. The mean old ewe on the top of the butting order keeps her place by intimidation and aggression. She will decide where she wants to walk, graze or lie down ahead of the other sheep. The rest of the sheep do the same to those sheep under them. When this rivalry and tension are going on, there is no rest and contentment. Every sheep is on guard to defend its own rights.

We hear an awful lot about *my rights* these days. We sing about doing it *my way*. Advertisers assure us that *I'm* worth it. Psychologists remind us to look out for *number one*. And we ask ourselves, "How can this attitude be so wrong when it seems so right?" Like in the world of sheep, there is a high price to pay when we seek to be number one. There's always somebody breathing down our necks to take us down. We must always be on our guard, striving with all our might to stay on top. Only when we know who we are as people of destiny are we able to take the low road on our life journey. Whether we are a corporate president or a parking lot attendant, maintaining a humble servant attitude is a sign that we are confident in who we are. The person willing to be second or even last is the person who will be nourished in green pastures. This is the place of peace. This is the place where you will be free from friction and life's stresses. Ultimately, freedom from friction has more to do with our attitude than our position in life.

Freedom from flies

THIRDLY, SHEEP WILL not readily lie down unless they are free from flies. In the case of sheep, it may be nasal flies, bat flies, warble flies or ticks - any of which will drive them to distraction and keep them from rest. I've seen my grandpa's sheep stomping their legs, shaking their heads and rushing into bushes for some sort of relief from pesky flies. This is where the shepherd comes in. He uses chemical repellents and dips, as well as providing bushes and trees where they can find relief from the irritation.

What's bugging you, Kelly? Is it someone at work who is out for your position? Is it the constant pressure of a mortgage and car payment? Or is it a fear that your body may succumb to the same disease as your friend's? The irritations of life keep us from enjoying the green pastures that the shepherd provides. As long as we keep stomping our feet, shaking our heads and running for cover, we'll never be able to lie down and rest in green pastures. During these times, we need to trust the shepherd to handle the irritations of life.

Giving up struggling is often the best thing that we can do, because it's at that point where our shepherd can take over and use our difficulties to teach us invaluable life lessons. It's like the opposing winds which an eagle encounters. Instead of allowing the winds to drag it down, it uses them to his advantage so that they lift him up to greater heights. One of the main reasons why the irritations of life are actually good for us is because they drive us closer to our shepherd and cause us to depend on his help. None of us were ever meant to live independently of God's care.

Kelly, even in my own life, I have seen how the shepherd has used the tough times I've gone through to shape me into who I am today. I remember an irritation which God used to teach me a valuable lesson from the days when I worked in the wholesale plywood industry. Although I was a manager with a fair amount of responsibility, my boss rode me very hard. He was a cranky man who was almost ready for retirement and he may have resented a young guy like me doing his old job. For whatever reason, even though he hired me, he didn't seem to like me very much.

Every day I would cringe as I saw Jack walk near my office. My stomach would tighten in pain with his constant criticism. No matter how well I did, he would always find some minute detail of perceived failure with which he could harass me. It got to bugging me so much that I began to dislike my job. I counted the days to his sixty-fifth birthday, but about a month before his retirement day arrived, Jack took an option of staying on for an extra year. I was devastated. That was the day when I knew something had to give. I had to make a decision to either quit my job or change my attitude.

It was a good job and I was counting my own days before a career move, so I opted for the attitude change. I decided that every day I would wake up and thank God that Jack was my boss. After all, he was the one who gave me the job. I also began thanking God for the lessons that I was learning from him. Besides his rich experience in the business world, I was inadvertently growing in my people skills and my self confidence because of the tension between us.

Within thirty days, everything was different. Jack didn't change, but I did. I began to see him as a man who was scared to retire. Work was all that he knew and he subconsciously resented the fact that his days were numbered, while mine were still ahead of me. The next year was better than any of the preceding ones and I actually felt bad when he finally retired. I wrote him a letter thanking him for all that he had taught me. The lessons that I learned under Jack are still serving me today. Kelly, you and I will be confronted by the Jacks of this world for the rest of our lives. Think of those nasty flies circling around our noses as gifts to us. They have been given to us as teachers to instruct us in the ways of wisdom, patience, courage and grace. Our attitudes regarding the irritations of life will either bring us to distraction or press us toward maturity and peace in the pastures of life.

Freedom from needing to find food

FOURTHLY, SHEEP CANNOT lie down in green pastures unless they are fed up. That's the picture the psalmist paints for us here. He makes me lie down in green pastures. The sheep in this verse have been satisfied by plenty of nutritious green grass. They're happy, full and ready for their afternoon nap in the sunshine.

When I write about being full and satisfied in reference to our life journey, I am not talking about our stomachs being filled with food. Rather, the sheep feeding on green grass is a picture of nourishing the person inside of us, which is our soul. Kelly, I can remember dinner times twenty-five years ago, when I was determined to make you eat your vegetables. Although you were only three or four years of age, you were just about as stubborn as I was as you sat and stared at those peas on your plate. That was a battle which neither of us won, but I tried my hardest to teach you to eat foods that were nourishing.

Eating healthy foods is important to sustain us physically, but even more vital to our long term health is soul food. Nourishment for our souls does not come from roast beef, potatoes and peas, but from intangible foods like good reading, healthy friendships, a right relationship to God and a positive attitude. Because our souls are eternal and our bodies are only temporal, feeding the inner person is of greater importance than a fat free physical diet.

Kelly, do the books and magazines that you read, contribute to your soul's strength and courage? Do the television shows and movies that you choose for your family, enlarge and challenge your inner world? Do the friends whom you hang around with contribute to or drain your positive energy? Is your relationship with your shepherd healthy? Does his counsel help you think wholesome thoughts and make wise choices? The menu of soul foods that is set before you and your family, every day, will determine the health of your inner world for years to come. As you discover and feed on these daily nutrients for your soul, you will find it increasingly easier to lie down regularly and rest in the green pastures.

Freedom from fear, freedom from friction, freedom from flies and freedom from having to find food are all daily blessings which our shepherd provides for us each day. The closer we follow him and the more intently we listen to him, the more time we will have to enjoy resting our souls in the soft green pastures which he has prepared for us.

Finding green pastures

PROVIDING GREEN PASTURES for either sheep or people does not happen by chance. They are the product of hard labor, time and skill. They require a shepherd who cares for his sheep. Kelly, do you remember the words that I spoke to you and Tom at your wedding ceremony? After that highly emotional tradition of me walking you down the centre aisle of our church, your mom and I stood beside you, and Tom's parents stood with him. Pastor Bob, your uncle, gave his introductory comments and we responded to his question, "Who gives this woman to be married to this man?" with our obligatory, "We do." Then we kissed you.

After we gave you away, I stepped up with you and Tom onto the platform and began the marriage ceremony. I remember saying to you both, as I fought back the tears, that we have all likely fantasized that our marriages would be colourful gardens filled with fragrant flowers. I said, "We have all dreamed of walking in our marriage gardens each day and basking in the beauty and peace of marital bliss. Those of us who have been married any length of time know that this is not always so. This wedding ceremony is not God giving you a beautiful rose garden, rather it is him giving you a plot of dirt, a bag of seeds and a few tools. Tom and Kelly, what you make of your marriage from this day on is up to you."

I explained to you, from my own experience, that gardening is hard work, "In our yard I've spent years raking and digging up rocks, but they keep coming, seemingly faster than the flowers. I have not only removed rocks, but I've had to pick at the hard ground, add new soil, fertilize, water and constantly re-till the ground to keep it soft. It's back breaking work. Only when the soil has been well prepared, do I plant the flowers. Each year it's the same."

"And then there are the weeds," I continued, " I'm not sure where they come from, but I know that if I neglect them for a couple of weeks, they're back again. A gardener told me last year that horsetail weeds have a root system that can crawl underground for up to two miles. No wonder it sometimes seems like a losing battle." An example of the weeds in our life are the unhealthy attitudes that we have fostered over the years. Anger over our parents' divorce, bitterness toward the opposite sex, lust for approval from others, undue attention to our physical appearance and disrespect for authority are a few among many of the poisonous weeds, which can destroy our healthy gardens.

I concluded my counsel with, "And that is marriage. It is a lot of blood, sweat and tears, but the work that you put into your marriage has many rewards. There is nothing as wonderful as walking outside on a spring morning and enjoying the fragrance and beauty of a well kept garden. In marriage, enjoying a cup of coffee together while talking about your day, walking hand in hand on a stroll in the cool of the evening, a healthy sex life and lovingly growing old together are more than worth the effort of removing a few rocks and weeds along the way."

Now that you and Tom have been married for a few years, you understand better what I was speaking about on your wedding day. You also understand, that just as beautiful gardens and good marriages do not happen by chance, neither do we benefit from the green pastures in our life journey if we don't take time for them. I'm thankful that our shepherd cares enough to provide them for each of us and he leads us to them. Of course, it's our choice whether or not we will follow where he leads us and whether we will enjoy the rest and nutrition of the pasture which he provides.

When these four conditions for the sheep to lie down in safety and security have been met, the afternoon rest time becomes a vital source of health for them. Although the verse reads, He makes me lie down in green pastures, the inference is that I, the sheep, have been satisfactorily fed and nourished in those same green pastures. For sheep, the lying down period is for both rest and rumination.

Sovereign foundations

THE FORMATION AND health of our souls, to a large degree, result from a combination of both nature and nurture. What we are born with and the family we are born into is not up to our choosing. They have been given to us by God. That's why I call them our sovereign foundations. The word sovereign tells us that we have been given by God, our designer, the starting material for our life journey. Children have no choice as to who is going to rear them. Some children are adopted; some are raised by step parents, single parents, foster parents or grandparents.

Let's consider your sovereign foundations, Kelly. First of all, you did not choose your mom and me to be your parents. (As a matter of fact, we didn't choose you either, although we are delighted with whom we were given). You were given to us sovereignly by God. You also did not choose your skin colour, size, temperament, weaknesses, strengths or a myriad of other winsome characteristics that you have. We say that you got your temperament and body shape from my side of the family, but actually you were given them by God.

You also did not have many choices in your early life experiences. We're told that most of our values and our character are formed before we are even five years old. These were, in a way, also sovereignly assigned to you because of the limited choices you could make. Many values, habits and tendencies that you now have as an adult were set before you even had an opportunity to make decisions for yourself.

The facts that you are a Canadian, speak English and have other nationalistic or ethnic distinctions were predetermined by your creator. Your social status as a child, intelligence, emotional stability, early nourishment, extended family, neighbors and early life experiences were all beyond your control. Those were your sovereign foundations, which

God had pre-chosen with your ultimate destiny in mind. All of those foundations were part of his plan to shape you and prepare you for your assignment in life.

Not far from our home are the beginnings of a house. Someone with great intentions poured the foundation and left it sitting for the past two years. I'm not sure if the city inspectors stopped the building process or if the contractor ran out of money, but there it sits. If I were to buy that property and begin building on the existing foundation, my choices as to the shape and size of the house would be largely pre-determined. The foundation has already set the direction for much of the future design of that house. Thus the shape of our souls is primarily determined by nature, better seen as our sovereign God. We then add nurture to what nature has given us. Nurture has to do with soul food - how we care for and nourish our souls in the green pastures to which our shepherd leads us.

Soul food to encourage your will

IN THE ANALOGY painted for us by David in his psalm, the green pastures that our shepherd makes us lie down in also become food for our souls. Just as the sheep are nourished with the lush green grass and lie down satisfied, so our souls must be well nourished before we will be content, refreshed and able to rest in the pastures which our shepherd provides. Every dimension of our soul requires some form of nutrients. These nutrients I call soul food.

This is how the various elements of our soul are fed. The king of our soul, Kelly, is your will. This is where you make your life choices. Every day your personal will makes thousands of decisions about what to say, think or do. Your will was nourished when you were young by the influences of those around you, by the discipline you received, and by the consequences of your actions. For example when you were a toddler, if your mom and I had let you make all the decisions in our home as to what television programs you would watch or what time you would go to bed; and as a child, how much you would practice the piano, what you'd eat and whether you'd go to school or not, you likely would have grown up to be a very self-centered woman. You may even have taken another life path all together. Rather than let you make your own choices before you were wise enough, we followed the shepherd's advice and trained you to go in the way which we thought was right, and you followed the path.

Gradually, as you grew in maturity, we increased your freedom to make choices for yourself. We're thankful that we did make those early choices for you and are delighted by the way you have turned out.

When your Uncle Dave and I were boys, we used to make wooden golf clubs out of young sapling maple trees. When a tree was only a year or two old, we would bend it near the base at a ninety-degree angle and hold it in position with a string fastened to the ground. The next year, we'd cut the tree below the bend and it would be set with a natural curve. Those sticks made perfect golf or field hockey clubs. The way our wills are shaped as children has a lot to do with the way they are set as adults. Of course, there are notable exceptions. Some children are shaped well when they are young, and yet still choose to go off track later in life. Others were shaped poorly as youngsters, but choose to get on the right path as they mature. Ultimately, our own wills decide which path we take as adults.

As maturing children, teenagers or adults, another way to nourish our will is by making good choices. Every time we make a choice in the right direction, we firm up our resolve to do right again. A simple example is my daily habit of drinking Ginseng tea. The first time I tried the tea I thought it tasted like dirt, but I decided that this would be a healthy habit to form. Now, a couple of years later, I still drink Ginseng tea every day, and I actually like it. My will has been shaped more firmly with every cup of tea that I have had.

Whether it is choosing to exercise regularly, diet consistently, control my use of the television or internet, or use encouraging and positive words, each time I choose wisely my resolve is strengthened for making other good decisions.

The same thing happens negatively. Only yesterday, I spoke with a man consumed by pornography. He told me that it began when he allowed himself to look at one pornographic movie all by himself in his hotel room. The more he polluted his will by watching the movies, the more his will was weakened. Now he is trying desperately to change his will by self-discipline because he sees how it has negatively impacted his marriage. It is a very difficult struggle for him, but I am confident that he will succeed.

Two good habits necessary to adequately nourish your will are to surround yourself with positive influences and to consciously and consistently make wise choices. Part of the strength that we receive during our times spent in green pastures comes from slowing down. We cannot make wise choices if we are always running, so our shepherd, from time to time, makes us lie down in green pastures.

Soul food to nourish your mind

OUR MINDS ARE nourished daily by what we read, what we watch on the television, internet or movies; by the music we listen to and whom we hang around with. The computer expression is *garbage in equals garbage out*. That's an easy concept to understand, but a difficult diet to consistently maintain. The rewards of a healthy diet for our minds are every bit as satisfying as following a healthy diet for our bodies.

Your grandma is a good example of a person who has a well-nourished mind Kelly. Although grandma is well into her eighties, she disciplines herself to watch wholesome movies, reads books that challenge her mind, takes courses on interesting subjects, practices her organ regularly, studies her Bible every day and takes notes on every sermon she hears. Because your grandma keeps her mind well nourished, she will likely retain her quick wit and memory for years to come.

Soul food to strengthen your imagination

OUR IMAGINATIONS ARE another area of our souls which need to be well fed daily. I was taught as a boy that my imagination could be used as the devil's playground if I allowed him entrance through my thoughts, but my king (that's my will) stands at the gate allowing or refusing his entrance. My dad was right when he said that what I read, the pictures I look at, what I daydream about, what I say about myself or to myself, are all within my control. For me, because I usually lie awake for an hour or so after hitting the pillow, my imagination is like a blank computer screen. Whatever button that I press with my will determines what dances across the screen of my imagination. When my soul has been well nourished, then I find it easier to use those relaxing minutes for positive exercises, such as setting the course for my future or thinking of stories to use in next Sunday's sermon.

When my soul has been under fed or malnourished, I've found that my imagination becomes an easy area of my life in which I can become sloppy. "After all," the devil whispers, "nobody can see your thoughts." The problem is Kelly, that an unkempt imagination usually filters through into our words and actions. Our entire destinies can be lost because of an undernourished or unswept thought life.

Soul food to fortify your emotions

EVERY PERSON IS an emotional being. Our feelings are a wonderful and necessary part of who we are as individuals. We were created to enjoy a wide range of emotional feelings from the highs to the lows, but that same range can either fulfill us or debilitate us.

Some people express their emotions very freely and others keep them under lock and key. Kelly, your emotional nature is similar to mine. We tend to be more reserved; we don't laugh as loudly, cry as hard, express anger as dramatically or get as excited as others. We see ourselves as calm, cool and collected, while others may see us more as detached and repressed. The truth is that the way we express our emotions has a lot to do with the temperament with which we were born.

Our natural temperament is part of our sovereign foundations. God decided before each of us was born what temperament that we would need to effectively fulfill our personal destiny. Every temperament has its natural strengths and weaknesses. We do not choose our temperament, but we are responsible for the nurturing, maturing and control of our natural weaknesses.

Temperaments can be divided into two basic categories - introverts and extroverts. Introverts are energized by being alone and become exhausted by being around people. Extroverts are energized by being around people and become exhausted by being alone. Kelly, you and I both tend to be introverted. That's not a good or bad thing. It was largely God's choice not our own, but it's helpful for us to know our temperament so that we understand how our emotions are to be nourished. For me, I need time alone to be recharged in my emotional batteries. If I don't have time by myself to think and to rest, I find that I become weary or irritable more quickly. It's like the cordless telephone in our kitchen. It must spend a certain percentage of its life on the hanger recharging or it will soon malfunction. When it gets rest for a prescribed time, then it functions properly as it was intended by its manufacturer.

For me, although I enjoy being around people, my natural tendency is to want to be quieter. I like being alone or with one other person rather than be in a large group. I would likely never go to a party if I didn't have to.

Of course, being a pastor presses me into both large and small groups all week long, and that has been very positive in stretching me past my natural comfort zone. As an introvert, if I don't keep pushing myself outward, my natural tendency would force me into a smaller, more self-centered world.

For an extrovert, he needs to work more on the being alone side of his life. We all must have quiet times of introspection as well as seasons alone with our shepherd in which we are recharged spiritually. Both introverts and extroverts have to find the healthy balance between being around others and being alone. People of either temperament can successfully and happily reach their own destiny when their emotional lives have been adequately nourished and disciplined.

It's important for us to know which temperament we have been given because the needs for our emotional nurturing will vary according to the way we have been wired. Every person is an emotional being and emotions have been given by our shepherd to each of us as gifts. What our parents and other early influences did to nourish or starve our emotions will often affect us for the rest of our lives. It's also helpful to understand the cyclical nature of our human emotions.

Emotional cycles

AS I UNDERSTAND the emotional makeup of human kind, we all have cycles. We each have high emotional days, where we feel good about life and ourselves; and we have low emotional days, when we feel less happy about life and ourselves. These low periods, we call depression and can be charted like this:

Cycle of Emotional Highs and Lows

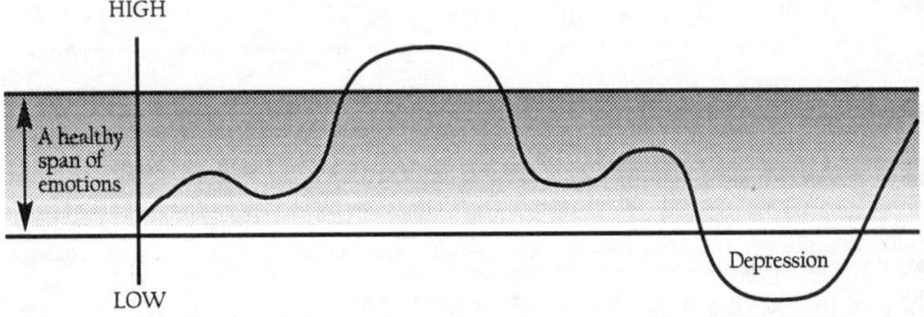

Often the up and down waves do not necessarily relate to the circumstances which we are going through. Everything may be good in our world, but we simply feel low; or conversely everything may be lousy, but we feel emotionally on top.

Both the highs and the lows in our feelings make our lives more interesting. It would be a very boring world if everybody were the same temperament. I was attracted to your mom because she was bubbly, talkative and high spirited. She was attracted to me because I was calm, cool and collected. We both love our differences and need each other to give balance to our own emotional nature.

Our highs and lows can either benefit us or debilitate us. Unhealthiness can come on either side of the continuum, when we do not express any of our emotions, or when we let our emotions rule us. It's important to know that balance is the key to health in the emotional part of our souls.

Our temperaments then, are assigned to us at birth by our creator. A person who is wired as an introvert will not likely be able to remake his personality into that of an extrovert, but whichever temperament we've been given needs our personal discipline. Every one of us has inherent and learned weaknesses. It's far too easy to cop out and say, "Well that's just the way I am. My dad was an angry man and that's the way I am too," or, "I can't help my tendency to worry and be anxious. God made me this way!" Each of us must take personal responsibility, within the parameters of our inherited temperament, to grow healthy through proper discipline and nurture.

The discipline for our temperament relates back to nourishing our will, mind and imagination in the green pastures that our shepherd leads us to. No one can make me say angry words, pull back in fear or not forgive. I alone am responsible for my actions and reactions. These are choices I make with my will.

What I choose to dwell on in my thought life will either solidify or change my emotional patterns. I spoke with a man this week who is experiencing ongoing depression. I have recommended that he see a medical doctor for whatever treatment is necessary to balance his inner chemistry, but there is more than an imbalance of chemistry in his soul. This man sees all of life through the colored lense of a victim. He interprets the words and actions of every person around him as a personal attack.

To level out his depressed emotions will take more than a doctor's prescription. He will have to nourish his will, his mind and his imagination at the green pastures for an extended season.

Encouragement versus discouragement

IN ADDITION TO discipline, every person also needs another vital nutrient for maintaining emotional balance in their souls. One of the healthiest soul foods that any of us can enjoy, which will nurture and strengthen our emotions is encouragement. Contrary to this, one of the most toxic soul foods that one can eat, which will poison and weaken our emotional stability, is discouragement. To be encouraged means to feel strong with enough courage to face whatever life brings us. To be discouraged is when that courage, necessary to handle life, is taken or drained from us. Spending time with an encouraging person gives us courage. We feel stronger for our being with him or her. A discouraging person saps our courage. We feel drained and weaker emotionally for our being with him or her.

Encouragement vs. Discouragement

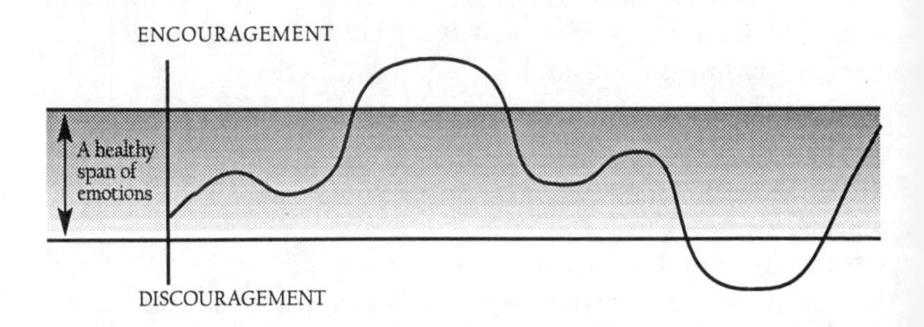

In the above diagram, the two solid lines show the range of healthy emotional balance. Most people's emotions will range from above those lines to below the lines, depending on their health, personal cycles, circumstances and relationships. Encouragement allows us to face and handle more stress and challenges, while discouragement debilitates us from handling those difficulties. There is nothing that feels as bad as discouragement and nothing that feels as good as encouragement.

As you know Kelly, I've been working on this book for about three years. The concept that the Lord is my shepherd and that he has a plan for my life has literally transformed my thinking. I find this psalm somehow influencing almost every counselling session and sermon in my week. But because the writing and editing has taken so long, I sometimes get discouraged with the process. I'm not one to show my emotions readily, so most people think of me as being happy all the time. A few months ago, after editing one of my letters for the sixth or seventh time, I sat down with a friend of mine to talk. She wasn't aware of my despondent feelings at the time and likely had no idea of how healing her words were, but she simply told me how beneficial that she felt this book would be to its readers. As she talked, my emotions were soaking up her words, and by the time we parted I felt emotionally refreshed and full of courage again. I'm constantly amazed at how satisfying and energizing a few words of encouragement can be. Encouragement to the soul is wonderfully refreshing, fulfilling and energizing.

In my experience, one of the most nutritious soul foods which I have benefitted from and that I need regularly is encouragement. In contrast, of all the unhealthy soul foods I have found discouragement to be the most toxic. I thank God for my parents, who had such a profound influence in my early years for teaching me the value of encouragement. Parents who are continuously teaching their children how to nourish their emotions give them a huge advantage later in life. I love watching you and Tom with your son, Alexander, and how you have already in his two years of his life been constantly encouraging him. Keep feeding him the same diet Kelly, and he will grow up with as healthy a soul as his mother.

Lessons from a toilet

THE OPERATION OF a toilet is a good illustration of the value of encouragement. The toilets we have in our homes have two main parts; the bowl that is filled with water in the front and the water tank at the back. Please excuse my frankness, but the metaphor works well. The process goes like this: once the toilet bowl has been used, we then pull the lever to release the fresh water from the tank. The clean water easily washes away the waste products and the process is complete. Now, consider what would happen if the tank at the back of the toilet were empty. When we pulled the lever, there would be nothing to wash the waste away. The smell would remain and even intensify.

The illustration below is one that you will likely not forget. Think of your emotional tank like that of a toilet. The tank part holds a reserve of emotional courage. When rotten circumstances come into your life, you simply flush them away by releasing your emotional courage reserve. Let's say that you go to work at your medical office and your supervisor is in a bad mood. She takes out her pent up anger on you because you are the first person whom she sees in the day. Of course you are hurt in your soul because of her abuse, especially since you did not deserve her rebuke. Because your emotional tank is full, (Tom has been considerate and kind to you; Alex and Max are growing and healthy; you are feeling good about yourself) you are able to easily flush away the hurtful words and are virtually unaffected by your boss's harsh words. You even have enough inner strength to say a gracious word to her later on that day. Of course the process drains you, but to prepare for more difficulties during your day, you simply need to refill your reserve of courage.

The Toilet - a picture of the value of encouragement

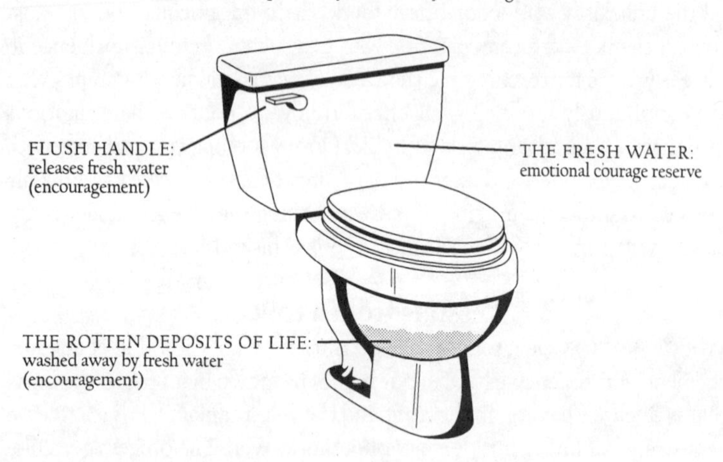

Now imagine that the comments of your boss were just one of a series of discouraging events in your day. You have been awakened in the early morning with a sick baby and can't get back to sleep, you can't find anything to wear in the morning, Tom is tired and snaps at you for running late, a guy cuts you off on the way to work, you diagnose your first patient and discover that he has a malignant tumor . . . and then your boss yells at you! Your emotional tank is going to need to be refilled with courage pretty soon because you're likely by this time to be running on empty.

Your sister Kristy, as a school teacher has many stories which illustrate the value of a parent's consistent encouragement. Even as early as grade two, children whose emotional tanks have never been filled by encouragement act out of their hurt. Kristy told me of a young boy in her class who, in the first week of school, was already the terror of the school. He would do anything to get a reaction from his classmates or the teachers. In his dysfunctional little mind, even negative attention was better than no attention to help fill his empty tank.

I love the way Kristy responds to challenges such as this little boy. Right from the beginning of her year, she saw his potential, as well as his hurt, and began to feed him with lots of encouragement and love. As the semester passed, he became Kristy's little buddy and would literally hang onto her whenever possible. It was truly amazing to see the changes in his behavior, how his attention span and his learning skills both improved dramatically as the year progressed. He simply needed someone to generously pour encouragement into his emotional tank.

A parent's primary job

IF PARENTS ARE serving their children well, they are readily encouraging them by constantly filling up their children's emotional courage reserve tank. Keep in mind Kelly, that it takes seven positive encouraging words to balance only one discouraging word. This may help us to understand why some children face life well able to handle adversity, while others face every day with no reserve whatsoever and are overwrought by even small obstacles.

Psychologists tell us that a child largely develops these character skills and emotional strengths before he or she even begins school. How important it is for us as parents to be refilling our children's tanks several times every day. Even as you and Kristy have become adults, your mom and I feel that it's our ongoing responsibility and privilege to keep encouraging you and your families.

As a pastor, I see men and women every week who were seldom, if ever, encouraged by their parents. Instead, they were continuously discouraged by emotionally abusive parents or relatives. As adults, they face daily pressures with an empty tank and their emotional lives are cluttered with wastes, which they are incapable of flushing from their systems.

To take the metaphor a step further, some parents have not only neglected to fill the emotional tanks of their children with encouragement, but they have sucked them dry with discouragement. Added to the inadequacies of an empty tank, these parents have figuratively taken a hammer and smashed their children's reserve tanks. Imagine a toilet with a broken tank; even when sufficient water is poured into the tank, it leaks out as fast as it enters.

Now, take the man or woman who has not only an empty tank, but a cracked one and place them in a marriage. The spouse tries everything to meet his or her partner's emotional needs, but it is never enough. Physical food alone is insufficient to feed the starving emotions of a broken person. We need nourishment and healing in our souls to adequately prepare us to fulfill our destinies.

When we arrive at the *restoring of our souls* stop on our journey, we'll discover how to get past this emotional sinkhole. For now it is enough to understand how important it is for each of us to encourage our children, spouses and friends as often as we can. Each one of us has a large ladle which we carry with us every day. Using our ladle, we either add to a person's emotional tank with our encouraging words and actions, or we dip into it with our discouraging words and actions.

The rest areas of our life

WE'VE SEEN IN this stop on our journey Kelly, that green pastures are the places where we are nourished in our bodies and souls. These are the rest areas of life, which will make it possible for us to be successful throughout the balance of our journey.

Remember Honey, when you and Kristy were young and we used to stop at the highway rest stops from time to time, in order for all of us to get refreshed? We would get out of the car, use the restrooms, have a snack and run around a bit. We always kept a ball or a frisbee in the car to throw around on our breaks. As a result of those rest times we were all much happier for the next part of our journey. We need green pastures to nourish our souls, just as much as we need rest stops to nourish our bodies.

If there's anything that our modern American generations need Kelly, it's to learn the value of the green pastures of life. As I wrote earlier, we're pretty well informed about how to keep our bodies in good shape, but we've got a long way to go to fully understand the value of soul food. I pray for you and your family that you will be thoroughly nourished in the green pastures of your life journey; that you will be free from fear, free from friction, free from flies and free from the need to search for food. I pray that your shepherd will not have to press you to lie down in green pastures, but that you will purposefully and regularly choose to lie down in quiet rest; and that each one of your family's emotional tanks will be filled to overflowing with love and courage. Amen.

Love Dad

CHAPTER FOUR

Quiet Waters

He leads me beside the quiet waters.

THE SHEPHERD LEADS us beside quiet waters for the purpose of refreshing, nourishing and refocussing our spiritual centres. By disciplining ourselves to take regular sabbath rests, we are better prepared for the more challenging part of the journey, which lies ahead of us.

Dear Kelly,

In this letter Kelly, I'm writing to you about a third dimension of who you are - your spirit. As important as nurturing and caring for both your body and soul are, this third part of you, your spirit, must take its place as your highest priority. Because our spiritual dimensions are often neglected and undernourished, it's vital to know how to promote and maintain health in your spirit.

A well satisfied spirit finds its nourishment beside the quiet waters. In this fourth point of the shepherd's psalm, the author underlines one of the most basic requirements of any sheep - clean, refreshing drinking water. His metaphor emphasizes our human need for daily nurture of our spiritual life. We'll see how this happens beside the quiet waters. I believe that a well satisfied spirit lays a foundation for a healthy soul, and a healthy soul in turn will form a framework for a strong and useful body.

When the three parts of who you are; spirit, soul and body, work together in mature harmony Kelly, you will successfully complete your life journey and fulfill your predestined purpose.

True peace

I REMEMBER A SERMON that I heard when I was a teenager about true peace. My pastor described a painting contest, which was once held for local artists. They were instructed to paint a picture which portrayed peace. From among the dozens of entries, three finalists were chosen. One of the paintings was a pastoral scene. It featured a contented looking cow in a lush viridescent meadow, happily chewing her noon meal. There were soft green trees in the background with colorful birds chirping on the branches. The sky was a warm azure and cumulus clouds floated lazily over the pasture. It was the kind of picture that stirs within me the desire to live the life of a farmer. The judges must have felt the same way because it won third prize.

The second painting was of a vacation wonderland somewhere in the tropics. In the picture, a young couple romantically sipped champagne on the grassy hill overlooking a dazzling crystal waterfall which flowed into a cool, clear refreshing pool. There were delightful displays of God's creative genius - beautiful flowers, lush plants and blue sky with a soft summer sun, which warmed the entire painting. In the shadows and colours, one could almost smell the tropical fragrance and feel the gentle breeze. But as beautiful as it was and as much as the painting reflected an idyllic peacefulness, it only won a second prize ribbon.

The painting, which proudly wore the blue ribbon, was entirely unique among the entries. It was of a raging storm so vivid that one could almost hear the howling winds and breaking branches. There were trees bending, leaves whirling, rain pounding and lightning flashing. The tones were greys, browns, heavy greens and blacks - hardly the colours of peace. At first glance, a viewer would have thought that the painting was placed in the contest by mistake, but then upon careful scrutiny the artist's point became clear. In a crevice of the rugged mountainside hid a large female eagle, a magnificent bird. Cuddled under her wing was a tiny eaglet, sound asleep, totally at peace. The picture was entitled Peace Amidst the Storm. To the judges and to me also, the painting reflected true peace.

This story brings us to the second stopping place on our life journey.

It is a peaceful place of spiritual rest called the quiet waters. The word *rest* has an interesting etymology. Its origin is from a nomadic period of history when a rider would arrive at his destination and dismount from his horse or camel to rest from his day's journey. Its roots reach back to the word house, which is where we rest every evening. You'll notice that our modern words *arrest* which means to stop, and *restore* which implies inner healing, are also related to the word rest. The way this word has arrived in our current usage helps us to gain insight into how resting beside the quiet waters is an important place along our life journey, when we stop what we are doing, dismount from the driving forces of our life, and are restored in the inner chamber of our person.

In the last letter that I wrote to you, I discussed the necessity of our souls being nourished in the green pastures. Here beside the refreshing clear water, we will be nurtured in the deep recesses of our spirits.

Enjoy your stay at the quiet waters Kelly, for as long as you are able. I have travelled down the road of life long enough to understand that the peace we enjoy here is preparatory for the difficult days ahead. Life was never intended by our shepherd to be lived only in the green pastures or beside the still waters. You've likely already discovered that our shepherd provides these places of nourishment to give us strength and endurance for the coming challenges ahead on our journey.

The missing link

SHEEP, JUST LIKE YOU and I, require plenty of water to live. Their bodies, on the average, are composed of about seventy percent water. Without a regular intake of water, a sheep's health and strength would be in serious jeopardy. Dehydration of the tissues could result in life threatening damage. A sheep's intense physical need for water is a good picture of our spiritual need for God.

Even though some of our human characteristics can be compared to those of certain animals, one of the most significant elements of our nature, which separates us from cats and dogs, is our spiritual nature. We, unlike animals, have a deep thirst for spiritual life which cannot be satisfied by physical, mental or emotional pleasures. It is difficult to diagram our human make-up because a human spirit, soul and body are not clearly divisible, but the diagram following will help you to understand my point.

Every human being has a God-given thirst for a personal relationship with their creator. Just as the shepherd is vital to his sheep's supply of water, so our shepherd is the only one who can satisfy our spiritual thirst. The statement, *he leads me beside the quiet waters*, suggests that without our shepherd, who leads us to the thirst quenching waters, our spirits would dry up and ultimately die.

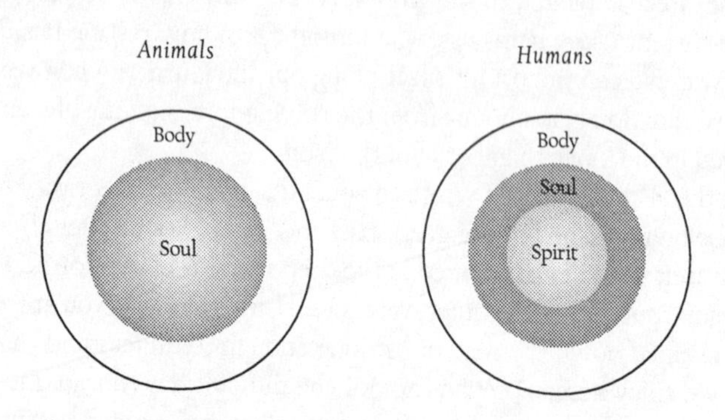

Kelly, you grew up through school, work and church with dozens of friends. Even though many of your friends would not see themselves as church goers, I don't know one of them who would deny believing in God. And that's typical, because in both the United States and Canada, the population by a large majority are believers in God. In our last Canadian census, only thirteen thousand people out of twenty-eight million registered as atheists. About eighty-seven percent of us believe in the Judeo Christian God. Three thousand years ago, King Solomon wrote that all of mankind have been created with eternity in our hearts. There is a dimension deeply implanted in each of us, which longs for a relationship with a power that is greater than ourselves.

Last week, I spoke with a man who appears to have everything. He is about forty years old, has a beautiful wife, two well adjusted children, his own company which affords him every trinket a family could ask for, and good health to enjoy it all. It was a humbling experience for him to sit in my office and say, "There's something missing." He had already tried to fill the gap with more work, more stuff and more friends, but none of those things were bringing him the fulfillment that he so desperately wanted.

I explained to him that there is another dimension to human life, which cannot be filled except through a relationship with our creator. This man didn't want the perfunctory religion with which he had grown up. He needed a living, practical, fulfilling relationship with his shepherd. He needed that spiritual dimension in his heart filled with something eternal, rather than with something temporal. This is how our physical need for water parallels our need for God. Only a personal relationship with our shepherd can satisfy our inborn spiritual thirst.

He leads me

TAKE NOTE OF these three words, he leads me. There are two pronouns and one verb. The two pronouns he and me, refer to the Lord, my shepherd, and to me, his sheep. There is a leader and a follower. Both are necessary to complete the progressive action of the verb to lead. He leads me.

First, we need a leader. Without his leading us to the quiet waters, we would die of thirst in the wasteland of life. Secondly, we need to follow him. I'm not sure why it is, but we like sheep, have this perverse tendency to refuse to follow the leader. Even though we know that the Lord always wants what's best for us, we often tend to choose our way over his way.

One of my favorite writers is Phillip Keller, a shepherd by vocation, who wrote *A Shepherd Looks at Psalm 23*. In his book, Phillip describes a typical scene that he witnessed one day of some sheep that were being led down to a picturesque mountain stream. Even though there were crystal clear, snow fed waters nestled within a forest of green trees, he noted that several of the sheep stopped to drink from small, dingy, mud filled pools beside the trails. The puddles were not only churned up with mud, but were also polluted with the urine and waste of sheep who had passed before them. This water was contaminated with germs, which could eventually destroy the sheep with parasites and disease.

When we think about the sheep drinking that water we cringe inside. How could they do that? Don't they see the sparkling fresh water that the shepherd is leading them to? Why don't they trust the one who loves them and has their best interests at heart?

You've always been a good follower Kelly. Your nature as a child was always to please and follow the rules. Your sister Kristy, lived a little further on the edge than you did. If we said to be home at eleven at night, she would push it to eleven-thirty. If we said that she couldn't go to a certain place, she'd counter with an argument, "Well, why not? My friends are all allowed to go!" Even as a toddler, when we were in a shopping mall, you would hang onto your mom's leg, while little Kristy would wander off and hide in the clothes racks where we couldn't find her. I guess there's a little rebellion in all of us which seduces us into going to where we shouldn't go and keeps us from going to where we ought to go. It's the same spiritually as it is physically. We tend to chase after the things that we think might satisfy us, rather than to follow the directions of our shepherd, which will ultimately bring fulfillment.

The fact is that the only way we can have our spiritual thirst satisfied is to follow our shepherd's lead. I've seen many of my friends try to fill the spiritual vacuum of their lives with physical pursuits. Travel, sports, hobbies, cars, homes or fine foods will all satisfy us physically and even emotionally to a degree, but they will never quench our deep inner thirst. Learning, achievements, arts, culture or music will satisfy our souls, but they will never fill our spiritual vacuum. Our human spirits can only be satisfied as we closely follow our shepherd's lead. The psalmist David described his own spiritual thirst in another psalm, as a ravenous deer panting after water. He wrote, "that's how I thirst for you Lord." He concluded from his own experiences of failure, as well as success, that only God could satisfy his spiritual thirst.

You might ask the question Kelly, "How does God lead me to the quiet waters so that I can satisfy my spiritual thirst?" The simple answer is, through difficult times. When I say simple, I mean that it's easy to say - but to actually understand how our shepherd uses difficult times to lead us to the quiet waters is worthy of some thought. Let me explain by way of illustration.

The cycles of life

LAST WEEK, not far from our home, I noticed that a temporary carnival had been set up in the mall parking lot. Among the variety of colorful rides, I saw the one which I dreaded most of all. Just watching it brought back memories from at least twenty years in my past when you, Kristy, your mom and I would go to the amusement parks. We've been to Disneyland, Disney World, Magic Mountain and several other famous attractions. In each of those parks I've had the distinct delight of riding with both of you girls on just about every ride possible. For you especially Kelly, it was always the faster the better. Now it's time for my true confession.

Of all the rides that we went on, there was really only one which scared me from the inside out. It wasn't the fastest, darkest, highest or the wettest ride which shook me. It was the old fashioned Ferris wheel. The huge Ferris wheel at Magic Mountain in California must go up a hundred feet (it certainly felt that high to me). The problem with being a dad, especially of two girls, is that we always have to look like we are in control. At least that's what we dads think. I remember distinctly sitting between Kristy, who was eight and you, who were ten. My arms were around you both as we were heading up the back end of Magic Mountain's gigantic Ferris wheel.

Another thing about men is that we have an inborn perverse desire to frighten girls. It's part of our makeup. Boys do it with spiders and snakes, but as men we are much more sophisticated; so as we were rising higher and higher on the Ferris wheel, I subtly rocked the chair that we were seated in. You girls cried on cue, "Daddy, don't do that!"; then you cuddled up more closely to me. You thought that your daddy was so fearless.

Going up the backside of the ride was not so bad. I could handle that because all the way up I could easily see the large I-beam frame, which held our chair securely in place. But then as we rounded the cycle to the top of the ride, all visible means of support were suddenly gone from my view. It seemed that we were sitting on top of the world, while our whole foundation rocked mercilessly back and forth. Then each time we came again to the top of the ride, the sadistic operator would stop the machine with a violent jerk to let another person on. The chair we were on felt like it was rocking faster than any of the others. Now who was scared? I wrapped my arms more tightly around you girls, as you giggled with glee. You didn't know it, but I wasn't holding you closely to protect you; it was for my own well being. The ride going down the front of the Ferris wheel was not any better than at the top. All the way down, I could not see any of the steel structures which were designed by some genius engineer for our safety. I rocked and cringed all the way to the bottom of the cycle. The ridiculous part of the ride was that once we finally made it safely down to the bottom, we immediately began the ascent again; up and down, round and round the Ferris wheel sailed, while the carnival lights and music danced around us.

To me, the Ferris wheel is an accurate metaphor to picture the cyclical nature of life. The upside is not too bad. When my job is secure, marriage is happy, children are obedient and health is good, I feel like I have a solid support structure and that I am in a safe place. During those seasons life is actually a fun ride, but as sure as the journey goes up, it also comes down. The downside, where we can see no visible means of support, is designed by life's engineer for a purpose. These are the times when we learn to trust our shepherd. We discover the truth of where our security really rests; and it often isn't where we think it is. Our families, jobs, savings and possessions are all wonderful gifts, which are right to enjoy; but if they are our only support system, then we will fall apart when they are gone. I have personally cried with hundreds of men and women who have lost jobs, marriages, houses or children, and because of their loss, felt like life was over for them.

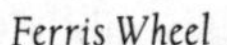
Ferris Wheel

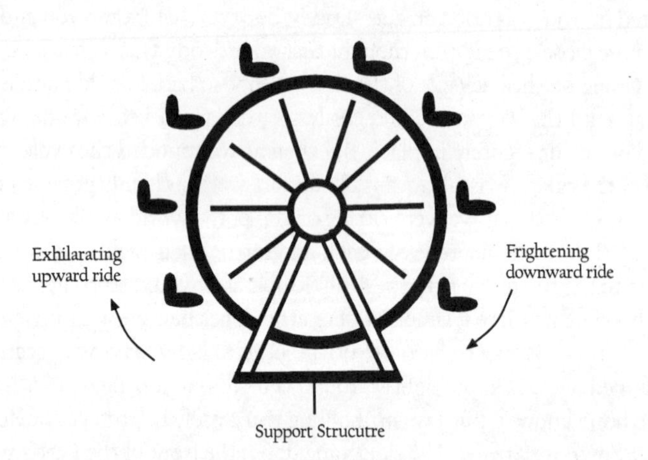

Usually it's when one or more of those steel girders are removed from our lives, that we come face to face with our need for a transcendent support system - something beyond ourselves. Those are the times when we ask the big questions: Is there a God? Is he aware of me and my problems? Does he care? Does God really love me? Can he do anything about my loss? Who, where or what is my ultimate security? We will only grow in our spirits when we step out of our comfort zone and into faith. If we play it safe our world will stay far too small. We will never discover our true security in life as long as we are seated comfortably in our easy chairs.

Stepping out into faith

KELLY, YOU AND TOM are at a very wonderful, yet precarious stage of your lives together. Both of you have worked hard and God has blessed you. At a rather young age you have reached a commendable level of success. You enjoy relative luxury, a healthy and happy marriage and family life, as well as personal and spiritual maturity and balance. My caution to you both is to be careful not to fall into the subtle trap of depending on any of those physical or emotional blessings as your foundation. Our natural human tendency is to do so, but keep your focus on your true source, the Lord your shepherd. Without your dependence upon him, everything else, which you enjoy now, would begin to lose its attractiveness. I am certainly not saying that you are in danger of losing any of the blessings, which you have now; but I do know from experience that our shepherd predictably presses us beyond our present security to a place where we are forced to trust him alone, and to discover for ourselves in what we are placing our trust.

Remember Harrison Ford in Indiana Jones and the Last Crusade? Dr. Henry Jones, played by Ford, was hot on the trail of the holy grail and his enemies were only a few feet behind him. In a dramatic scene near the end of the movie, he came to the edge of a cliff with nowhere to go but down. About fifty yards away, on the other side of the gaping chasm before him, was the cave where the ancient cup was hidden. With his enemies behind him and his destiny in front, Dr. Jones stepped off the edge of the cliff. As quickly as he stepped forward, an invisible beam of light spanned the gorge. Jones looked like he was walking on air as he gingerly ran the fifty yard dash across the invisible bridge of light. His enemies followed him, but because they lacked faith, the unseen support was no longer there and they plunged to their deaths.

The beam of light appeared in response to the faith of Indiana Jones. His security, the solid path along which he had been running, came to an end. Only when the professor reached the end of his physical support system, did he discover his transcendent spiritual security.

To us, following a shepherd whom we can't see, down a path that we have never travelled before, takes just as much faith as it did for the professor to step off the edge of the cliff and onto an invisible bridge. Such trust is forged only on the down side of the Ferris wheel because faith grows only in difficult and challenging times. That's the way the Lord designed us to mature in our spirits.

Life has a rhythm to it

AS WE'VE SEEN by our ride on the Ferris wheel Kelly, there is a rhythm to our life journey. Up and down, up and down our pathway runs. If we stop to think for a moment, we'll note that there are similar rhythms in many expressions of creation. Day and night continue rhythmically; the circling of the earth around the sun and the seasons are also designed by the same creator with a rhythm. Even men and women have rhythmical cycles to their lives. Not only do we have physical cycles, but we have emotional and mental cycles as well. There are natural high days when we can see visions of grandeur from the mountain top; and there are valley days when we hardly want to get out of bed and face life. Both, the days on the mountain top and the days in the valley, have distinct purposes in our life journey. Our creator made all of his creation to be rhythmic. Everybody understands our human need to stop and rest each night so that we will have the energy necessary to function in the daytime. Rest well at night, work effectively during the day. That's how we were created to maximize our potential.

The downward cycles of the Ferris wheel ride of our lives are designed by our shepherd to press us toward the refreshing quiet waters that he has provided for our spiritual nourishment. Usually, the more challenging the ride down, the faster we run to the waters of life.

The next concept, which we learn from the Ferris wheel illustration, is that we must continuously return to the bottom of the ride to get off or get on. The idea of getting off the ride introduces us to the sabbath principle.

The sabbath principle

JUST AS WE were originally wired by God to stop for a portion of every twenty-four hour cycle, so we were also designed to stop for a portion of our weekly and annual cycles. A clock has a second hand, a minute hand and an hour hand all specifically designed by its creator to rhythmically rise and fall on time. So we were created to rhythmically rest and run in daily, weekly and annual cycles.

Our daily rest periods are our sleeping hours. Our weekly and annual rest periods are called by the shepherd, sabbaths. Although we often mistake the word sabbath for a synonym of Saturday or Sunday. It really doesn't mean either. Back in Genesis, the first book of the shepherd's life handbook, we can see his intention for all of mankind. Right at the beginning, after God made the world and everything in it, he took a sabbath. It says that God rested (that's the word sabbath) from all the work he had done. The word sabbath means to quit, stop or take a break. It is not a spiritual word. It simply refers to our non-use of time.

Before we can understand the concept of a regular weekly sabbath Kelly, it may help to look at a twenty-four hour day from our shepherd's perspective. You know how it is with me, how it takes a loud ringing alarm clock to rouse me from my sleep. That's how many people begin their day. Before dawn's light, we hesitantly rise from our slumber, turn on the lights and stare into the mirror for a while until we begin to focus. Our day of busily going about our business begins slowly and gradually picks up speed. It ends after dark when our bodies are wasted and the television programs are over. We then crawl into bed for a few hours to catch up on our sleep, before we begin it all over again the next day. On and on the cycle goes.

Life's rhythm was not designed that way. In the sacred writings of Moses we read; *And there was evening and there was morning, one day...and there was evening and there was morning.* Even today, the Jewish understanding of a day is that it begins at six o'clock in the evening and ends twenty-four hours later at six the following evening. Their weekly sabbath begins Friday evenings and ends Saturday evening.

Because we westerners imagine our days beginning at six or seven in the morning with bacon, eggs and coffee, we have to make an adjustment to understand our shepherd's rhythmic plan for our life. The way it was intended to be was for evening to begin our day. When we awake in the morning and rush out the door with coffee in hand, we tend to think that our day is just getting started. We are ego-centered enough to believe that we actually are the initiators of what we are setting out to do each day. We pray, "Lord please bless my plans for this day."

I love the way Eugene Peterson explains the concept in his book, *Working the Angles.* He says that when we wake up, we walk into a day's destiny already half over. The basic plan is already established, the assignments have been handed out, the people whom we are going to meet today are already in motion. It would make much more sense for us to begin our day by asking our shepherd, "Where do I fit into your plans today? Make my life a blessing to you as I work toward the destiny you've already set into motion." The biblical concept is that there is a rhythm to life. We go to sleep and God begins His work. We awaken and are called into a world that we did not make and in which we ultimately have no control.

When we quit our day's assignment Kelly, the shepherd's work does not cease. We prepare for sleep with a sense of satisfaction, yet even in our rest periods the Lord continues his work. We will join him again the next morning, half way through the new day, when we are refreshed and ready for our allotted assignments. Our work will settle into the larger context of his work. Our human work is honorable, but only makes sense when integrated into the rhythms of our creator's plans.

Remember the Sabbath day

I'VE BEEN WRITING to you Kelly, about the cyclical nature of our lives. Our creator created us to enjoy these up and down, rest and run rhythms in twenty-four hour, seven day and fifty-two week cycles. Our days, weeks and years were all designed to be cyclical. The creator made our weekly cycles to include one day of rest for every six days of work. He called that seventh day the sabbath or stop day.

It's so easy to see our lives in terms of our accomplishments - How many hours do I work? How much money do I make? How many things can I acquire? How many places can I travel to? Before we know what has happened to us, we forget that we belong to the Lord. He is our shepherd; he has a plan for our lives and we are only truly successful if we are walking toward his prepared destiny. The moment that we begin to see our life journey as what we do, rather than who we are, we violate humanity. We are human beings, not human doings.

That's why the Lord our shepherd made us the way he did. Sabbath keeping is a gift from our creator to us. They are stopping and resting points on our life journey that are vital to our existence. These resting places are to preserve the image of God which he placed in each of us, and they also help us see life from his higher perspective. They promote balance between what we do as humans and what we are as sons and daughters of God. We were intended to begin our day with a twelve hour rest time to orientate our spiritual centres around the creator. In our week, after repeating this cycle six times, we were intended to end it with one sabbath day to refocus and recharge our spirits again.

Sabbaths are given to each of us to remind us that our real security is having our shepherd in his rightful place at the spiritual core of our lives. Only then, when our spirits are well centred, can we be truly effective in fulfilling his plan throughout the balance of our hours and days.

Keeping a safe balance to our lives

EVERY ONCE IN A WHILE, my old Oldsmobile begins to wobble as I drive down the freeway. When this happens I drive in to see my friendly mechanic to have the wheels of my car balanced. He places them on a spinning device to determine where each wheel needs weights to bring it back into balance. Our weekly sabbaths are like my mechanic's spinning device. That twenty-four hour period is necessary to help us keep the balance between who I am and what I do. These are the thirst quenching stops at the quiet waters that our shepherd leads us to.

It really doesn't matter on what day we take our weekly sabbath; only that we keep it regularly. Before you were born Kelly, most Canadians were able to take Sunday as a rest day. The Lord's Day Act protected the sanctity of the first day of the week. Over the last several years however, because many businesses chose to remain open on Sunday, millions of people have to work on what was once a traditional sabbath day. I, as a pastor, also have to work on Sundays. To compensate, your mom and I always take Monday as our weekly sabbath. The day of the week that you choose for your sabbath Kelly is not the issue. What's important is that you set aside one day out of seven to stop working, to rest and to refocus your spiritual centre. This is what the sabbath principle is all about.

It's important to note that we are not only taught to set apart one day out of seven as a day of desistance, but we are also commanded to work on the other six days. Maintaining a healthy self-image, as well as our fulfilling our destiny, requires proper use of all seven days. Happily resting and diligently working are both important values to maintain throughout our life journey.

We also need to understand that this sabbath day requirement is not for God's benefit, but for our own physical and spiritual health. To desist or to stop our work, and do nothing productive is mandatory to our spiritual wholeness. In order to fully benefit from the quiet waters, which our shepherd leads us to, we need to keep our sabbath day with regularity. It is at the heart of our rest beside the quiet waters. True spiritual peace is a product of disciplined rest habits as well as healthy work habits.

What does it mean to rest

KELLY, I KNOW that you and Tom are now at an age in life when you are seeing more clearly your need to rest. Tom is advancing quickly in his career as many people do in their early thirties. You are trying to balance keeping your home, raising your children and working part time. It's a busy time for both of you. During these pressing seasons of life, many of us have a tendency to push aside the necessary rest times. "We'll take a break next year when we get a raise," "If we can sleep a couple of extra hours on Saturday, it will make up for the hours we missed this week." "We don't have the money for a vacation this year, so we'll work hard now and enjoy ourselves later." Even in your twenties and thirties Kelly, although you may not feel exhausted, rest is an absolute necessity.

When I was part of our high school band, I played the tuba. Before every concert, our band went through a regular ritual. Our conductor, Mr. Thompson, would give us all a short encouraging pep talk making sure that our eyes were focused on him. He then would wait until our instruments were in tune with one another and with his tuning fork. To bring us into harmony he would strike his tuning fork against his music stand, set it down and hold the microphone up to it. Then each section in the band would ensure that our C majors sounded the same as his C major. His tuning fork set the standard for all of us.

When we stop for a rest beside the quiet waters, whether it's daily, weekly or for an extended vacation each year, the objective is for these resting times to accomplish the same three goals as our band master set. They are to refocus our eyes on the shepherd, make sure that our spirits are in tune with his spirit and be encouraged. Only then are we ready to move along on our life journey to the next stop.

Finding refreshment at the quiet waters

THINK FOR A moment Kelly, how you personally find rest for your spirit. Do you take time daily, weekly and annually for spiritual renewal? As surely as your car needs a regular tune up and your body needs an annual physical checkup, so your spirit requires these rest periods beside quiet waters to bring refreshment and restoration.

What we do to restore our spiritual centres will vary from person to person. It will also vary according to what stage we are at on our life journey. Sometimes, you simply need to sleep. You may feel guilty taking a nap by the fireplace in the mid-afternoon because your self-esteem has always been pumped up by what you've produced, but a fifteen minute nap, an hour rest or an early night to bed may be just what your exhausted spirit is crying out for.

You may be refreshed by reading a good novel, watching a love story on video, having a bath or doing your nails. That's okay! You know what does it for you. Pamper yourself for a while. For others, nature may help them to refocus. Hiking in the woods, going for a run, strolling through a park with your kids or trimming the rose bushes in your yard will give you the lift you need. Just make sure it's not work. This is your time to stop producing, doing or accomplishing anything. Remember that taking a sabbath means to stop!

Make sure that your sabbaths include times of meditation. Even cows understand the concept of meditation. We can learn from them. Have you ever watched cattle out in the pasture, idly standing or lying down, staring into space, chewing their cud? They are redigesting some of the grass that they ate earlier through one of their seven stomachs. That's where we get our word cogitation. It suggests the idea of thinking about something over and over for an extended period of time.

For me, I begin my meditation process by focusing on the shepherd. I find it easier to meditate after reading a psalm, a proverb or another passage from the Bible. It helps me to keep focus. While the meditation time is guided by my shepherd, I often feel a release of buried thoughts, concerns, hopes and memories from the deep recesses of my being. Sometimes, inspiration flows in those moments. Sometimes my shepherd reminds me of someone for whom I should pray or maybe even a person whom I need to forgive. As I sit meditating, a variety of thoughts appear on my spiritual screen. I've had to learn to sift through them and sort the worthwhile thoughts from the worthless thoughts. That's why it is important for us to be aware of the guiding hand of our shepherd during our times of meditation. Meditation can be practiced while lying on a couch, sitting drinking a cup of coffee, driving in your car, walking through a park or pruning rosebushes. Whatever helps you relax is likely a good place to rest beside the quiet waters.

Prayer also should be a valuable part of our sabbath times. Simply imagine that you and God are sitting down for coffee, and then start talking to him just as you would to a friend whom you've invited over. Don't worry about the words you use. God isn't stuck in the seventeenth century - he speaks the same language you do.

What's pressing in on you? What are your fears? What are you thankful for? Ask him for direction, wisdom and strength. God loves to listen to and answer the prayers of any sincere person. By the way Honey, you and Tom are at an ideal stage in your lives to be teaching your children how to take sabbath breaks. Just like you are teaching and modelling good eating and exercising habits for your children, you can teach them the spiritual discipline of sabbath keeping. I know that you maintain Sunday as a family day, taking your family to church, laughing and playing together in the afternoon and praying together at bedtime. Keep using those intimate family times around the dinner table and while preparing for sleep, as teaching moments for your children. The good habits that we learn as small children usually hold us steady through the difficult years yet to come.

Whether we are single, married, at home with four kids, working two jobs, going to school or retired, we seem to find time to do what needs to be done. There's a wise old saying that you will always have time for those things you put first, and resting by the quiet waters needs to be put first. At this place of quiet waters, our spirits are refreshed and refilled, and we are better prepared to effectively and efficiently produce for the next six days of our cycle.

Kelly, we have established that when the Lord is your shepherd, you are in good hands. We have grasped the idea of how necessary it is to have your soul well nourished in the green pastures. I've emphasized how important it is for your spirit to be regularly rested and tuned to the shepherd's voice at the quiet waters. We not only need to understand this principle, but we need to actually practice it! As you and your shepherd move forward to the place where your soul will be refreshed, and then down the specially prepared path ahead of you, you are in for an awesome adventure. You will experience exhilaration and joy, as well as apprehension and sadness on your journey. Through it all, you will grow in maturity, wisdom, inner strength, courage and fulfillment. And throughout your journey, I'll be there for you, Honey, whenever you need me. I love you.

Love Dad

CHAPTER FIVE

A Stop at the Hospital

He restores my soul.

EVERY PERSON IS born disconnected from their centre. Our shepherd's plan is to reconnect us to our rightful centre so that we can begin the process of restoration, which ultimately promises wholeness and fulfillment of our intended destiny.

Dear Kelly,

Do you remember when you were about six years old, and I would read nursery rhymes to you? My all time favourite has always been Humpty Dumpty.

Humpty Dumpty sat on a wall;
Humpty Dumpty had a great fall.
All the king's horses and all the king's men,
Couldn't put poor Humpty together again.

I don't know who wrote this profound poem, but I understand it has survived from the middle ages when riddles were used to teach life philosophy. I'm not sure what the poet was trying to teach, but to me Humpty Dumpty is a picture of all of us. His personal tragedy is mirrored in every life that has ever existed - even yours and mine.

Several years ago, you and I sat cross-legged on the floor of our church sanctuary. All the chairs had been removed for our annual Kid's Day Celebration. There were a couple of hundred energetic children, with several of us adults and a few of you teenagers supervising. I was having as much fun as the kids were. Lunch was over and we were sitting together on the floor watching a movie about Humpty Dumpty. Forgetting that I was there to watch the children, I was gripped by Humpty's sad story.

The cartoon first introduced the oversized egg and his friends. They were a pretty ordinary bunch. One fine spring day, Humpty went to his mom and asked if he and his buddies could go play by the big wall at the edge of town. Mom gave her permission, with an explicit warning that they were not allowed to climb the wall. She explained that it had been built for their protection. When the young egg asked what she meant, his mom's eyes widened as she described the unknown dangers that lurked on the other side. There were ancient rumours of monsters, who lived in the darkness beyond the wall and who loved to eat scrambled eggs. Humpty and his buddies were sufficiently scared and promised that they would stay away from the wall.

The moral of the story was something like children obey your parents, but I, along with the kids, was caught up in Humpty's adventurous spirit. Early in the story it was evident that he was an egg who liked to test his limits, so it wasn't surprising to me that climbing the wall before them posed a clear temptation.

Just as I had suspected, as the eggs were playing football in the shadow of the huge outside wall, one of the more athletic among them threw a long high pass. Over the top of the wall the football went. Humpty and his buddies stared at each other in silent fear. There was a hush that settled over the children and me as we watched Humpty volunteer to climb the stairs and take a look over the wall. The other eggs tried to warn him, but he wouldn't listen. He was moved by a curiosity that had plagued him for a long time. There were "oohs" and "aahs" as he waddled up the steps toward the summit. What was on the other side of the wall? Was it really as frightening as his mom had said? Even if he couldn't get the ball, Humpty just wanted to look where he wasn't supposed to go. When he finally reached the top, the children and I leaned forward in suspense. The music set the mood and even I was frightened by the sudden turn of events.

Humpty Dumpty was now standing on the top of the wall, but not too securely. He was so fearful inside that his shaking body made him wobble as he walked. The eggs below yelled up to their hero, "What's it like Humpty? What's on the other side?" For the first time, he bravely ventured a peek into the awful darkness and just as he did, a hideous monster lifted his ugly head from the thick black fog. Humpty was terrified, but as he pulled back, his footing gave way and down he tumbled.

It was a miracle that he fell on the inside of the wall. Falling on the other side would have made him an instant breakfast treat. There he lay on the ground, cracked and crippled. Humpty couldn't move. The rest of the story involved an ambulance, a hospital, his parents, doctors, the king's horses and the king's men. No one could put Humpty Dumpty together again!

The children and I had learned well from the story to obey our parents. Just as we tried to teach you when you were a little child Kelly, moms and dads certainly know better than their children do about the serious consequences that await them beyond the walls of obedience. To me though, the story of Humpty Dumpty held a deeper message. It was a graphic picture of every human's desire to wander off the path that has been prescribed for us.

Our wheels are a little off kilter

I SEE THIS bent nature illustrated every time I go grocery shopping with your mom. My job is to wheel the basket while she picks out the food that we need. I'm not sure how it happens, but I often seem to get the grocery cart with one wheel that has a mind of its own. When I want to go straight ahead, it wants to turn to the left and when I want to turn down another aisle, the wheel refuses to move. I have to laugh at the self-willed baskets that I choose because they are so much like I am. My shepherd says "Go to the right," and I suggest we rest for a bit. He says "Keep walking straight ahead," and I want to veer to the left.

What has happened to us back in our human history that has twisted mankind so badly? How do our children learn to lie when no one has ever taught them? Why is the first word a child usually learns to say without being coaxed "No"?

Kelly, what I have to write to you in this letter is a primary key which will unlock the mystery of our life journey. This key is the understanding that every person is born disconnected from their centre and that everyone of us is dysfunctional at the core of our being even before we begin to walk, talk and think.

As I have mentioned in a previous letter, in every person there is a spiritual centre called our spirit. It sits at the very core of our souls. Our spirit could be compared with the throne room of a king's palace or the oval office of the White House. It is the control centre of everything we are and influences everything we think, say or do. The question which must be asked of all of us is: Who sits on the throne of my life? Who is my boss? Who holds the final vote in any decision that I make? I believe that there can only be one of two answers. The right answer should be the shepherd, but the alternate choice is me. Who is the boss of my life? Is it the shepherd or is it me? Is it his way or my way? There are only two choices.

Alexander is almost two years old as I write this letter to you Kelly. I know that you have been discovering over these past couple of months that he, like every other child in the world, was born self-centred. Although the Lord our shepherd knows Alex and holds considerable influence in his life, Alex doesn't know the shepherd. It may be a few years before he begins to understand that there is a God who wants to sit on the throne in the control room of his life.

You are seeing evidences of his self-centeredness as he begins to talk. Like every other two year old, among the first words he has learned are "no" and "mine." Somebody wrote these ten laws that toddlers live by:

1. If I like it, it's mine.
2. If it's in my hand, it's mine.
3. If I can take it from you, it's mine.
4. If I had it a little while ago, it's mine.
5. If it's mine, it must never appear to be yours in any way.
6. If I'm doing or building something, all the pieces are mine.
7. If it looks just like mine, it's mine.
8. If I saw it first, it's mine.
9. If you are playing with something and you put it down, it automatically becomes mine.
10. If it's broken, it's yours.

One of your and Tom's most important jobs as parents, just as it was your mom's and my responsibility, is to teach your children about the good shepherd and the place that he must have in their lives. The reason it's so important is because without that teaching and training they will remain disconnected. You are the primary influencers in their lives. The best time to shape them and direct their pathway is during these first five years. I've been watching you and Tom as you've been parenting, nurturing and loving your children. You are doing a terrific job Honey, and I have no doubt that they will learn very early to make the Lord, their own personal shepherd.

A broken image

I KNOW THAT this concept of our being disconnected from our spiritual centre right from the time we are born, is a tough one for parents to grasp, but it is true. The sooner that all of us understand our dilemma and our need to be reconnected, the better off we will be on our journey. Our shepherd's intention has always been that life is a school. A school with its curriculum of learning to move us from self-centredness to shepherd-centredness. As we mature from grade to grade through the school of life and become more shepherd-centred, we slowly learn that self-centredness leads to dissatisfaction while shepherd-centredness leads to fulfillment.

Some people whom you may know Kelly, are thirty or forty years old and still have not discovered this key. They are still struggling to open the door to fulfillment in their life journey by focusing on themselves. They scream by their actions, "Look at me!", "Talk to me!", "See how smart I am!", "See what I own!" All the while fulfillment eludes them. What's happening in this picture? Why doesn't their key of self-centredness fit into the door and open the way to satisfaction?

A couple of years ago, as I was in the bathroom going through my morning ablutions, I opened the cabinet door and our hand mirror fell out. When it hit the ceramic tiled floor it broke. There were a few slivers of glass on the floor, but most of them, although shattered, remained intact within the plastic frame.

I looked at the dozens of broken pieces in my hand and saw myself. You can imagine the distorted picture in the mirror in front of me. The colour of my face was the same, but there were cracks and lines where none had been before. My left eye was off to one side, while the right one wasn't even in the frame. As I looked at the broken reflection, I saw in my mind's eye another picture of life. I saw that every person is broken in some way, just like my image in the mirror. If I were to try to fix my hair or shave my face using that distorted image, it would be a very difficult, if not impossible, assignment. We have a world of broken people, broken marriages, broken families, broken hearts and there is no whole human image for us to model ourselves after. Our heros are broken too. We even use the terminology, "We broke up," "She broke my heart," or "I'm broke." Everyone of us can relate to brokenness in some way.

When I talk about brokenness, Kelly, I am not referring to our physical bodies. With diet plans, health clubs, designer clothes, plastic surgery, hair implants and dyes, our bodies are looking better than ever. But the outside of our bodies denies our inner brokenness. Our souls are in bad shape and we need to be repaired.

As I said before, the primary key to unlocking the mystery of our life journey is understanding that we are all born disconnected from our centre and that everyone of us is dysfunctional at the very core of our being. Because this premise comes from the opposite side of so much of today's pop psychology (which declares: I am okay. I am number one. I am somebody. Me first), I need to underline this with a double red line! Yes we do have a purpose! We were created with a destiny! There is meaning to our lives! But before we can discover that purpose, destiny and meaning we have to get reconnected to our spiritual centres.

Communism didn't work

COMMUNISM LASTED ABOUT seventy years in the Soviet Union. It didn't work because it was built on a false foundation. A basic premise that Karl Marx held was that man is born good and honest. Marxists believed that it is only the self-centred philosophy of capitalism which perverts our innate goodness. Capitalism, according to Communist dogma, teaches and promotes selfishness; therefore if they could eradicate the satanic Capitalists and their twisted philosophy, mankind's inborn goodness would rise to the surface. Man would love his fellow man and all would be right and well with the world. The founders of the Communist belief system figured it would take about one generation to retrain the population by blocking out all communication from the perverted capitalistic nations, stopping the deluded teachings of religion and promoting the communistic precepts to all the people.

After a generation had passed, they expected that the natural good man and woman would arise and that all mankind would then work harmoniously in a system truly built for the common people. Peace and love would prevail. But history has proven the fathers of Communism wrong. Their philosophy collapsed because it was built on the faulty foundation which said that mankind is naturally good. They came to see that selfishness and corruption reared the same ugly head under Marxism as it has under every other system of government. They discovered after seventy years that mankind, rather than having a tendancy toward goodness and love, leans toward selfishness.

Why are we so selfish? Why do we want to do it my way? Why did Humpty Dumpty not obey his mother? How did mankind become so broken? And how can we get fixed? Who can we call to reconnect our spiritual centres? The answer Kelly, has already been given to us in Psalm Twenty-three; The Lord is my shepherd... he restores my soul. Before we look at the process of restoration and answer these large questions, we must go back in history to the place where we first went off track.

Back to the beginning again

WHAT HAPPENED TO our forefathers that broke us so badly? Once we've determined the cause, the cure will be more apparent. To help give us insight, we will look at the shepherd's handbook. The first book in the Bible is called Genesis, which simply means the Beginning. In the Genesis story, we are introduced to the beginning of mankind, the beginning of the world, the beginning of our brokenness and the beginning of our creator's solutions. I know that you know this story backward and forward Kelly, but I want to underline a few basic truths which will help me explain later how he restores my soul.

The plot line includes the introduction of God, the creation of our first parents, God's explanation of their children's destiny, the seduction of the serpent, Adam's and Eve's failure, their resultant brokenness of soul and God's solution to their crisis. Their story is our story.

Let's begin with Adam and Eve in the garden of delight, (that's what Eden means). Their first visits with their shepherd were instructional. He taught them: "Everything here is for your enjoyment. There's work for you to do and doing that work will bring you fulfillment. I've got a destiny for each of you and for your children, but you must follow my instructions. Rules are for your own good. They will protect you from evil and guide you in the life journey which I've prepared for you. The first rule is: don't eat from that tree over there, but all the other trees are good for food."

Fairly simple instructions we would think. Humpty Dumpty's mother thought her instructions were simple too. "Don't go up on the wall. I'm telling you this for your own good."

When you were a preschooler Kelly, your mom would say to you; "You can play in the yard, but don't go out on the street." When you were a teenager, we'd say, "As long as we know who your friends are and we know where you are, you can stay out until eleven o'clock at night, but call if you are going to be late for any reason. It's for your own safety. We give you rules because we love you!"

I suppose that a shepherd could tie his sheep up to a tether and they would never wander or disobey. Parents could lock their children in their bedrooms and they would have to stay put. And God could have done the same with Adam and Eve. He could have taken their privilege of choice away by not giving them a free will. If their souls had been tied to a giant tether or if they had been locked in their bedroom, Adam and Eve could not have chosen to reject their shepherd's counsel. They would have had to obey what they were instructed. They would have never strayed into dangerous territory and all of our destinies would have remained intact. But our creator chose otherwise. He gave us the right to choose and the wisdom to make wise choices. What more could we have asked?

Days passed, perhaps months, and it was going great. Adam and Eve were fulfilled in their assignments and in their relationship. They were totally in love. Nothing was hidden from each other or from their shepherd. They were naked and had no secrets. Every day the Lord their shepherd would visit his sheep. They would talk, laugh, learn and play together. Life could not have been more delightful or satisfying for Adam and Eve in the garden of delight.

The shining one

AND THEN ONE DAY everything changed. It happened on a warm, sunny afternoon when Adam and Eve were out on a stroll in their garden. Suddenly, a beautiful shining angel stood before Eve and spoke to her. Adam was standing silently by her side. "Do you see the succulent fruit growing on that tree over there? Doesn't it look delicious? Why don't you taste some of it?" Eve was very aware that the Lord had told her not to eat the fruit of that tree.

The shining one, the devil in disguise, was saying to the first woman,

"Why don't you just try the fruit? I think you'll like it. It looks delicious. Go ahead, eat the fruit. God's holding back the best from you."

The shining one may have said to you as a teenager Kelly, "If your parents really loved you, they'd let you do what you want. They wouldn't limit your freedom with all those silly rules." He has spoken to me from time to time, "If your shepherd really loved you, he wouldn't keep the things that you want away from you."

Eve was deceived. Because she believed the beautiful angel, she stepped over the line and it felt kind of good. I remember as a boy on the way to school that my friend and I crawled under a fence and stole some apples from a neighbour's tree. Apples never tasted so good as those stolen ones, so I understand Eve's enthusiasm as she talked to her husband about what she had done.

Adam, who was with Eve, was not deceived. He knew it was wrong, but he ate the fruit anyway.

A memory from my past

WHEN I WAS FIVE years old I had a friend named Jerry. If you can believe it, I was a good boy, but my friend was trouble. One day, as Jerry and I were walking up Twentieth Street on our way to kindergarten, he turned to me and smiled. There was a big pile of sand on the corner where a house was being built. The sun was warm and the sky was blue. Jerry turned to me and said with a sly grin, "Let's not go to kindergarten today. Let's stay here and play in the sand."

I was shocked at the suggestion and replied, "Are you kidding? My Mommy would spank me if I didn't go to kindergarten."

He said something that had never crossed my mind before. "She won't ever find out. We'll play here for the morning and when Michael and Billy walk past us on their way home from kindergarten, we'll go home. Your mom will never know the difference."

I don't remember if it was a rush from my early wild side or Jerry's intimidation, but I did what he suggested. We had a wonderful time and when the other kids came by, we simply brushed off the sand and walked home. It was the perfect plan. I can still remember walking into the kitchen and in my best form, yelling "Hi mom, I'm home." Your grandma was in the dining room vacuuming when I arrived. She called me in and turned off the vacuum.

"How was kindergarten Barry?" she asked. I didn't realize that she was giving me an opportunity to confess and say that I was sorry.

"It was a good day mom," I lied, "Mrs. Jacks was in one of her funny moods again."

Having failed to get the response that she wanted with her first approach, she tried again, but less subtly, "You didn't go to kindergarten, did you Barry?" Red faced, but knowing that she had been home with my three younger siblings and that she couldn't possibly have seen me, I blurted, "Yes I did." That's when my doom was finally sealed.

"Mrs. Jacks called, Barry. She told me that you weren't at kindergarten today!"

In a few moments, my red face matched my red bottom and I learned the first of many lessons on the virtues of obedience and honesty. I don't remember if Jerry got away with his crime or not. For his sake I hope that he didn't. Only at the point when we understand that we really are broken and off centre, will we begin to take steps toward wholeness and centeredness. The sooner that Jerry and I were taught this life principle the better off we were.

Everything changed

AND SO IT WAS with Adam and Eve. After they ate the fruit, which their shepherd had forbidden, everything changed forever. We pick up the story shortly after their disobedience, when the Lord came by for his regular afternoon visit. It was evident that things were different that day, because instead of Adam rushing out to meet the Lord he was nowhere to be found. He was hiding.

"Adam? Adam, where are you?" the Lord called. Like my mom did to me when I lied to her about going to kindergarten, the shepherd was giving his wayward sheep an open door through which he could return back to the right path. If Adam had just come out of hiding, admitted that he had broken the rules and been truly sorry, there would have been immediate forgiveness. I know the shepherd. He loves to forgive.

The fig leaf dress

BUT ADAM DIDN'T confess or apologize and there was another hint of what was going on inside Adam's soul. When Adam ultimately did come out of hiding, he was covered in a fig leaf dress. Who was now on the throne of Adam's and Eve's souls? In the beginning, Adam and Eve had been created God-centred. Now they had become self-centred.

When I think about our centres, a picture comes to mind of a bicycle wheel. In a bicycle wheel there are three main parts - the axle, spokes and rim with a rubber tire. A wheel that is built according to plan will successfully roll along and take the cyclist wherever he intends to ride.

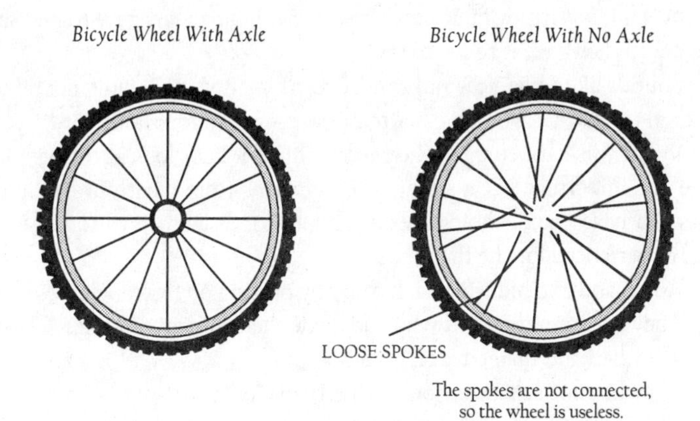

The spokes are not connected, so the wheel is useless.

Kelly, think of the wheel as your life. When the axle, spokes and rim are all in their proper places, then your life can roll purposefully along and go where it is supposed to go. That is my view of a successful life. Now when you picture the wheel, imagine that the axle, which represents God, is missing. With no axle the wheel cannot be connected to the bicycle and therefore the bicycle cannot go where it is supposed to go. Here's a picture of the wheel with a rim and disconnected spokes. Obviously it cannot be a successful wheel without an axle at its centre.

Adam and Eve are the parents of all of us. When they chose to disobey their creator, they disconnected themselves from their centre. Rather than remain God-centred as we were all intended, they chose to be self-centred. By choosing their own way rather than God's way, our ancestors cut out the axle of their lives. They were no longer God-conscious, but became instead self-conscious. Watch what happened right after they removed God from the centre of their lives.

After Adam finally crawled out of hiding clothed in his fig leaf dress, the Lord gently addressed him again. "What's going on here Adam? Obviously, something pretty serious has happened!"

Adam replied, "I heard you walking in the garden and I was afraid so I hid myself."

"Did you eat from the tree that I told you not to eat from Adam?" the Lord asked, gently giving Adam another opportunity to confess and say that he was sorry.

"Well it wasn't my fault Lord. It was that woman you gave to me. She ate it and then gave it to me to try."

Sounds like a five-year-old child, doesn't it? "It was her fault, not mine. And on top of that, you gave her to me so it's really your fault Lord."

What was happening in the garden of Eden? Let's look at the big picture. It's important because the reverberations from what our first parents did have been echoing throughout history, right up to today. Fear was experienced for the first time.

Adam and Eve hid from each other by putting on fig leaf clothes.

They hid from the Lord who had made them and loved them.

They lied and blamed each other.

They became self-conscious rather than God-conscious.

The axle had been removed from the wheel and it was therefore no longer able to fulfil the purpose for which it had been made. Unfortunately for Adam and Eve, as well as for us, the story gets worse before it gets better. The Lord turned to Eve to ask her what the facts were, but she had already picked up on Adam's tune. "It's not my fault. The shining one told me to eat the fruit. It's all his fault!"

And so it has gone on for thousands of years. "It's not my fault. It's somebody else's. I'm just an innocent victim!" We've learned from Adam to pass the buck. We're so self-conscious, it seems to us that we would die if we were to take responsibility for our own choices. So we keep blaming others. It's the government's fault. It's my parent's. It's society's. It's God's. It's anybody's fault but my own.

Now what does the shepherd do?

WE, LIKE HUMPTY, have fallen and are broken on the inside. Following through with the bicycle wheel analogy, when the axle is gone, there is nothing to connect the spokes to any longer. The spokes can be compared to various dimensions of our life - our time, money, leisure, work, marriage, family, relationships, sex life, recreation, spiritual life etc. Like spokes which are disconnected from their centre axle, every part of us suffers when we become disconnected from our rightful centre.

All of us were made to be shepherd-centred, like a bicycle wheel is made to be axle-centred. With our centre gone, there is an emptiness on the inside, which can never be filled by anything except by God himself. That's how we were made. Business success, fame, money, loving relationships, pleasure, good looks, self-esteem are each wonderful, but they will all fall short of satisfying the emptiness that is in the depth of our disconnected souls.

We need repair. We need to be restored and that's what the shepherd immediately set out to do. He laid out the plan of restoration for all of us when he challenged Adam and Eve to first of all admit their failure, and secondly to turn back onto the right path. Here again in Psalm Twenty-three, the shepherd underlines his willingness and ability to restore our broken souls. He makes a positive promise to his sheep; He restores my soul.

Why are you cast down?

AS A SHEPHERD, David was very familiar with one of the plights that every sheep faces. He writes about it in another psalm when he asks, "Why are you cast down, oh my soul?"

Being cast down is a sheep's worst nightmare. It often happens when the sheep is least expecting it. On a warm summer afternoon, a well-filled sheep lies down on the soft grass for a snooze. He wriggles on his side trying to find a comfortable resting place and before he knows what has happened, his body begins to roll over into a low spot in the pasture. Unable to stop himself, his well-rounded body turns upside down into the depression. He is what the shepherd calls, cast down.

Unlike a horse or a bull, which can kick his heavy legs until it has righted himself again, a sheep has relatively small legs and cannot turn himself back upright. Rather, the more he kicks, the deeper he works himself into the hollow. Unless he is rescued by his watchful shepherd, a cast down sheep will die.

My old shepherd friend told me that sheep often get themselves into this deathly position and this is one of the main reasons why they need constant care. That's why David chose sheep as an analogy of humankind.

We, like sheep, were never intended to live life without an intimate connection with our shepherd. Think of a man lying on a hospital bed hooked up to a kidney machine. His life-blood is flowing through the machine in order to be purified and ready for use. Now, as horrible as it is to imagine, think of an evil enemy coming alongside and unplugging the kidney machine. If no one were around to help that man on the unplugged life-support system, he would eventually die. It may take an hour or a few days, but he's in the process of dying. He needs to be plugged in, in order to stay alive.

That's the way we were made also, Kelly. We were created to be plugged in to God, our shepherd. When the plug was pulled out because of Adam's and Eve's disobedience, humankind began to die. We desperately need an outside, transcendent force to help us get plugged into our life source again.

On the sheepfold, a cast down sheep is easy prey for a cougar, bear or coyote. So are we when we are cast down in our souls. We are open to all kinds of attacks from the enemies of our soul. Our intangible inner person, which is our soul, is much more vulnerable to attack than our body is. The author of the couplet, Sticks and stones will break my bones, but names will never hurt me, was wrong. In addition to our willfulness, every one of us has been damaged in our souls by careless name calling, slanderous comments, gossip, lies, putdowns, shame, anger, fear, broken promises or rejection. We've all felt the pain and brokenness from both direct and indirect assaults on our souls. There is nothing quite so painful as a broken heart or soul. Thankfully, our shepherd understands what a broken or bruised soul feels like and so he is always on the look out for hurting sheep.

He makes us new again

THE STORY IS TOLD of a shepherd who had a hundred sheep. As he was counting them he noticed that one was missing, so he left the ninety-nine sheep and searched for the one which was lost. Just like the one cast down sheep is at the heart of the loving shepherd, so the shepherd of our souls is looking to restore cast down people.

When the shepherd finds a cast down sheep, he immediately rolls it over. Then straddling the bawling animal, he rubs its legs to restore their circulation. Meanwhile, the shepherd speaks gentle, loving and encouraging words to the sheep. That's how he restores its soul.

Note the verb *restores*, Kelly. The word means, to renew; to bring back into existence or use; to bring back or put back into a former, original state. The tense of the phrase, he restores my soul, is present progressive, which tells us the process is happening now and it's also ongoing. There is a beginning point and an ongoing process.*

After the first critical encounter with the shepherd, the process of restoration continues throughout our life. Every part of David's psalm describes a part of this life process. In our life journeys, the green pastures, quiet waters and right paths are all vital to our soul's restoration. Every day our shepherd purposefully leads us into situations, conversations and experiences, which are intended by him to be part of our restoration process. It may be a time when we are freed to rest in green pastures, an encouraging word from a co-worker which comes like cool water on a hot day, or an adjustment in our life direction onto a new path.

I just returned from a breakfast meeting, which came about because an old acquaintance crossed my path by chance a couple of weeks ago. The meeting could well have a life changing influence on the future plans of our church. All the circumstances of my life, as well as the lives of the men I met with, have been momentarily intertwined by our shepherd for a larger purpose. In the process, each of us will have our visions clarified, our characters sharpened and our pathways illuminated - all parts of the process of restoring our souls.

I'll write to you in the next four letters about how our shepherd specifically uses the shadows of death, his rod and staff, and the presence of our enemies for the purpose of restoring our souls. There is a long, challenging road ahead of us Kelly, but in order to successfully fulfill our destiny we need to be restored again. We must become shepherd-centred and we cannot do this independently from the shepherd's help. All the king's horses and all the king's men cannot put us together again. It will take the King himself to restore our souls to wholeness.

There remains one final thought before we move into the heart of David's thesis. We've learned from both Adam's and David's stories that sheep cannot survive without the shepherd, but we'll also see that the shepherd will not restore our souls without our cooperation. He will not violate the free wills which he has chosen to give to each of us. Let me explain with a story.

The violin, the bow and the violinist

A FEW YEARS AGO I had the pleasure of officiating at the wedding of your sister, Kristy and her husband, Jeremy. In your wedding ceremony Kelly, I used the garden metaphor, but because Kristy is a musician, you'll remember that I used a musical metaphor in their wedding ceremony. I described a violin and its bow, and explained that neither one without the other was intended to be complete in itself. Even though the violin and the bow were each made to be different and are two independent pieces, their creator crafted each of them to be complimented by the other. Unless a violin and its bow were positioned in the master's hands and skilfully played together, the two instruments would lie on the shelf forever and never fulfill their joint destiny. The violin and bow serve as metaphors for the husband and wife in a God-centred marriage, but also illustrate the harmony that our shepherd intends for each of us to enjoy in our personal life journey. Think of the bow as representing your life choices and direction, and the violin as God's plan and purpose for your life. When they both are submitted to the touch of the shepherd's loving and skillful hands, the harmonious music which results will bring joy, health and peace to all who hear it!

Let the music play on Kelly! May you and your family continue to enjoy harmony in your souls as you and the shepherd work in concert throughout your life journey. There will be moments of disharmony along the way, as you are learning to understand and submit to his plan, but the final health in your soul that will result from diligent practice will be well worth the effort!

Love Dad

* In our Christian faith, we have words for that beginning experience such as being born again, becoming a believer or being saved. I have written a booklet as an addendum to Life Journey which explains how to navigate this crucial intersection of life. It is called Life Centre and is available by writing to the address listed on the back page.

CHAPTER SIX

The Right Path

He guides me in paths of righteousness for his name's sake.

THE LORD, OUR shepherd, guides each of us down a uniquely prepared pathway toward our destiny. Our daily choices lay between following that right path or digressing from it. The consequences will either be enjoying or missing out on the opportunities and challenges prepared for us along the way.

Dear Kelly,

You were on the platform with me awhile ago, when I was honored with a gold watch commemorating twenty years of service as the founder and senior pastor of our church. Nobody knew this, but as one of our board members was presenting the gift to me, my mind was fast forwarding twenty years into the future. I could see myself passing my engraved watch onto one of my grandchildren one day. The reason that I was thinking of my grandsons is because, as much as I love my career as pastor, I value my position as a dad and papa even higher.

The greatest responsibility that God has entrusted to me has been to guide you and Kristy on the right path for your own life journeys. That privilege ranks higher than any other work that I have done in my life, and it always will. This letter is about that subject, the right path. When David wrote; *He guides me in the path of righteousness*, he simply meant that our shepherd's job is to guide us on the right pathway throughout our lives. As a father, I see my job as an under shepherd. I am working under the oversight of my shepherd to help Kristy and you walk down the path that has been uniquely prepared for each of you. You and Tom have the same assignment for your children. To me, there is no greater privilege or responsibility in life.

In Psalm Twenty-three each word is full of meaning and has value. However, this sentence; He leads me in the right path, is the very heart of the entire psalm. In this letter to you I'll lay out the implications of the shepherd's leading you for your personal life journey. I'll explain how following that specially prepared pathway, as difficult as it may be at times, will ultimately serve you best. In contrast to that, you'll see how digressing from that pathway can defer and even stop you from fulfilling your intended destiny.

The path of righteousness

THE RAW FACT of life Kelly, is that most people throughout history have been pretty messed up. Our forefathers have infected the entire population with their brokenness, and we are doing the same as they have done. We live in a world of broken people, broken families, broken international relationships, broken economics, broken justice system, and broken environment.

In the same way as Humpty Dumpty's shell was broken beyond repair after he fell, so was all of mankind. Our fall broke us through and through, and as it was in Humpty's case, only the King himself can restore us to our original whole state. Some of us feel that our souls have been so badly cracked or broken that nothing could ever repair us. The truth is however, that our shepherd offers to not only repair us, but to give us a brand new start on our journey.

I wrote to you earlier about how the shepherd repairs our broken souls. The verb tense that David chose to use is significant; He restores my soul. The word *restores* is a present, active, progressive verb which tells us that there is a continuous process that has been going on, is still going on, and will continue to go on as long as we live. We are in restoration mode.

Our good shepherd promotes this restoration process by preparing a special pathway for every person. Before you were even born Kelly, he already knew the place and circumstances of your birth, and the personal obstacles and privileges of your upbringing. Therefore he paved an individual pathway, with experiences and stopping places along the way, designed to facilitate your personal healing, and to prepare you for your ultimate purpose. This process of restoration is different for each of us. Each of our lives has been exclusively designed by our shepherd to accommodate our unique needs and idiosyncrasies.

This pathway which he leads us on is simply called the path of righteousness by the psalmist. Righteousness is the state of being right, so therefore the path that he describes is simply the right path for us. It's the way our lives were intended to go according to the shepherd's master plan for humanity. Although all of mankind is on a similar type of journey; the route, terrain and experiences we enjoy or dread along the way will be unique for each of us. While on the road to that predetermined destiny, there are myriads of choices for us to make.

Let me explain with an example. Before either of us were married, your Uncle Dave and I travelled across the Atlantic Ocean on a passenger ship, the SS. Carinthia, from Montreal to Liverpool. Each passenger and crew member on the large ship was on the same journey, headed for the same destination. However, during the overall voyage, each person had a distinct schedule with their own daily choices and responsibilities. The captain, cooks, purser and passengers each had their reasons for taking the trip. They had their specific daily tasks they wanted to accomplish throughout the ship and they were often unaware of one another during the day. Even Uncle Dave and I made many different choices during the six day journey across the Atlantic Ocean. He loved playing shuffleboard and tennis, while I preferred the library and the theatre. Although all of our paths went in many directions, the ship kept on sailing forward toward its intended destination under the captain's orders.

So it is with us. We are all participants in this journey called life. From birth to death, the pathways that we choose are our own. Like on the ship that we took to England, even though the direction of the journey was predetermined, there was still freedom for every person on that cruise to make a thousand personal choices each day. Of course every choice that we made was followed by a natural consequence.

The first half of life

WHEN I THINK about pathways, two memories come to mind, which will help me to explain to you Kelly, my understanding of life. The first memory is from a trip that I took with your mom three years ago. We were driving from the flatlands of Saskatchewan, over the Rocky Mountains, back to our home in Coquitlam. We began our eighteen hour journey early in the morning as the sun was just rising. The prairies were flat as far as the eye could see. The road skipped easily over the flatlands and it seemed that we could have driven our Oldsmobile in any direction we wanted to without difficulty. A new road could have easily been made wherever we chose to travel.

I've often thought of how those flatlands in Saskatchewan could be compared to the early adulthood stage of our lives. It's where you and Tom are now on your life journey. I remember how wide the opportunities were before me when I was in my teens and twenties. In those years of early adulthood, I believed that I could do almost anything. There seemed to be no obstacles before me. If I were a diligent student, willing to put in the time, effort and money, I could have been a doctor or a dentist. If I had liked the outdoors, I could have trained as a fireman or a farmer. If I hadn't wanted to work, I could have chosen to sleep all day and party all night until my limited resources ran out. At that point in my life, I felt like I was the master of my own destiny. I could do what I wanted to do when I wanted to do it.

Reflecting back on that car ride across the prairies, I remember how by mid-morning as we approached Calgary, I could see in the far horizon ahead the beginning growth of tiny foothills. From that distance of fifty to sixty miles, they seemed as if they were only one or two feet high. Those little hills remind me of when I was in my thirties. At that stage of my life journey, I began to see that there really would be an end to my journey some day. Little obstacles, like those miniature mountains ahead of us dotted my personal horizon. My grandparents' dying, increasing financial pressures, growing family responsibilities and a few failures along the way, led me to the realization that not only was life serious and challenging, but also that it would not go on forever.

As we travelled closer toward the foothills, they seemed to be growing into actual mountains. Within a couple of hours, the Rockies loomed in the path directly before our Oldsmobile. From my perspective they seemed to be impassable. I think of those enormous mountains as the dark mid-life years that we often experience at about forty to fifty years of age. In this stage of our journey, we sometimes feel as if the die has been cast; the road has been laid. Many of our choices are seemingly over and we see ourselves doomed to a grey life of mediocrity for the rest of our days. Like the Rockies which loomed before our car, we feel because the end is in sight that our personal freedom is fading fast. Many people, whom we both know Kelly, have made foolish grasps to regain their youth at this point. They dye their hair, nip and tuck their sagging bodies, buy youthful clothes and a peppy sports car to try to slow the process, but life keeps moving forward.

The second half of our life journey

I REMEMBER GETTING closer and closer to the impenetrable Rocky Mountains. They were directly in front of us blocking our path. Sometimes, during our midlife or menopause season, it seems like the good days are behind us, while only weakness and loss lie ahead. The truth is that when it seems like the journey is all but over, the best is yet to come in the second half of our life journey.

On our trip, just when we thought that the road would end and that our path would be blocked by the mountains, hope reappeared. A narrow path began to come slowly into focus. What we might have seen as the end of our journey, had now become a gateway to a wider world, better than we could have possibly imagined. The opening in the Rockies, called Kicking Horse Pass, which leads to the world famous Lake Louise, are symbolic to me. Life does get better after fifty. The mid-life obstacles are not the end of the journey after all, but are instead the beginning of a new chapter in our life story.

One can only imagine what the early pioneers thought as they crossed the crest of the Rockies and saw the western side of our continent for the first time; land that is now California, Oregon, Washington, British Columbia, and the beautiful Pacific Ocean. What an exciting adventure it is Kelly, that awaits those who persevere in the last half of their life journey.

Life is like a game of football

A GOOD ANALOGY to further explain this second stage of our life journey is a football game. Your husband Tom will relate to this one. In the first half of the game, the team does its best to gain a few points on their opponents. Yet when half time comes, regardless of whether they are ahead or behind, it's time for a new strategy. The coach has carefully observed and analyzed his own team's strengths and weaknesses, as well as their opponent's. He draws out the game plan for his team, encourages and sends them out to win the last half. During the second half, although the team's strength has diminished, their wisdom has increased with experience, so therefore strategy becomes the key to success. How the last half of the game is played determines whether they are ultimately successful or not.

Attitude and wisdom, as well as effort, become the deciding factors.

Having passed the fifty marker in my own life a few years ago, I've seen the other side of the mountains. If my friends from the prairies will forgive me, it's the most beautiful part of the journey so far! In the second half of life, it's not going to be our youthful good looks, amazing flexibility and unbounded zeal that gets us to the finish line. It's going to be knowing who we are, why we are here and where we are headed that spurs us onward to finish our journey successfully.

The road you are travelling on in your life journey Kelly, will not be the same as mine or anyone else's, but there will be some similarities. You too will go through various passages along your journey; the excitement and freedom of early adulthood; the dawning understanding of possible obstacles in the future, as you move through your thirties; the frightening emotional turmoil of finding purpose in your mid-life years; and the joy of discovering the wonders which await you in the second half of your life. Kelly, you will experience each stage as you are led down the right path by your shepherd. Knowing what lies ahead helps us to get through those difficult passages; and certainly knowing who you are, why you're here, and where you are headed, will also help keep you on the right path.

The musings of a dreamer

THE SECOND MEMORY that comes to mind, which has helped me understand life, is of a dream that I had in the fall of 1996. This dream was very personal to me, but sharing it will help illustrate the concept of a right path. It will also introduce the idea of a personal destiny, which I'll write about in a future letter.

Normally Kelly, my dreams seem to come as I'm falling asleep or just before waking up in the morning, but this time it was in the dark of the night. Suddenly in my sleep, I was fully aware of a picture in front of me. The picture was like a slide projected on a screen, maybe six feet square. The scene which appeared in my dream, I had seen before on flights over the Coast Mountain Range, on the British Columbia side of the Rockies. In the picture, there were tall evergreen trees everywhere with logging roads like bunny trails, winding throughout. The terrain was very hilly, like goose bumps on freezing skin. There were a few snowcaps on the higher mountain peaks. You and Tom have flown several times over the mountains of Washington, Oregon and British Columbia and so you know the scene I am describing. Just before the vividness of the picture woke me up, I was very aware of these words which were emblazoned in neon white across the screen; *Stick close!. I've been this way before.*

I didn't understand the meaning immediately, but I jumped out of bed wide awake, drew the scene the best I could and wrote down any thoughts I had so that I wouldn't forget its message. I've thought about that picture many times since that memorable October night. I, like you, am on a journey, travelling down a road which has never been travelled before. There have been times when it would have been so easy for me to think that I were lost or that there were no design or destination to my path; but the message to me in my dream was that my shepherd knows exactly where I am at all times. I have never been out of his sight. He knows exactly where I have come from, where I am now and where I am headed. There is a design, a destiny and a right path for me, just as there is for your life.

Stick close! I've been this way before.

I told a few friends about my dream, one of whom owns an international map-making company. Bryan's office has impressive state-of-the-art computers, which help design roads through uncharted areas for logging companies and government agencies. He presented me with a large picture taken over our British Columbia interior, which almost exactly replicates my vision. I have it hanging on my office wall as a reminder of the promise of my shepherd. He knows where I am going and how I will get there.

While the interpretation of my dream is very personal to me, the general picture is applicable to everyone. Our shepherd knows each of his sheep, and he has a plan for every one of us; Stick close. He's been this way before. Sometimes the road is a super highway and there's no stopping us as we speed down life's freeway. Other times it's a winding side road which seems like a detour. Then there are the days and months when we seem to lose sight of the trail all together and we feel like we are lost.

Kelly, neither you nor I have any idea of what you and Tom will experience in the years ahead of you, but I am sure of this: Your shepherd has promised that he will always be right beside you, as well as ahead of you and behind you. You and your family are in good hands as long as you stick close to him. He's seen your tomorrow already and has the right path for you already prepared. It's going to be a wonderful and fulfilling journey each step of the way. There will be some obstacles. You can be guaranteed of that, but on the other side of each obstacle is added wisdom and promise.

On a plane to Cincinnati

A SHORT TIME after I had that dream in the fall of 1996, your mom and I were on a flight from Seattle going to Cincinnati. Somewhere over the hills of Yellowstone Park, as I was looking out the window, I could see the thickly blanketed trees below, just like in my dream. There were thin lines, probably hiking trails, which wound throughout the park. I put my imagination to work and pictured a hiker standing a hundred feet off the main trail. He was lost and had no idea that he was so close to the trail that he had wandered away from. All he could see from his perspective were towering trees looming on every side of him. Every way the hiker looked seemed to be the same. Adding to his anxiety were the lengthening shadows of the setting sun and the crying of animals in the distance. The hiker in my imagination was lost and frightened. I could feel his hopelessness. Would he ever find his way back to the well marked trail?

From my perspective, thirty-five thousand feet above the hills of Yellowstone Park, I knew exactly where the trail was which would lead him back to homebase. It wasn't very far from where he stood. He wasn't lost at all from where I sat. If only we had some way of communicating, then I could easily guide him back to the safety of the trail.

Thinking again of my dream, I thought how similar this all was to the way it is with my shepherd and me. He sits above time and space. He knows exactly where I am at any given moment, where I should be and how I should get there. All I need to do is stick close because he's been this way before. In another letter, I'll explain the way he communicates with us and how we can communicate with him.

From time to time Kelly, as we walk down the path of life, we wonder: Am I headed in the right direction? How did I stray from the main road? Can I find my way back again? Am I going to make it through the maze of trees which seem to be blocking my way? Where am I going, anyway?

These two memories help to remind us that there is a right path for each of us. Although that path may be difficult for us at times, our shepherd knows the way that we should go. He not only knows the right way, but he is constantly there to guide us through the frightening passages, to encourage us when we feel we are lost, and to provide us with enough strength and wisdom to help get us back onto the right path again if we have wandered off.

People are a lot like sheep

THIS SIMPLE STATEMENT by David; He guides me in the path of righteousness, was reflective of his own experiences as a shepherd. He had led his sheep down enough paths to know that they were both willful and stubborn. Not only do sheep have minds of their own, but the minds that they do have are not particularly bright. They often get themselves into life threatening messes because of their many poor choices. David understood sheep and that's probably why he wrote this psalm with them in mind.

Sheep are creatures of habit and because of that, they often make the same mistakes that they may have succumbed to only hours before. Like people, they easily fall into ruts which can be destructive to their own health and welfare. For example, sheep will graze in the same areas of pasture until they are ruined. They will eat the grass to the ground, walk about in their own manure and not have the sense to know when to move on. This causes devastation of pastures and it spreads disease from one animal to another. They not only destroy their environment, but they also destroy themselves in the process. That's why sheep are one type of creature who need to constantly be led by a shepherd. They require more care and guidance than any other animal, and if left to themselves, they will die. A good shepherd is always looking ahead for new green pastures. He keeps his sheep moving every day. Even the paths which they take under his leadership vary because of the sheep's tendency to form ruts as they walk from pasture to pasture. By changing courses regularly, even the sheep's waste products become fertilizer for future grass growth, rather than disease promoting cesspools. Wise shepherds know how to take even the negatives and turn them into positives.

Sheep can be compared to people because we also tend to make poor choices, which can be threatening to our soul's health. We return very easily to the well-worn ruts of our lives. This keeps us from discovering the newness that each day has to offer. The best choices that we can make at any point on our journey are to resist going our own way and to follow the shepherd where he is leading. He is a wise shepherd and knows the right path which will take us to greener and better pastures.

Getting out of the ruts of life

IN MY OWN LIFE journey, there have been a few memorable pivotal points when my shepherd has had to jar me out of my comfortable ruts. One rut was the familiarity that I had with lumber and building products when I was in my early twenties. My dad began taking me to his lumber yard before I was a teenager. He often talked about how he wanted his three sons to take over his building supply business. To follow in my dad's career footsteps would have been an easy path for me because handling lumber was second nature to me.

As honorable and profitable as your grandpa's business was Kelly, it was not the right path for me or for my brothers. The shepherd had a totally different path for each of us to take. In my case, he had a particularly forceful way of revealing his plan to me. On two occasions, which I will never forget, my shepherd pushed me around a new career corner.

The first time was very difficult for me emotionally, but at the same time it made my choice to leave the building supply business easier. I was fired from the lumber yard where I was working and I was forced to find another job! After a few months of searching and interviews, I ultimately took an office job. For the first time in my life, I began wearing a suit and tie to work. It was, for me, a frightening career change, but in retrospect it was one of the best moves of my life.

The second time that my shepherd jarred me out of my comfortable rut was after ten years in the business world. The job that I took after I was fired from the lumber yard was at Canadian Forest Products. Over the years that followed my career change, I became very familiar with the wholesale plywood industry and with managing staff. I thoroughly enjoyed all aspects of my job.

I knew though, especially in the last couple of years, that my shepherd was calling me around another sharp corner. The call to become a pastor had actually been shaping in my thinking for over a decade, but on July 1, 1980, I knew that the time had come. Again, financially and security-wise, the choice was difficult; but on the other hand because I knew it was right, the decision process flowed smoothly.

In each of those two pivotal points in my life Kelly, I needed my shepherd's guidance. If he had not pressed me those two times, I might still be piling lumber and packing cement today. My shepherd knew my future and my destiny better than I did. He knew the right path that would ultimately lead me to greener pasture on my life journey.

His name is at stake

THE MOST IMPORTANT job of any shepherd is to have a predetermined plan of rotation for his flock. It takes a large percentage of his time to properly prepare for the sheep's weekly journeys. The reason that he gives this job so much time is because his reputation as a good shepherd is at stake. David writes; He leads me in the right paths for his name's sake. The shepherd's name, like our names Kelly, is who he really is. I recall a very simple lesson, which your grandpa taught me while he was working in the garden. I was about ten years of age and I remember him snipping off a Black-eyed Susan and taking the flower in his hands. "Barry", he said, "this flower is like our lives. It's here for a short time, brings a lot of pleasure to people and then it dies. Every one of us makes out of our lives what we choose. Each choice that we make affects our life reputation. A good reputation takes a long time to form, just like this flower. From a tiny seed, it had to send down roots, develop a stem and leaves, and finally open up its petals. These yellow petals with a black centre is the flower's reputation. This is why it is named a Black-eyed Susan."

As he said that, my dad deliberately ripped off one of the petals, then another and another. He then said, "By removing these petals, I've just made three choices which have changed this flower forever. Notice how it has lost its original beauty. Now, say I change my mind and want the flower to be as it was before I made my three choices. Can I simply put the three petals back where they came from?" Of course my answer was, no. "And that," he said, "is like life. Some choices that we make affect our reputations forever."

The lesson was not lost to me. Even though the conversation took place over forty years ago, I remember it as if it were yesterday. Reputations are hard to come by, but easy to lose. A good name is like gold on our life journeys. Your own name, Kelly; our family name, Buzza; and the shepherd's name, Jehovah; are all on the line as you walk down the path of righteousness. In this psalm, David underlined the fact that the

Lord's name, as the shepherd, is at stake. This principle of maintaining our shepherd's good name is so important that it ranks as one of the Ten Commandments; You shall not take the name of the Lord your God in vain.

We may think that this precept refers only to our language and the way we verbally use the words, God or Jesus, but there is a deeper implication. By my saying; " I am a Christian", or "I am a follower of the good shepherd", or "I am a God-fearing person", I am identifying myself as a representative of his. Now everything I do, say and think, reflects on the good shepherd to those within my circle of influence. If I behave honourably, his name is respected; but if I behave dishonourably, his name is brought into reproach. We are, in effect, ambassadors on assignment on planet earth, living out the master plan of the great shepherd. No wonder he takes his job so seriously. Our shepherd has a right path for each of us, which when followed, will give us a good reputation as well as preserve the namesake of our shepherd. Your name, Kelly, which is your reputation, is invaluable and so is your shepherd's name. The way we live our lives; how closely we follow our shepherd's lead down the right path; and the attitudes with which we turn corners on the path; all have a profound effect on our names, as well as our shepherd's. A blemished name or reputation will greatly debilitate our success and our positive influence on those around us.

The shepherd has a plan and a purpose

FOR A SHEPHERD to fulfill his responsibility of leading his sheep well, he needs to have a keen awareness of the terrain: Where are the green pastures? Are they accessible? Are there clean, cool waters on the way? Is the journey dangerous? Are there wild animals nearby? How long will each day's journey take? Are the sheep ready for the change? Where will I lead them the following week? Where will they end up as the winter weather approaches? The shepherd must see not only the next few days ahead, but he must also have a strategy for several months in the future. Meanwhile, the sheep, confident in their shepherd's wisdom, simply need to follow where he leads.

Amazing as it seems, they don't even do that well. They still resist change and fall into old habit patterns easily. Even though they have experienced their shepherd's wise leadership and sense that he knows what he's doing, their stubbornness often pulls them back to their own ways. The shepherd must constantly watch out for sheep who lag behind or who try to make their own paths in unhealthy, dangerous places. No wonder people are often compared to sheep.

The most obvious examples that come to mind are those of us who have addictive personalities. Whether the addiction is pornography, alcohol, prescription drugs or gambling, I've seen far too many acquaintances fall back into patterns which they knew all too well were extremely destructive. I spoke with a beautiful young woman just last week, who has struggled for years with a cocaine addiction. She has seen how it has torn apart family relations, left her sleeping in a skid row gutter, led her into dangerous and illegal circumstances, and has all but destroyed her clarity of thinking. With the help of our Twelve Step program and a forgiving family, this young lady had shaken herself free of drugs for almost a year. Then last week, facing a challenging confrontation and decision, she turned back to her drug demon for the comfort which she knew it could not deliver. There she sat in my office, crying, shaking and wondering if she could pull herself out of it again. Addicts are not the only ones subject to falling into old habit patterns; you and I are too, Kelly. I have to discipline myself constantly to keep myself from wandering back into poor eating or sleeping habits, destructive thought patterns or ruts of unproductive speech.

A good example of this is how I have needed to discipline myself again in going to sleep earlier. I know that I function better on eight and a half to nine hours sleep. During the past four months, because of a demanding schedule, your mom and I have been getting to bed later and have only been getting about seven hours sleep. Through experience, I have come to realize that too little sleep affects my moods, my productivity and my health; and I know I could have countered it by going to bed earlier, but I didn't. Now I've reached the point where I am light headed, exhausted and easily attacked by germs, so I have been forced back to my right schedule. If I had been wise, I would have corrected the problem when the cycle was just beginning. I have ended up losing more time than I have gained because I stayed up far later than I should have every night.

A journey down the road of life

NOW KELLY, let's shift from the shepherd and sheep metaphor to a more suburban one. The principle remains the same; Our shepherd predetermines our destinies, and cares for, as well as guides, his sheep on the path which he prepares. In the picture that we have just looked at, we are the stubborn, habitual, happy-go-lucky sheep, whom our shepherd, the Lord, wants to lead to significance and success.

In another metaphor, more suitable to our suburban understanding, we will be the drivers on the road, which is our life journey. The Lord will be the travel agent, who lays out our daily travel agenda. When your mom and I are planning to take a vacation together, we usually make an appointment with the British Columbia Automobile Association. The agents there are extremely helpful in the forming of our travel plans. They provide the maps, show us the easiest and the most scenic routes, identify the places where we may want to stop along the way and point out a number of interesting tourist sites on the roads which we choose to take. By the time we leave their office, we have each day's journey all marked out with the number of miles to our destination and the time it will take to get there. This is like how our shepherd lays out your life journey map. He knows better than anyone, which paths are safe, which hold hidden dangers, where you will learn the most valuable life lessons, how long you should linger at a stop before moving on and even when to detour off the main road for a life changing alternate route.

Remember when your Uncle Dave and Auntie Carol played that game for each of your cousins' grade twelve graduations? Each time, David and Tanya, along with you and Kristy and their friends would go on a wild adventure. Auntie Carol would take weeks to plan the whole day extravaganza. She did the prep work of scouting out, in the greater Vancouver area, several fun places to see and things to do. Then they drew a map and made clues for you kids to figure out. You all had to follow a prescribed course, racking up points as you proceeded. At one stop on the journey, you had to park your cars and hop on a bus from one point to another. Money was provided in envelopes, which could only be opened upon arrival at the particular destination. When you got off the bus, you were directed to walk a number of blocks North, turn left and then proceed two blocks West, counting telephone poles as you walked. After lunch at McDonald's, you crossed the Burrard Inlet on the Seabus and ended up at Lonsdale Quay in North Vancouver. On each leg of the journey, you accumulated points by watching for certain signs or spotting particular items in defined stores. After a game of miniature golf, a few more food stops, and a round-about ride home, you arrived back at their house exhausted, but happy. That's when the winners with the most points received their prizes.

In the game, your Uncle Dave and Auntie Carol were the shepherds, predetermining the journey which you were going to take. That journey is a great example of the right path. It's a picture of all of us who walk down our personally designed pathway. Following or not following the directions and rules determines our success or failure. In the game, arriving home safely with the most accumulated earned points was the ultimate goal. For all of us travelling on our own life journey, our ultimate goal is to finish successfully, which is to fulfill our destiny to the best of our ability. We will arrive one day at the finish line and our points will be counted to see if we finished well or poorly, and to see if all that we have done has been worthwhile or worthless.

Following, is a simplified map of a typical life journey. Several observations from my own experiences will help give clarity to show you how this predetermined journey works.

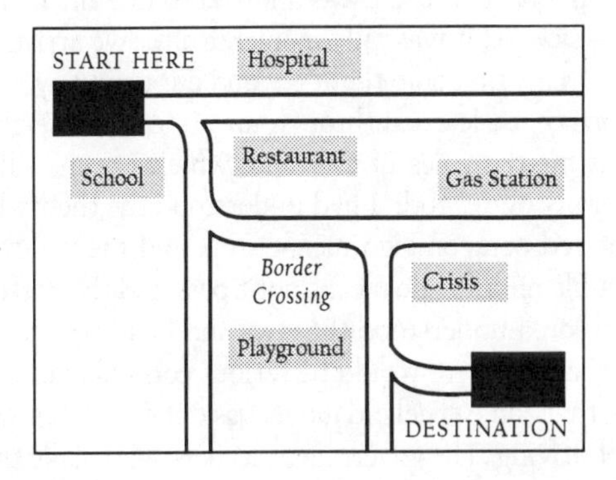

There are rules to follow

SOME OF US LOVE rules and some of us fight against them throughout our entire lives. You were an easy child to raise, Kelly. You wanted to know the rules and you were happy to stay within the parameters which we set for you. You have been a parent's dream, so I don't have to explain to you the value of rules. They exist to help us stay on the right path and to successfully complete the course ahead of us. Following the rules makes our life journey much easier and happier, but learning that concept often requires a few painful negative experiences.

When I was fifteen years old, the most important goal of my life was getting to my sixteen birthday, so that I could get my driver's license. In British Columbia, a teenager used to be allowed to get his learner's license sixty days before that milestone birthday so on December 22, 1962, I was in the long line-up to write my exam. I'd had the driver's education booklet memorized for the previous six months; I had already paid one hundred dollars for my 1952 BSA motorcycle; and it was all repainted and polished, sitting and waiting for me in our carport. That was all the incentive that I needed to be well prepared for the driver's examination.

First, the inspector tested my eyes for color blindness and distance perception, and then he tested my reflexes on a mock car chassis. The exam was multiple choice, based entirely on what I had been studying for months. It was a snap and I walked out of that office with my learner's permit in hand. My mom had driven me to the test, but I drove her home. Never again would I be driven anywhere by my mom. I was now a man - at least so I thought. Because I was allowed to ride my motorcycle with just a learner's license, it was only moments after we arrived home that I took off to go on my first solo flight beyond our driveway.

The lessons that I learned through my sixteenth to eighteenth years forever taught me the rules of the road, which I eventually discovered were there for my own good. I had understood the theory behind them. Of course the red octagon sign meant stop, and the yellow sign meant yield. The double middle line meant don't pass and the dotted line meant pass with caution. I understood the laws and I had been warned repeatedly to obey them or there would be serious consequences. Having rules did not mean that some cruel old judge was out to see if he could squeeze the fun out of driving. The government leaders who make the laws really have our best interests in mind.

For years before I got my license, there had been a back and forth battle of words between the courts and motorcyclists regarding mandatory use of helmets. In my young mind, there was no greater freedom then riding the back roads of our beautiful province in the warm summer sun with the wind blowing through my hair. I was willing to put up with the flies and the danger just to have the right to ride without a helmet on. After all, I reasoned, it was my skull I was risking. Shouldn't I have been allowed to decide for myself?

Nevertheless, the law had passed earlier that year, so for two months I had been grudgingly wearing my helmet. It just didn't seem fair - at least until that April morning of 1965, when my helmet saved my life. I was eighteen years of age when I had my first major motorcycle accident. I was going to work from the suburbs to Vancouver, travelling west on the Lougheed Highway. Maybe I was not as alert as I should have been early on that dark Saturday morning, but I don't think I could have stopped in time anyway. The man driving his car from the opposite direction turned a sharp left in front of me without even signalling. He obviously did not see me coming. At about fifty miles an hour I crashed head on into the side of his speeding Plymouth. My motorcycle folded underneath me and I shot like an arrow over his car, landing headfirst on the road beyond him. He drove off, intending never to be seen again and I lay bleeding in the middle of the road. Either people were in a hurry to get to work or they just didn't care about guys in black leather jackets, but no one stopped to help me. I had to drag myself and my badly wounded bike off to the side of the road. After I called my workplace, someone came by and drove me to the hospital.

We learn through struggle

THREE VALUABLE LESSONS were learned the hard way. One was to not only care for myself, but to watch out for the other guy also. The police later found the driver drinking at a nearby hotel. There was a large dent in the side of his car parked outside. The man told them that his car had been stolen; and because I couldn't identify him in a police line-up, he got away with no charges. Even though the other driver was totally at fault, caused me severe pain and cost me many dollars for motorcycle repairs, my shepherd actually used him to help me mature in my character. Of course the accident was not caused by or even planned by my shepherd, but he was aware of it long before it happened.

The second life lesson I learned from the seemingly negative experience was how to forgive someone even when they are totally wrong. My attitude after the accident determined whether the incident would promote my growth or hinder it.

And thirdly Kelly, I learned the value of rules and laws. Obeying them has served me well many times in life since that day. Laws and rules bring order to our lives. Order brings peace. The very rules that we resist are the same rules which allow us to drive our cars in safety and security. On the road there are signs to read, lines to stay within, rules of courtesy to keep and police officers to insure the laws are obeyed. The rules are there for our own good. Following them brings peace; breaking them leads to destruction. Thank God for the law which forced me to wear a motorcycle helmet against my will. My life journey almost ended at eighteen years of age when it should have been just beginning.

There are many rules which exist for the health of our souls, just as there are many rules for maintaining the health of our bodies. For our bodies' sake, we obey rules which pertain to our sleeping, eating and exercising habits. Rules for our souls' sake pertain to areas such as morality, virtue and piety. I hesitate listing a set of rules for our souls because there are so many, but we do find a summary statement in the Bible, which encompasses all of the rules for maintaining the health of our souls. Jesus was the one who said; "You shall love the Lord your God with all your heart, and with all your soul, and with all your strength, and with all your mind; and your neighbor as yourself." He further taught; "Do this and you shall live." The antithesis of his statement is that if we don't follow the above rules, we won't enjoy the health which we were intended to have in our souls.

Stopping places along the journey

ON THE LIFE journey map, you probably noticed several stopping places along the way. Each of them has been designed by the shepherd to either keep us on track or to press us back on track when we have wandered off the right path.

Our family has taken many trips together and we have experienced the benefits of each of these stopping places. Remember our long drives to California? We enjoyed lunch breaks, bathroom stops, shopping adventures, beach times and refuelling stops. We have also seen or experienced flat tires, accidents, road repairs and engine breakdowns on our journey. On the diagram, notice that I've drawn a few of the different places along our life journey where stopping is important.

You'll see a school, which represents places in our life where we learn; a gas station, which represents places where our energy is refuelled and we are encouraged to go forward; a hospital, which symbolizes those stops in life where we are healed, either in body or soul; a playground, which is a place of rest, fun and refreshment; a crisis point, which often becomes a boundary event that forces us to turn a corner in life. There can be good crises, such as getting married or having a baby; or bad crises, such as contracting a serious illness or having an accident. Each stop serves a useful purpose in our character growth. You'll see a restaurant, which represents the daily nourishment we need in our souls, such as loving friends or family, or even a good book. Of course the ultimate stop is death. Even that becomes a doorway to a greater hope than any of us can fathom.

Let's consider each of these stopping places. In a previous letter Kelly, I referred to your sovereign foundations. You did not have any choices regarding your mom and I being your parents, being born in Canada, speaking English as your first language, having blonde hair, having a phlegmatic temperament, being highly intelligent or growing to be five foot four. Those were sovereignly assigned to you at your conception. Like you, each person has a personal sovereign foundation. My belief is that our shepherd has uniquely designed even our prenatal histories. Although he doesn't cause certain things to happen, such as alcoholic parents, birth defects or unplanned pregnancies; he uses all these things for good later on in our life journey. I'll come back to this subject when we cover; *He anoints my head with oil.*

Schools, gas stations and playgrounds

SCHOOLS ARE A LIFE-LONG part of our journey. We can learn every day, from every person we meet and every circumstance we encounter. I love to watch young children and listen to what they teach. Terry, one of my associates, told me a story about his four year old son. One day, he was hiking with his son through the woods. Brody watched his dad carefully as he took each step. Terry didn't realize how strong his influence was until they came to a fork in the path. They stopped and wondered out loud which way to go. In his youthful innocence, Brody looked up at his dad and said, "You choose the best way to go dad, but remember I'm right behind you." The lesson is one to note for every one of us who is a parent. If we're listening, we can learn life lessons from anyone.

Restaurants and gas stations are the stopping points where we get refuelled. Whether it's dinner time, a vacation, seminar or church, there must be the green pastures in our lives when we take something in so that we have something to give out. Our bodies, souls and spirits need to be regularly nourished to help us stay on the right path.

Playgrounds are not just for children. Every one of us needs play times because they bring refreshing. Fly a kite, build a sand castle, have a party, pick daisies or write poetry. God gave us one in seven days for a rest-from-work time, but every day should have its sabbath moments. Kelly, I know how you love to put together decorative photo albums. Those are valuable hours, not only for your family memories, but also for your soul's health.

Serendipitous experiences

YOU HAVE HEARD of the word serendipity, but I'll tell you the story of how it was derived. Serendipities refers to those important times in our lives that happen by the way. We don't plan on them. They are lying along the side of life's path and we will never discover them if we don't stop to play.

In the ancient fable, the king of the Serendip Empire called his chosen men to his side. He commissioned them to find an old palace treasure that had been stolen and hidden many years before. His men began their journey stopping at many places along the way to ask for directions or to rest. The discoveries that each soldier made on the way to his destination, such as learning how to weave a cloth, rescuing a child from a lion's clutches, falling in love with a beautiful maiden and hearing ocean sounds in a sea shell, were called serendipities. The ultimate lesson that the king's men learned was that the real joy is in the journey. How many of us rush down the highway of life so quickly that we fail to experience the joys of a playground?

I mentioned earlier about the vacation that Uncle Dave and I took in Europe when I was nineteen. We travelled on our motorcycles through several countries and gathered some of our most valued life memories together. The best thing that happened to me that summer was a serendipity experience at the train station when we were leaving for our trip. That was when I met a pretty young teenager named Susan, who later became my wife and your mom. If I had not planned that vacation and had not been at that train station on that day, my life may have been a totally different story and you might not be reading this letter today. That was one wonderful serendipity experience which has continued to bring delight to me for over thirty years.

Hospitals, crises and boundary events

HOSPITALS ARE PLACES of healing. You'll notice that both, the word hospice and the word hospitable, come from the same root as the word hospital. Each of the three words gives us a different perspective on healing. A hospice provides a place for weary travellers to sleep, clean up and be refreshed. Hospitality is warm, loving, caring friendship for a visitor; and a hospital is a place of repair and healing for brokenness or sickness.

Nobody wants to go to the hospital, but thank God for the doctors and nurses who serve us there. The cool waters can be playgrounds or they can even be a hospital stay. Some of the greatest lessons of life are learned while we are flat on our backs in hospitals. We all need times of healing for our bodies, souls and spirits. They are parts of our life which seem unpleasant for the moment, but often help us to turn important corners in our life journeys.

A couple of years ago, your mom went through two operations. We spent a fair amount of time together in hospitals over those months and we are thankful for them. During your mom's hospital stay, she realized that she had to make several life adjustments in her eating habits, as well as her thought patterns over the months which followed. You've learned in medical school Kelly, that a high percentage of disease is caused by or exacerbated by anger or fear. Some doctors believe that as much as seventy-five percent of disease is related to our way of thinking and our emotional health. Your mom is exuberant, winsome, sanguine and melancholy, with many more strengths than weaknesses. However, she would be the first to admit her propensity toward anxiety - especially when it comes to the health of her family. Thanks to a very painful and difficult battle with her digestive organs, we both are relearning how to think about ourselves and take care of our health. We eat more nutritiously, take better care of our souls and bodies, and our faith is growing. It was a matter of necessity, taught to both of us by our unplanned visits to the hospital. As unpleasant as they may be, even stops at the hospital are important on our life journeys.

Crises are difficult times. As a pastor, I am often called on to care for people's souls during crises. Divorce, accident, death, sickness, financial failure, teenage pregnancy, run-away children and loss of a job are some of the most devastating and challenging times of our lives. We'll look at these types of crises more thoroughly in the next two letters that I write to you, but for now, know that our shepherd allows them for a purpose. He doesn't often cause the crises, but uses them to teach us lessons to force us back on to the right path or to quiet us down long enough for us to hear his voice.

Ten memorable stopping points in your life

KELLY, IT MAY be a helpful exercise for you to identify some of the pivotal points in your life, maybe over the last five years, that have served as schools, restaurants, gas stations, playgrounds, crises and hospitals for you. Try and list positive effects which have come out of each stop. Some of them may have seemed negative at the time, but you will likely be able to find some benefits gained from each of the stopping places as time has passed.

Finally, boundary events are those places that force or at least press us into turning a corner in our life. Sometimes an incidental meeting, a sentence in a book, a sermon or an accident can change the direction of our life forever. You'll be able to identify several boundary points in your own life over the course of the last decade.

All of these stops in our life can be compared to a giant dot-to-dot puzzle in the desert. We move the pencils of our experiences from one dot to another to complete the puzzle. Every day we live another line, trying to make sense of the larger picture. There is a picture, drawn by our life designer, but we can't see it because the winds of circumstance have blown sand across the surface of the paper. All we can do is trust our shepherd, who has already seen the completed drawing, to guide us each day from experience to experience, down the path of righteousness. At one point we turn a corner. At another we slow down. And yet at another we stop for a while. One day the design, which was there all the time, will become very clear to us. It will all make sense at last.

Kelly, I have no idea what lies on the path ahead of you and your family. I do know that there will be green pastures and quiet waters for your refreshment, as well as dark valleys to promote your maturity. I don't know when they will come or what form they will take. There is however, one thing that you and Tom can be very sure of. You can know for certain that wherever your life journey takes you, if you follow your shepherd down the right path, he will ensure that your way is marked by increasing maturity and fruitfulness. Along the way to fulfilling your life purpose, you can also be sure that goodness and loving kindness will accompany you. It will not always be an easy road Honey, but it will always be a satisfying and worthwhile road.

Love Dad

PART III

The Shadow Of Death In The Valley Of Life

CHAPTER SEVEN

A Walk on the Dark Side

I walk through the valley of the shadow of death.

EVERY ONE OF US must pass through the dark valleys of death and loss at times in our lives. During those difficult seasons our shepherd's intention is that we be pressed into maturity and fruitfulness by the pain which we experience.

Dear Kelly,

There are some difficult sections of the road on our life journey that every parent wants to save their children from experiencing. I vividly remember a day when you, Kristy and I were hiking along some wooded trails on one of our summer vacations. You were almost six and Kristy was only four and a half. Along the trail, I spotted a bear that had been dead for a couple days. I'm not sure why it was lying there, but as I neared the carcass, I noticed that it had been half eaten. Its side lay bare and thousands of maggots were feasting on the exposed flesh. It was a nauseating sight and I thought that seeing it would cause you some fear and perhaps even nightmares so, to protect you, I led you both away from the carcass.

It wasn't until about a year later, when we found a dead bird in our back yard that we sat down and had our first discussion about death. A little while after that your grandpa died and you girls went to your first funeral. Exposure to the valley of the shadow of death is very difficult for all of us, but nevertheless it is a vital part of our maturing process.

All throughout your life Kelly, while living under our care, your mom and I felt that we needed to shelter Kristy and you from experiencing the pain of the dark valleys. We never did know exactly when to protect you or when to let you suffer a little. We recognized that one day, both of you girls would have to learn about the harsh realities of life, but we didn't want you to experience more than you could bear in your young years.

Now, several years later, you've been exposed to death, sickness, divorce, failure, loss, accident, abuse, war and disaster. You've seen them on the television news, in movies, in friends' lives, at work and at school. You understand more, with each passing year, that the valleys of the shadow of death are a reality in every life. You have also come to realize that although valleys are difficult, they are a necessary part of our life. None of us wants to pass through the dark days, but all of us must. It's inevitable. The valleys of the shadow of death are where we become aware of the presence of our shepherd and where we are pressed into maturity.

In this letter Kelly, I want to explain to you how our shepherd uses the dark days and the challenging valleys to promote growth in our lives. Although we pray for our paths to bypass these critical areas, they are an important and beneficial part of every life journey. You'll want to hang on closely to the shepherd as we wind downward into the valley ahead of us.

Life flows from the valleys

EVERY SUMMER YOUR mom and I look forward to visiting our friends in Southern California. From their beautiful home in the hills of La Cresenta, a person can see on a clear day, past the city of Los Angeles to Catalina Island. It must be eighty miles of scenery. I love to go for morning walks up the hill just above their home and sit on a large rock outcropping, where I have time to think and pray. There's something about being on a mountain top which inspires me. Vision flows easily.

There are no farms on that mountain. The hills are dry and barren, except for landscaped areas, which have been watered at great expense. All of the bountiful California produce comes from the valleys. Although the mountain tops are wonderful to enjoy and the view is spectacular from the high peaks, growth always takes place in the valleys below. As difficult as they may be, our life journey would be meaningless if the pathway did not wind down through the valleys of the shadow of death.

A friend of mine, who is watching his nineteen year old son struggle through the last hours of his cancer plagued journey, said to me a couple of days ago, "God's promise of his presence is not simply to take us to the valley of the shadow of death, but to take us through it." He was quoting the words from Psalm Twenty-three to encourage both their son, David and themselves. Even though I walk through the valley of the shadow of death, I will fear no evil, for you are with me.

Our journey that I have written about in my first letters Kelly, has so far been very positive. We've been enjoying green pastures, quiet refreshing waters and a scenic walk down the road of life. We've been hiking down this pathway called the path of righteousness, which is simply the right way for each of us to go on our own personally designed journey. But now, it's time to take a turn downward along the mountainside into the shadowy valley.

Each of us has set foundational beliefs which serve to hold us steady on stormy days. We consider them to be the solid ground of truth that we walk on. There are five of these axioms, which if we believe them, will contribute to our balance as we descend into the valley below us.

My uniquely planned life journey

THE FIRST IS THAT every person has a predetermined journey planned especially for them. We either believe that humans are cosmic accidents with no purpose or that there is a master design to the universe. If we are of the former persuasion, there's nothing that I or any other person can say which will give meaning to our lives. If there is no creator, then human life has little value or purpose. If there is no shepherd, then our families and acquaintances are simply meaningless accidents who have aimlessly wandered in proximity to our empty lives.

If, however, we believe that there is a God who has made us and who has the whole world in his hands, then our lives begin to make sense as being purposeful journeys. I believe Kelly, no matter where you were born, what colour your skin is, what your IQ is or how much money you have, you are a uniquely created child of the God of our universe. He knows who you are. He loves you and he has a purpose and a design for your life.

My journey was planned before I was born

THE SECOND PREMISE is related. The life journey that you are living right now Kelly, was planned before you were even conceived. Whether or not your mom and I planned your birth, the good shepherd did. He was not surprised by your arrival and neither will he be surprised by your death.

Your days were numbered long before you were born. David, the song writer who wrote the Twenty-third Psalm, was reflecting one day on God's all-knowing nature. He writes; *For you created my inmost being; you knit me together in my mother's womb, I praise you because I am fearfully and wonderfully made; your works are wonderful, I know that full well. My frame was not hidden from you when I was made in the secret place. When I was woven together in the depths of the earth, your eyes saw my unformed body. All the days ordained for me were written in your book, before one of them came to be.*

Kelly, because of your occupation, you know better than I do of how a baby looks in their mother's womb. As an ultra-sound technician, you see preborn babies at every stage almost every day. You're usually the first one to discover whether the baby is a little girl or boy. But long before it is even possible to take an ultra-sound image, God is fully aware of every approaching birth. He knows how many fingers and toes we will have. He knows our potential weaknesses and strengths. He has prepared our sovereign foundations and he has already planned our entire life journey.

David was inspired to write; *Even while I was a fetus with no shape, you had already charted my course. You had every page of my diary already numbered.* Sometimes, in my morning quiet times I think, "Today is day number 18,715 in God's record of my life." Then I pray, "Lord, help me to make the right choices today, so that I will be aligned with your plan for my life and fulfil the purpose that you've already determined for this day."

You or I do not know how many days we have left on this planet to accomplish our assignment. All we know for certain is that we have this moment. But the shepherd who is guiding us through this life journey has already ordained the exact number of days that there are left. No wonder David ends his 139th psalm with this prayer; *Search me, O God, and know my heart; test me and know my anxious thoughts. See if there is any offensive way in me, and lead me in the way everlasting.*

Dad and mom are my primary shapers

THE THIRD PREMISE to understand as we begin our descent into the valley, is that our parents or guardians, during our pre-school years, are the major influencers in our life direction. Child psychologists differ in their estimates, but most would agree that what happens the first five years of a child's life shapes them for a lifetime. Our sense of humour, work habits, attitudes, spiritual awareness, learning aptitude and self-concept are all largely set in those early years.

It follows then that our early caregivers set the tone for much of our soul's health for the rest of our lives. David's son Solomon, who was renown for his wisdom, said; *If we train a child to go in a certain direction when he is in the formative years, when he is older, his life compass will be set, and he will not deviate from that pathway.* Three thousand years after Solomon spoke this proverb, social scientists are concurring. He also said that we parents have a choice to train our children in either one of two basic life directions. Our two choices are either prudence or perversity. Prudence follows God's pre-planned journey, while perversity leads us away from it.

There is only one qualified guide

FOURTHLY, BECAUSE our shepherd has pre-planned each of our journeys, he is the only one who is adequate to act as our guide through both the hills and valleys of life. In the next couple of letters we will look at the two ways our shepherd leads us - with his rod of discipline and with his staff of wisdom. It's sufficient for us at this point to know that he is aware of each one of us at all times, even at this exact moment. He knows where we have come from and where we are headed. He also knows the thoughts that are in our minds, even before they become words or actions.

We get to choose our own path

THE LAST PREMISE we must understand Kelly, is that each of us has the freedom to make personal choices. All day, every day we are choosing to speak or to be quiet; to be kind or to be rude; to go one way or another, to obey traffic laws or disobey; to eat certain foods, or not; to go to bed or watch a movie. These choices will either keep us on the right path or they will move us off that path into a dangerous, or at least unproductive, place in our life. Every choice that we make has a corresponding consequence. Some are all-consuming while some are minor, but each one builds upon the other to make our journey purposeful or futile. Consider the choices which most of us have of getting married or remaining single, or of whom we choose to marry. Life will never be the same after we make that choice. Consider the choices which we have to produce a child or several children. Either way, everything changes after each choice. Even small choices, as to whether we confront a co-worker, retaliate after a hurtful comment or ignore a difficult situation, have corresponding consequences. Each choice that we make is a corner on our pathway which changes the circumstances, as well as the scenery, of our life journey. Stop for a moment and think of the corners that you've turned in the last year or even weeks, which are making a significant difference in your life today.

A personal trip through the valley

A BRIEF OVERVIEW of a decade from my own life might help you see how my own choices and their responding circumstances have significantly affected my life course.

In the year following my graduation from high school, my mom (your grandma whom you never met) died of cancer. Although that event was not by anyone's choice, it changed our family dynamics forever. Mom and dad had six children ranging from twelve to twenty-one at the time. Dad sold his lumber business after mom died and I chose to remain working for the new owners (I also chose to go to Bible College at the same time in the evenings). It was obvious to me, as well as to my new employers, that driving a lumber truck was not my God-given destiny. I made several serious errors in judgment during those years. One time, I forgot to put the boom of our forklift down and unwittingly ran into a twelve by twelve cedar beam which was holding up the warehouse roof. The entire building almost caved in on top of us. The end result of my series of poor choices was that I was fired. I remember the knot in my stomach as I drove home to tell your mom the news. We had just bought our first house, you were a newborn baby and we had no promise of further income. For me, it seemed like we were in the depth of the valley of the shadow of death.

It even got darker in the valley as I began my job hunting expedition. Since I had started working for your grandpa as a teenager, I'd never had to go through the humiliating process of interviews before. Rejections upon rejections piled up for the next four months. Unemployment benefits at that time were only fifty-two dollars every two weeks and I was getting very discouraged. Finally, a friend suggested that I take a different tact and try for a job in the business world. My comfort zone was in the building supply business and so I was very nervous about launching into a white collar office job. After a few applications and frightening interviews, I chose a job which changed the course of my life forever. My new business career lasted ten years, until I felt I was sufficiently mature enough to step out and become a pastor. In that decade of working in sales and management, I learned life lessons that I never would have experienced or even imagined, in either the lumber business or in college. Some of my most valuable life changes came because I was forced out of my comfort zone and forced to make the choices that followed. Lessons about business principles, relational skills, leadership and friendships were all on God's predestined agenda. My walk through that valley, including my good choices and my bad ones, brought me to the other side a new man.

Everything I am now is different because I chose to move out of my dad's care, go to Bible College, get a job, get married, have a baby and begin a white collar job, all by the time I was twenty-five years of age. Most of the determining factors in the decade of growth that I just described were the consequences of my own choices. Others were caused by outside circumstances. Through it all, my shepherd was guiding me down the path of righteousness, over mountain trails and through the valleys, toward my pre-planned destiny. Consider your own life over the last decade Kelly, how circumstances and choices have shaped you into the woman that you are today.

A right way and a wrong way

ONE FURTHER WORD about choices before we descend into the shadows is that if there is a right path to follow, we can assume there is also a wrong path we can choose to follow. Our freedom of choice is a priceless gift from our creator to us, but it places much of the responsibility of fulfilling our pre-assigned destiny on us. I ultimately have no one else to hold accountable for my life choices except for myself. One day I will stand before my maker and I will have to give an account of all that I have done with all that my shepherd has blessed me with. He is fully aware of my sovereign foundations because he chose them for me. My shepherd is the one who initially set me on the path that he wanted me to follow. He also knows every choice that I have made along the way, which has led me either closer to my destiny along the right path, or further from that destiny along the wrong path. I alone make the daily choices to submit to my shepherd's leading or to resist it.

I have just finished reading Charles Templeton's life story, *Farewell to God*. Charles worked alongside Billy Graham in the late 1940's and early 1950's. They were both fiery, effective young evangelists with a common call on their lives. In those years, Charles felt that he needed more education and so he chose to go to Princeton University. He encouraged his friend to go with him, but Billy chose to pursue his call as an evangelist. He felt that evangelism was his God ordained destiny.

Each of their choices at that juncture changed both of their lives, as well as millions of others whom they have influenced. Charles Templeton attended the liberal Princeton University and began a journey which changed him from a Youth for Christ evangelist to the author of Farewell to God, a book which sadly recounts his journey away from his shepherd, toward self-reliance. Billy Graham was catapulted into world renown by publishing giant William Randolf Hearst and has been on America's list of the ten most respected leaders for years. He released his life story, *Just as I Am*, recently. Although each of them have notoriety, their choices led them in almost opposite directions.

An illustration in one of Billy Graham's books reinforces my point of how important our choices are. Almost two hundred years ago, two Scottish brothers, John and David Livingstone were choosing their life pathways. John's primary goal was to make money and become wealthy. David's was to propagate the Kingdom of God. On his burial site at Westminster Abbey, an inscription reads; For thirty years David Livingstone's life was spent in an unwearied effort to evangelize. In an old edition of the Encyclopedia Brittanica, after a long entry outlining the renown work of David Livingstone, John Livingstone is listed only as *the brother of David Livingstone.* Both brothers were born into similar sovereign foundations and began making personal choices from that starting place. John, who chose to make money his primary pursuit, died and left it all behind. David, who chose to make a difference in his world, received not only the admiration of millions, but also a healthy eternal reward. Our choices make a world of difference in the way we finish the course of our life. There is a wake that is left behind every one of us on our life journey. That wake can either give or take away life from those who follow behind us.

Kelly, I suggested to you earlier that you have a choice to believe the above five premises. Believing them will serve you well, as a secure handrail to hold on to, as you begin your descent into the valley of the shadow of death. At times in your life journey ahead, it will be very dark and cold and the winds will be blowing very hard. It would be easy to lose your footing or even your direction, if you did not have the security of knowing that: you have a predetermined journey planned especially for you; this life journey was fully mapped out by your shepherd even before you were born; your mom and I were the primary influences in your life course and you hold the same authority in your and Tom's children's lives; because your shepherd knows your past, has his hand on you right now and has already seen your future, he is the only adequate guide that exists to lead you through the valley ahead; and finally you have freedom to make your own daily personal choices which will either keep you on the right path or take you off that path into possible danger. Now with these basic premises holding us secure, we're ready to begin our journey down through the dark valley.

The shepherd prepares for his sheep

A GOOD SHEPHERD, like David, was well acquainted with this dangerous trek through the valleys. Each spring a shepherd would begin the long journey with his sheep, up to the high country toward the lush summer range. In the autumn, early snow would chase them back down through those same valleys before the cold winter season set in. The valleys were difficult and dangerous, but the trek was ultimately necessary for the health of the sheep. Of course the shepherd would never lead his sheep where he had not already journeyed before. He was well aware of the swollen rivers and the potential for avalanches or rock slides. He knew the poisonous plants, the waiting places for wild animals and the dangers of a sudden sleet or hail storm.

Safely arriving at their destination, either the grassy table lands in the springtime or the rich well watered lowlands in the fall, made the sheep's bi-annual trek worth the challenges. Remaining on the snowy mountain tops through the winter would be too cold for the sheep and staying in the valleys throughout the summer would keep them from enjoying the lush green pastures of the plateaus. Reaching either destination made the dangerous trek through the valleys a necessary part of the sheep's life.

The treachery of the descent through the valleys would increase as the sheep were led through steep walled canyons. The high rock cliffs cast long, cold, dark shadows over the flock of sheep as they walked and crafty predators would wait in hiding for their tasty prey. Coyotes, wolves, bears and cougars were ravenous after a long cold winter. Rock slides and avalanches were an ever-present danger and sudden sleet or snow storms were always a possibility. A wise shepherd knew the skies and was ready to protect his sheep from the cold. Sheep are easily drenched by sleet and because they have thin skin, are susceptible to pneumonia and other respiratory illnesses. Death in this valley was a real possibility for every sheep. Shepherds knew it well and stayed very close to their sheep on their bi-annual journeys.

Kelly, I'm not saying that your life is in danger as you go through your own valley experiences; but I am alerting you to the threat on your soul as you go through the dark, cold seasons of your life. Your mind, emotions and will all come under attack during these times. That's the way your shepherd designed your life journey. As I'll write later in detail, we tend to grow in both strength and maturity as a result of our going through struggles. Opposition builds character - that's the purpose of our shepherd's leading us down through the valley of the shadow of death.

King David's own life journey

KING DAVID SPENT his youth as a shepherd and therefore thoroughly understood this principle that opposition builds character; but it was likely not until he was a successful older man that he reflected back on his days of caring for sheep and clearly saw their journey as a metaphor of life. When David was thirty years old, he moved into the assignment for which God had been training him during his life on the sheepfold. He was crowned the King of Israel and led his people from being an oppressed nation, through forty years of conflict, to becoming the greatest nation this world has ever known. Under King David's rule, Israel reached to its widest boundaries ever in its four thousand year history. When he died, he turned the throne over to his son Solomon, who enjoyed the golden years of Israel's history - forty years without conflict.

During David's seventy year life span, he experienced many times over every phase of the life journey which he describes in Psalm Twenty-three. In the third letter that I wrote to you Kelly, I made reference to the rhythmic ebb and flow of our human emotions. We go up and down from day to day and from month to month. David's experiences in his life journey led him both up hills and down valleys. His shepherd led him on paths especially prepared for him through green pastures, quiet waters and dark valleys. I'm sure that he wished at times along the way that he could have just curled up and died, but he writes that there were other times when he danced with inexpressible joy before the Lord. This psalm covers the whole spectrum of his life journey.

Winter, spring, summer and autumn

A METAPHOR WHICH will help you understand the value of your journey's ebb and flow is the annual calendar with its four seasons. As you know, because you've lived all your life in British Columbia, we have four distinctly different seasons here. Winter is rainy, bleak and dark and we often have cold snaps when ice and snow pressure us to stay inside as much as possible. The normally green landscape becomes brown, frigid and flowerless. Night falls at around 4:30 in the evening and the sun doesn't rise until after many of us are already at our workplaces. There are no signs of life in our gardens and the once colorful deciduous trees appear to be dead.

Springtime always follows wintertime. Usually, by the end of February there are crocuses popping up through the once frozen soil. Little birds, that we thought would never return, appear on trees and there are days in early March when brave men walk around in shorts and t-shirts. As Easter arrives, new life is everywhere. Pink and white blossoms are on the trees, and daffodils and tulips colour the gardens with renewed hope. Children once again play in the cul-de-sacs while moms and dads chat on their porches. Along with the sunshine and flowers, we sense another change - there is a hope of new beginnings.

Summer follows spring and always brings fruitfulness. Yes, there are weeds to pull, lawns to mow and mosquitoes to swat; but the sun shines brighter and the days are longer. People are happier in the summer weather. They spend more time outside with their families, go for runs in the park, cook with barbecues and swim at the beaches. To most of us in British Columbia, summer never seems long enough. As quickly as summer heats up our world, it turns into yet another season.

Autumn is the same every year. The flowers begin to wilt and the lawn's growth slows down. The green leaves change into a beautiful rainbow of colors. The evenings are cooler and the sky lights up with gorgeous sunsets. Summer has ended and winter is once again on the way. And that Kelly, is life. Winter, spring, summer and fall. There's no stopping it. As surely as winter follows fall, so spring will follow winter. Life keeps moving and change is constant.

Don't be surprised by the valley times Honey. Your shepherd is not picking on you. Life is not necessarily fair. The valleys of the shadow of death in your future are every bit as predictable as the last twenty-nine winters that you have lived through. Let every new springtime be a reminder to you that just as there has always been an end to winter, there will also be an end to the dark valley seasons of your life journey. Even more important than the promise of their ending Kelly, are the promises (which I'll write about in my next three letters) of great growth and fulfillment while you are in the midst of the valley of the shadow of death.

King David understood life

DAVID UNDERSTOOD the ebb and flow of the seasons in his life. For seventy years he experienced the difficult winters as well as the fruitful summers. His journal reveals the hills and valleys of his life journey. As a boy, David was an athlete and a musician. His reputation on the harp won him an audience in the king's court and his poetic genius was renown.

Although David was trained as a shepherd on his father's ranch, his career path took him to the battlefields as an able general and administrator, and ultimately to the throne as the greatest king in Israel's long history.

As a young man, David became friends with Prince Jonathan, the king's son. It was during that time that he won the admiration of his country by killing the infamous giant, Goliath. The maidens danced and sang their song of praise to the young hero. Life for David was exhilarating. His experiences led him to the mountaintop of emotions.

But what goes up, always comes down again. The upshot of their applause was that King Saul became violently jealous of this young soldier and David had to spend several years running for his life as a virtual fugitive. He hid in caves, ate what he could find and cried out in despair to his shepherd. He often felt alone and wished that he were dead. At one particularly low point, David pretended to be insane, so that he would be cared for by his enemies rather than be killed. That dark winter season was a humiliating failure in his life, but spring was not far away.

When King Saul (who was his father-in-law by this time) died, David was anointed as the new king of Israel. His reign was difficult, but successful. Military victories were summer high points along the way, especially his recapturing Jerusalem as Israel's capital city, but mid-life was a dark downward spiral into winter for the melancholy king.

When he was about forty-five years old, David had an affair with the wife of one of his best soldiers. He might have got away with it too, if his lover Bathsheba hadn't become pregnant with his baby. Things moved from bad to worse. In a desperate effort to cover his tracks, David brought her husband Uriah back from war to spend the night with his wife. Uriah, to David's further shame, was too loyal to his king and refused to enjoy a night with his wife when his fellow soldiers were yet out on the battlefield. David's deceitful plan had failed, but rather than admit his guilt, in a desperately dark moment, he ordered his friend and neighbor to be placed on the front lines of battle where he would surely be killed. According to plan, Uriah was shot and killed; and after an appropriate time of mourning, Bathsheba and David were married.

His return to the path of righteousness and back into the sunshine of spring was long and winding, but he finally got it right with his shepherd. It seems, however, that David never really did fully recover from those two mid-life winter seasons. Absalom, his handsome and articulate son, tried to steal the throne from the king in his later years. David would have crawled into a corner and let it happen if it had been up to him, but his general took the matter into his own hands and had Absalom killed. David never forgave himself for his failure as a father.

The last season of his life was also a great disappointment to King David. He wanted nothing more than to build a temple in Jerusalem in honour of his God, but his shepherd, the Lord, had other plans. He said "No" to David, but "Yes" to Solomon, David's son. This great man was one of the most revered and prominent kings in history, certainly in Israel's story, but when he reflected back, as an older man, on what he had written about walking through the valley of the shadow of death, we can be assured that he had actually experienced what he wrote.

What carried the psalmist David through the valleys of the shadow of death? How did he hold on through the dark days? We know quite a bit about both his feelings and his faith through those challenging seasons because David kept a journal. On one of his low days, while he was hiding in a cave for his very life, he wrote: *I cry aloud with my voice to the Lord; I lift up my voice to the Lord for mercy. When my spirit grows faint within me, it is you who knows my way. In the path where I walk men have hidden a snare for me. Look at my right and see; no one is concerned for me. I have no refuge; no one cares for my life. I cry to you, O Lord; I say, You are my refuge, my portion in the land of the living.*

In another psalm he wrote: *The enemy pursues me, he crushed me to the ground; he makes me dwell in the darkness like those long dead. So my spirit grows faint within me; my heart within me is dismayed. Let the morning bring me word of your unfailing love, for I have put my trust in you. Show me the way I should go, for to you I lift up my soul. Teach me to do your will, for you are my God; may your Spirit lead me on level ground.*

Three points to ponder

KELLY, YOU'LL NOTICE three things about David's journal entries. First, even though he felt like he was drowning in the waves of adversity, he knew that he was firmly anchored to the shepherd. His foundation was unshakable. There's an old parable about a man who built a beautiful home on a sandy foundation. When the storms came, as they always do, the foundation gave way, the house fell and was destroyed. Another man built a similar house on a foundation of rock. When the storms came, the winds blew and the rain beat on his house, it stood firm because it was built on the rock. If our lives are built on the solid rock of trust in our shepherd's plan, it doesn't matter what kind of storms come at us, we will endure and not fall.

I have a good friend who endured a very unhappy marriage which ultimately ended in divorce. She was left with her two children and very little else. The only material thing that she had left was her small old house. Shortly after her divorce, that house burned down to its foundation. Then there was nothing left. As we talked last week, Carol told me that when her house burned down and there was nothing else to hold on to in this world, she was left with only her trust in God's goodness and his love for her. Now ten years later, she looks back on that difficult valley as one of the times of greatest growth in her life. Her shepherd had allowed everything to be taken away from her - her marriage, her security and her home. He didn't cause it, but he was there all along to guide her through the dark valley. Today, Carol is a new person. She is happier than she has ever been in her life, married again for the past eight years, has a beautiful daughter named Sarah, has found her life purpose. Life changed for Carol while she was in the valley of the shadow of death. She didn't give up and continues to enjoy the fulfillment that comes from being on the right path, anchored in her shepherd's plan throughout the winter storms.

The second observation which we make from David's journal is that he knew how to pray. There was no religious formality to it. He simply believed that his shepherd was not only always present, but was also listening to his crying and caring about his plight. Prayer for David was a simple honest call for help. His life journey took him to the heights of wonder as well as to the depths of despair, and even though he was not always aware of it, his shepherd was consistently there to lead him through every experience. The key word in this section of his psalm is *through*. He writes: *Even, though I walk through the valley of the shadow of death, I fear not evil.* The dark valleys are not intended as stopping places, but as passageways to growth and fruitfulness.

Thirdly, David made a daily choice to follow his shepherd's lead or to reject it. When he successfully made the choice to stay close to his shepherd, he grew through the valley seasons with much less effort than when he chose to go his own way. It is true that we also grow through our failures, but choosing to follow the shepherd in the first place and learning from the mistakes of those who have gone before us is the faster and easier way to maturity.

Kelly, I said earlier in this letter that my desire as a dad has always been to protect you from as much adversity in your life as I possibly can. During the years that you were growing up in your mom's and my care, we did our best to keep you on the right path; but over the last few years, I've come to grips with two truths which have helped me lessen my protective hold on you.

One is that adversity will come, regardless of how we keep up our guard and how closely we stay with the shepherd on the right path. There will always be a certain amount of opposition in every life. I think that if I were to have the opportunity of raising you and Kristy again, I would let you fall a few more times before picking you up. I would let you work on your homework assignments a little longer before jumping in and rescuing you. I would let you make a few more mistakes before reacting quickly and doing a job for you. That is how our shepherd models parenting for us. He is always there close by to make sure we learn from our failure. He keeps loving us no matter what we do or how well we do it. His plan for us is always for our good, maturity and fruitfulness, but he knows the pathway to a successful and fulfilled life winds through many dark valleys along the way. It's not only alright to go through the winter season - it is a necessary part of the shepherd's design for our lives.

The second truth that I've learned over these last years is that pain is a gift. The pain and opposition that we experience throughout our life journey is given to us to help us grow. I'll write more about this in my next two letters to you, but the bottom line is that no matter what life challenges us with, we need to fear no evil because the shepherd is always with us. He is present even at the hospital bed, by the graveside, in the line up at the food bank, at the point of our worst failures, in our loneliest midnights and in the natural disasters that we fear so much.

Kelly, your mom and I love you very much and we always will. We pray that you will stay very close to your shepherd as you walk through the valleys ahead and that you will always be aware of his love and care for you.

Love Dad

CHAPTER EIGHT

No Fear

I will fear no evil, for you are with me.

WHEN WE WALK through the dark valleys, fear is a natural reaction to the evil that surrounds us. However, when we walk with our shepherd, who is always with us, we experience and grow in wisdom, character and maturity. We also learn to walk in alignment to his plan and purpose for our life.

Dear Kelly,

I don't think that either of us can even guess what went through the mind of seventeen year old Cassie Bernall, just before her life was snatched from her. You've seen the news coverage from Littleton, Colorado too many times to not have heard about her bravery in the face of death. She was in the Columbine High School library on Tuesday, April 30, 1999, reading her Bible, when the two young gunmen, Eric Harris and Dylan Klebold, invaded the room with murder on their minds. According to the survivors, one of the masked boys pointed his rifle at Cassie and asked, "Do you believe in God?" She paused, maybe knowing that her answer would determine her fate, and then answered, "Yes, I believe in God." Before she could consider the boy's second question, "Why?", the gunman shot her dead.

I will fear no evil, for you are with me. I believe that Cassie Bernall, the junior with long blonde hair, who loved her God more than her life, understood what David meant by this statement. I can only imagine the jolt of fear that raced through her veins in that brief moment as she was forced to make a decision between life and death. Standing in the very presence of evil, Cassie made an instant choice to honor her shepherd and to deny her fear. She joined the honor roll of millions of martyrs before her, who knew that their shepherd's plans for them encompassed much more than the moment through which they were living.

Kelly, I thank God that we have not ever had to face the same challenge as Cassie did on that black Tuesday, but I pray that if we ever did, we would make the same choice as she did to trust our shepherd more than ourselves. He really does know best and he really does love us. In this letter Honey, I want to explain what it means to stand in the centre of a very dark valley and to not fear the evil around us. The key to our experiencing this possibility is in our understanding of the fact that our shepherd really is with us all the time. Dark valleys are a part of every life, so to help you prepare yourself for the inevitable shadows ahead on your life journey, I'm writing about two things: what are the possible causes of valley experiences and what are the choices I can make in response to them.

Into the shadowy valley

AS YOU KNOW Kelly, your mom and I watch the news every evening, often before we go to bed. I have found over the years that it has become increasingly frightening. Three youths were murdered in a campground in our beautiful British Columbia interior, breast cancer is on the increase, little babies are being abused by their parents, fires are burning hundreds of acres of forest devastating our province's number one industry, our elected officials are slandering one another, financial doom is apparently on the horizon. As if we didn't have enough shadows in our own valley, we fill our eyes and ears with other people's tragedy. Maybe there is some kind of warped comfort in knowing that we're not struggling through life alone. Someone else is going through worse pain than we are.

We all have our stories of life's hardship to tell. I have just finished doing a video interview with a young man in our church. Darren was born into a dysfunctional home, lost his mom in the early years and was tossed from foster home to foster home. He ended up a few years ago living on the streets of Vancouver's skid row. Amazing as it seems, he was in the midst of that difficult season when his life journey turned a delightful corner.

Through sovereign circumstances he landed a good job, met a beautiful Asian lady in our church and a few months later married her. They have a young son now and all of Darren's hopes and dreams are being fulfilled. At the same time that his life was on the upswing, Darren began experiencing some unusual pain. He went to the doctors who discovered that he had multiple tumors growing on many of his major organs. Over the past ten years he's had ten life threatening operations to remove tumors from various parts of his body from his brain to his kidneys. His story makes my walk through the dark valley seem like easy street.

In an earlier letter Kelly, I wrote about my fear that I felt on the ferris wheel when you and Kristy were young. This part of our journey through the valley of the shadow of death can be compared to the downside of the ferris wheel ride where we can't see the steel guides which are supporting us. The seat we are riding in has crested the top where the view has been magnificent, and we are now on the downward swing where it looks as if nothing is there to hold us up. We feel alone, insecure, frightened and in danger. We can take comfort though in knowing that we will make it through, because as I wrote earlier, spring always follows winter.

It is in these dark, shadowy valley times that we learn to trust our shepherd as he guides us through our life journey. We've been happily walking down life's right paths, stopping to rest at the green pastures and the quiet waters. He's been restoring our soul, but now everything is beginning to change. Checking out Psalm Twenty-three again, we see that we have not only moved into the dark and dangerous valley, but our relationship with our shepherd is becoming much more intimate here.

The good side of a bad season

IN THE PSALM which we have been using as a life map, David has been referring to the shepherd as the Lord or He. He guides me. He leads me. He makes me lay down. Do you see how all of the pronouns are in the third person? Third person pronouns speak of a relationship, but a distant one. He or she is someone slightly removed from us. In this section of the psalm, however, David switches pronouns. No longer does he refer to the shepherd as *he*; he now becomes *you*. The author has moved from using a third person to a second person pronoun. It's now you and me Lord. I am not alone after all. You are with me in this valley of the shadow of death. This is one of the miracles of these dark winter seasons. It is here in these valleys of life that we are often brought face to face with our spiritual need. Because we are pressed out of our comfort zones, we become increasingly sensitive to our relationship with our creator and shepherd.

Kelly, you know that as a pastor, I have many opportunities to talk with people, both at their happiest and at their saddest points of life. I love to counsel young adults as they move toward marriage. One of the highest privileges that I have is to stand within eighteen inches of a starry eyed bride and groom on the platform on their wedding day. I say to the groom, "Now, look into your bride's sparkling blue eyes and repeat after me, I, William, take you, Julia..." There is nothing quite like the emotion that I, as well as they, feel in that sacred moment as I pronounce them husband and wife.

Another aspect of pastoring, which I love is when I dedicate babies. In our church tradition, a dad and mom stand on the platform with me and we publicly bless their newborn child. What an honor it is for me, at a Sunday service, to hold the gorgeous baby up to the congregation and admire God's creative genius with them. There are always cheers and sighs from proud family members and friends in the church. I can't describe the joy I feel as I talk about God's love for these little ones and his pre-ordained destiny for their lives. I'm privileged to be asked to pray for his blessing on both the parents and the child. I will never forget the day when you and Tom, as well as Kristy and Jeremy, asked me to bless your sons, Alexander and Jacob, in our Sunday morning service.

You can understand why I love officiating at weddings and baby dedications, but it may seem strange to you that I also enjoy being a pastor at funerals. When I say that I enjoy it I'm not referring to the sadness and loss that we all feel when a mother, sister or friend dies. I understand the difficult grief process. I find though, that there is often a miracle that happens at funeral services. There is no other time quite like it. The miracle is what happens to people's souls when they are in grief over the loss of someone whom they have dearly loved.

Just a few months ago, I held a six-foot-four leather clad, tattooed Hell's Angel in my arms, as he cried over a buddy who had been killed in a motorcycle accident. I have watched the hardened teens, as well as sophisticated business tycoons, weep in front of the caskets of their mothers. They for the first time have come to grips with the sad truth that opportunities to say "I'm sorry" or "I love you" are over.

I've spoken with atheists at wakes, who are wondering if they will ever again see their brother who just died of cancer. Our souls are soft ened by funeral services. People are jerked from their jobs, which they couldn't seem to get time away from a moment before the death. Life routines suddenly seem meaningless when death arrives at our door. Now the questions are eternal ones: "Where is my mom now?", "Why did God let this happen?", "How will I survive without my husband?", "Will I ever see my son again?"

In the valley of the shadow of death we are brought face to face with God. These experiences open windows along our life journey, when it's just you and me Lord. We look our shepherd in the face, and he is looking right back at us.

I will fear no evil

AND THAT KELLY, is the good part of a bad season. If the tragedy helps to open my eyes to the fact that I do have a shepherd walking beside me, that he really is aware of me and that maybe there is a higher perspective than I've been seeing, then maybe something good will come out of the valley of the shadow of death.

As I am writing this letter to you today Honey, your mom and I are waiting to go to an appointment that we have with the radiologist. You know that your mom's cancer, which was removed with a couple of operations two years ago, appeared in shadows on her recent mammogram. We have been waiting what seems like an eternity for this appointment for her to have a biopsy. Both fear and God are with us.

I sit here thinking of the verse that David wrote, I will fear no evil, for you are with me and need to understand the word evil. My dictionary describes it: morally bad; wicked; causing injury or any other undesirable result; marked by threatening misfortune or distress. Remember the pathway that I described earlier called the path of righteousness. This is the path that our shepherd has chosen for us to walk down throughout our life journey. It's simply the right path.Another way of describing our journey down this path is by saying that we are walking in the light. It can be compared to driving our car down a highway which is well lit by huge gas powered lamps. Then we pull off onto a side road into the darkness where there are no lights. If we think of God as light, then our journey down the right path, is like walking in that light. Unfortunately, we all have those self-willed twisted wheels that I described earlier which take us off the right path from time to time. When we get off the lighted path into the shadows and ultimately into darkness, we discover that this is where the evil lurks.

Evil is darkness. It is anything that diverts or keeps us away from the right path - the path of light. We are usually distracted by deception. We somehow are deceived into thinking that the grass is greener on the other side of the fence or that we will be happier outside of our shepherd's watchful gaze. We begin to believe that our shepherd's rules are restrictive or unfair, or that he really doesn't have our best interests at heart. That's when we are tempted to wander past the boundary fence, where evil waits to entrap us.

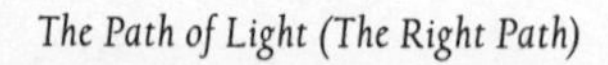

The Path of Light (The Right Path)

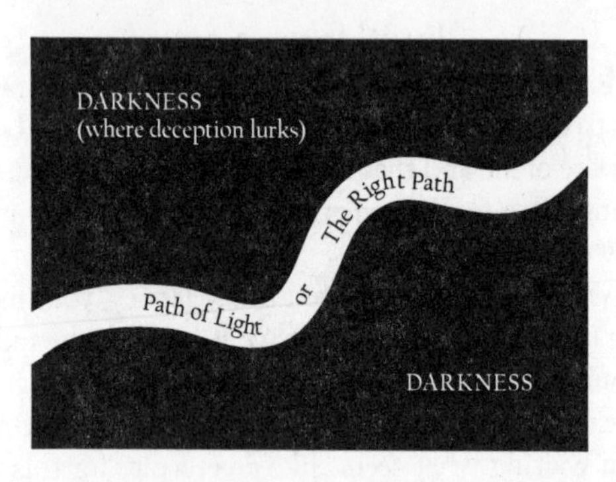

Humpty Dumpty was so frightened when he saw evil face to face on the other side of the wall that he fell and broke his shell. My intention in telling you about the reality of evil Kelly, is not to scare you, but to warn you. Just as Humpty's mother cautioned her young son to stay away from the wall for the sake of his own safety, so any good parent warns their children about the possible dangers which lurk beyond appropriate boundaries. My cautions are not so that you will fear evil but rather so that you would understand that it really does exist.

Walking in the shadow of evil

KEEPING IN MIND that there is real evil in our world, it is also good to know that sometimes evil is just a shadow. I remember when you were about eighteen months old. You had learned to walk during the winter season so we were inside the house for most of those dark months. In April, the spring rains subsided for a day and gave way to warm sunshine. I was outside in the backyard painting when you walked out through the door to play. Although twenty-seven years have come and gone since that day, I can see you in my mind right now as you excitedly walked toward me to help me paint. Then it happened.

You glanced down and saw something chasing you. At first you were too scared to move and your predator held its place. Then a second later, you worked up enough courage to take a couple of steps, but as quickly as you moved it followed you. As you literally screamed in terror, your mom and I ran to hold you. It took us a few minutes to calm you down enough for you to explain why you were so afraid. Then we realized that this was the first time you had ever noticed your shadow. It chased you wherever you moved. Your mom and I quietly laughed with each other as we held you in our arms and explained to you that your shadow could not hurt you.

Like your shadow Kelly, in many of the valleys which we go through, our greatest fears are only shadows. Fear itself is our enemy. At other times of course, evil really is out to destroy us.

The grip of fear

THERE IS SOMETHING about fear that grips us. We've all been held in its strangle hold. I can remember nights when you or Kristy, as teenagers, were out on dates or with friends. We had a rule that you were supposed to phone by ten or eleven o'clock to tell us where you were or if you were going to be late. More than once, one of you would forget to call and your mom would begin to fear the worst. One time, Kristy went out at about eight o'clock for a walk with her girlfriend and she said she would be back in a half an hour. It was a black winter night and by nine o'clock she wasn't home yet. Your mom was panicking and I was beginning to feel the grip of fear myself. Two young ladies walking in the dark were easy prey for some evil predator. By ten o'clock your mom and I were each in our own car, scouring the neighborhood. There was no sign of Kristy or Lisa anywhere. Even though I pretended to be calm, I was by this time as frightened as your mom. At eleven o'clock we decided to hop into one car together, because by then your mom was not fit to be left alone. We drove within a mile radius of the stores that we thought they would have walked to, but there was still no sign of them. When we came back home once again to check for them, we found Kristy in her pyjamas ready for bed. "Where have you two been?" she calmly asked, "I've been worried about you." After we cooled down, we learned that Kristy had been safe at home for the past hour. The grip of fear is all consuming, but sometimes it's only a shadow.

One would wonder why we entertain ourselves with ghost stories around the campfires or horror films at the theatres. Maybe we think we deserve to suffer a little or perhaps the adrenaline rush gives us a thrill. As if real life were not frightening enough! But whether the evil that we fear is only a shadow or is the real thing, in those dark terrifying moments or days, we are pressed into a place of trusting our shepherd. When all of the supports that have kept us buoyant are yanked from beneath us and it feels like we are stepping out alone into the black unknown, that's when our shepherd is ready to do his best work!

Where is our shepherd when we are consumed by fear?

THE QUESTIONS HAUNT us in times of fear, whether harassed by real evil or imagined evil, "Where is our shepherd?" and "Why isn't he there when we really need him most?"

You have heard the poem *Footprints* by Margaret Powers. In her poem, Margaret describes walking with God along the sands of the seashore in her life journey. She describes her conversation with God at the end of her life as he was reviewing the various experiences through which they had walked together. God explained that the two sets of footprints, side by side in the sand, were hers and her shepherd's. When the Lord finished talking, she had only one question for him "Lord", she said, "all through my life I see that there were two sets of footprints, side by side, in the sand. I can clearly see that you were walking beside me. But when I got to the most difficult stretch of my life journey, the valley of the shadow of death, there was only one set of foot prints. Why, at the time when I needed you the most, did you leave me? Why were you not beside me then?"

His answer to her is the same answer that he gives to us in similar difficult times, "I was with you throughout the entire journey. The reason that you see only one set of footprints on those most painful days is because it was during those times that I carried you."

Faith simply trusts the shepherd

FEAR IS THE opposite to faith. Where there is no faith, we leave the door open for evil to assault us with fear. Faith is simply trusting our shepherd regardless of whether or not we see him or feel his presence. It is based on the facts: God loves us; God promises to walk with us; he will never leave us, even in the presence of evil; and we are always safe and secure in his grip. The foundation of our life Kelly, cannot be the people around us, the money we have in our bank accounts, the security of our jobs, the right political party in government or even our good health. As history is quick to remind us, any of these things can change or be taken away from us. The only secure foundation that we can build our lives on is the truth that there is a God who made us, who loves us and is there to shepherd us throughout our life journey. On those facts we can place our faith, and in the presence of that faith, fear cannot find a foothold.

A woman in our church recently told me a story which underlines these truths. When she was a young girl her family was turned upside down by a very traumatic event. In those years of insecurity, her mother and father were very unhappy in themselves and with each other. She and her older brother felt the reverberations of her parents growing anxiety and lovelessness. Her dad became distant and angry and her mom reacted poorly.

As a five year old child, my friend spent many hours huddled fearfully in a fetal position in her closet. As an adult, as she was going through a twelve step healing program, those unhappy memories resurfaced. She clearly remembered the hours that she had spent in the closet trembling in fear. As her shepherd was guiding her through those painful memories during her healing process, he reminded her of conversations which had transpired during those times. He said, "Do you remember the reassuring voice that you heard while you were alone hiding in the closet?"

She answered, "Yes, I remember the voice which assured me 'You are okay, and I love you. You are safe in my arms.' That was my inner self speaking to me. It was a spiritual strength that came out of nowhere. It was the only thing that kept me from going crazy during those frightful times."

Her shepherd replied, "That wasn't your inner self reassuring you, it was me speaking to you. I was there with you in that dark closet."

A few years later, as a teenager, this woman's journey took her further into darkness and into the grip of evil. She ran away from home and ended up living on the streets. Drugs, alcohol and unhealthy relationships plagued her days. During one very dark day in that period in her life, walking alone on the streets of Toronto, she passed by an old stone church. A gentle voice in her mind urged her to go inside. She tentatively entered the building and knelt beside a pew near the back of the sanctuary. While on her knees she cried convulsively for a half an hour. Years later, while on her healing journey through the twelve steps, she was reminded by her shepherd of that voice which had urged her to enter the church. "That was my voice calling you back to me. I was with you on all those dark and dangerous days as you were walking the streets of Toronto and Montreal."

Even when I feel alone, frightened, unloved and worthless, You are with me. Your rod and staff, they comfort me. In another letter, I'll write more to you about our shepherd's rod and staff, and then describe how they bring comfort to us while we are in the valley of the shadow of death. But for now it's enough to understand that our shepherd is always with us.

Why am I going through this dark valley?

IN ADDITION TO the questions, "Where is God?" and "Why am I going through this most difficult valley alone?", many of us have asked the often unanswered questions, "Why is this happening to me?" and "What did I do to deserve this?"

Kelly, these questions will likely not be entirely answered during our life times, but I will give four general root causes for our life valley experience. They are our own choices, the choices of those around us, the vicissitudes of life and the shepherd, himself.

Our own choices

THE MOST LIKELY cause of our pain and one that often brings us into the dark valley is the consequences of our own choices. I choose the occupation that I give myself to everyday. There are good and bad things that go with my job just as there are with every other job. For example when I was a truck driver, there were many enjoyable experiences which I had, but there were also a few that I would have rather bypassed. One particular dark hour that I remember took place while I and a swamper were delivering a full truckload of wallboard to a house under construction. I had neglected to chain the five lifts of sheet rock down before I left. (Under normal circumstances a good well tied rope would have been enough. This house however was situated on the top of a very steep hill.) On the way up the mountain road, I clumsily shifted to a lower gear and almost as quickly, as I jerked the truck, the whole load slid off the back and scattered down the road behind us. You can imagine my humiliation as I phoned the office and told my boss that I had lost the entire load. Even more painful was my having to pick up the two hundred and fifty broken sheets and bring them back to the yard. That was one of the three incidents that ultimately led me to being fired from that company.

Another example of a consequence of a bad choice, much worse than my experience, is of a friend of mine who had parked his truck on a hill while going into a restaurant for a cup of coffee. Tragically, his truck brakes happened to give out at just that time and because he had inadvertently forgotten to turn his wheels toward the curb, his truck rolled unrestrained down the street and struck a little girl. My friend never drove a truck or anything else after that dark day.

You may call it ignorance or forgetfulness, but the fact remains that both of us chose to be truck drivers. In my case, I chose to tie my load down with a rope rather than a chain. The little girl died because my friend chose to park his truck on a hill without turning his wheels towards the curb. Both of our accidents could have been prevented by each of us making wiser or more thoughtful choices.

As a pastor, I often feel a sense of the pain of the men and women whom I counsel. It may be listening to a mother who has lost her son because he chose to commit suicide or confronting a dad whom I know has chosen to molest his daughter. Talk about valley experiences! Kelly, as a ultra-sound technician you have a highly responsible job. If you were to make an incorrect diagnosis and miss a growing cancer, or if you were to prematurely or carelessly tell a pregnant woman that her baby likely has Down's syndrome, you could cause great pain in several lives. Every day we have the potential of making choices which could result in our moving in a dark valley.

We also choose our life mates. I'm not particularly sympathetic of a man who complains about his wife's weaknesses. After all he chose to marry her. Often his wife's bad moods are simply a reflection of the way she is being treated by him. Again, it's because of our personal choices. We choose what we eat, how we exercise, our life styles and our bad habits. Often ill health is simply a consequence of those life long choices. I have a good friend dying of lung cancer. He was warned by his doctor ten years ago that if he didn't stop smoking his body would be in danger. He didn't quit, so at fifty he's walking through his last year of life.

There are millions of minor and major choices that we make throughout our life journey. Each has a consequence, which will keep us in the light on the right path, or lead us into the shadows under the influence of evil. Kelly, we can beat ourselves over the head for the rest of our lives because of poor choices that we've made in the past, but that isn't going to help. We can only turn things around by forgiving ourselves for our failure and then by learning from our mistakes. Yes, it is true that our bad choices lead us into troublesome circumstances, but hopefully we can use those memorable moments to help us make wiser decisions in the future. It's called learning from our mistakes. It is also called maturing!

The choices of those around us

THE SECOND REASON for our being side tracked in the dark valleys is because of the poor choices of others. Your mom's , Kristy's and your choices are intricately connected to me, just as anyone within my sphere of influence is affected positively or negatively by my personal choices. If I were to choose to violate my marriage contract and have an affair, not only would my life and my family's life be turned upside down, but also our whole church would suffer devastating consequences.

In the same way, every driver on the road who practices poor driving habits negatively affect, those around him on the highways. Politicians' and economists' choices affects nations. Advertisers, media news casters, television personalities and environmentalists all have influence in our life circumstances. In British Columbia, a large pulp mill with several thousand employees recently announced their closing. It happened because of changing environmental demands, poor management and an uncertain economy. Its repercussions will change that port city of fifty-five thousand people forever. Twenty percent of the city will be unemployed over night. House prices will plummet; restaurants, department stores, building supply businesses, furniture stores and automobile dealers will fall like dominoes behind the pulp mill's closing. My friend has lost his job at the mill. He and his wife will have to join the thousands of others trying to sell their homes. They will have to move to another city, find a job and start over again. None of this was their choice. We can sit at home behind locked doors and behave ourselves in every way, and yet we will still go through dark valleys. We cannot escape experiencing the consequences of the choices of those around us. And those around us in our circles of influences cannot escape some of the repercussion of our bad personal choices.

The vicissitudes of life

THE THIRD REASON for our experiences with evil in the dark valley is what we call life. We say, life happens; that's the way the cookie crumbles; or that's the way the ball bounces. Somebody contracts cancer and we say, "That's life." A volcano erupts and devastates an island, a hurricane howls through a seaport, a river overflows its banks or an earthquake shakes a city to rubble and we stand by helpless. The best we can do is help the survivors and repair the damage.

A good explanation for natural disasters is given to us in the Bible. When mankind fell off kilter in the begining, people weren't the only ones who suffered the consequences. When our parents, Adam and Eve chose to walk away from the love, protection and authority of the good shepherd, our world which we were assigned to as caretakers suffered upheaval. Our entire world order slipped into disorder when we chose to live independently of our creator and outside of his plan.

Our genes, as well as our environment, fell into disharmony with the music of our maker. Every day we eat the fruit of our broken planet. It's not our personal fault. It's our evil world reeling from the trauma of the cumulative choices of our ancestors throughout history; and the forecast for our future is not much better than our past has been.

Every nation, every city and every family is subject to the consequences that have been thrust upon us by those who have gone before us. Thankfully, by each of us deciding to return to the path prepared for us by our shepherd, we can begin where we are to turn around the futures of those who walk behind us. You will make a difference Kelly, in the people who are within your present circle of influence and also in those who will follow in the generation yet to come. Meanwhile, you and I will continue to mature and grow in our capacity to make wise decisions because of the challenge which we call life.

God himself

THE LAST OF our four reasons for our trying days is perhaps the most difficult for us to understand. The fact is clear that God himself causes some of our valley experiences. The reason we have trouble comprehending why God would actually cause us to go through the valley of the shadow of death is that our concept of pain is flawed. Most of us think of dark valleys, testing times or painful experiences as inherently evil. The truth is that they can either cause us to stumble or promote our growth. Pain can make us bitter or better. It can make us whiners or winners. The reason that I believe our shepherd leads us into and through the valley is because he tells us that he does. His reasons are often far greater than what we can see in the midst of our pain. Often they become clear ten or twenty years past the season of crisis.

Our Bibles are filled with stories of how the shepherd engineered challenging circumstances in our heroes lives to prepare them for something greater in their future. God purposely brought young Joseph through rejection, slavery, slander, imprisonment, loneliness, despair and loss for thirteen years in order to prepare him to be the Prime Minister of Egypt during some of the most important years of their history. He did the same with Noah, Abraham, Job, Jeremiah, Isaiah, Peter, James, John and Paul. The ultimate results were always well worth the difficult circumstances and pain that the good shepherd allowed or even caused them to endure.

Usually Kelly, the Lord our shepherd uses dark valley experiences from a combination of root causes. Our own wrong choices, the poor choices of others, the vissicitudes of life and God himself are all entered into the design that our shepherd has laid out for our life journey. Because he knows about each of these difficult circumstances long before they even happen, he is able to not only prepare us for them, but also to lead us through them and gain benefit from them.

After, Kelly, as we go through trials, whether caused providentially or as a consequence of our own poor choices, we tend to react with anger or fear toward God. We may even think in those times that he is upset with us or out to get us. But it's not so!

To help you in your love, respect and honor of your shepherd, who sometimes sets these bumps in front of you on the path of life, I want to explain to you the value of the valleys. Here are five benefits that flow out of the valleys of your life journey.

Pain is a gift

THE FIRST BENEFIT that comes from our dark valley experiences is the gift of pain. It is a healthy perspective for us to see pain, whether emotional or physical, as a gift. Is that hard to swallow? Dr. Paul Brandt in his wonderful book, *The Gift of Pain* does a commendable job of convincing his readers of the inherent value of pain. By the time I finished reading his work, which he wrote from his own experiences as a medical doctor in India, I began waking up every morning giving thanks to my shepherd for the gift of pain. Dr. Brandt uses leprosy patients as an illustration. Only recently has it been discovered that the ancient dreaded disease of leprosy is simply the absence of pain. He says that the only thing organically wrong with a leper is that he is unable to feel pain.

Imagine getting a small rock stuck in your shoe and walking on it all day. If you had leprosy, it would irritate your foot without your even knowing it was there. The resulting cut would become infected because of dirt and parasites, but because you wouldn't feel any pain, you would not take care to disinfect your foot. Deeper the infection would go ultimately causing complications, and in the end your foot would have to be amputated. Feeling pain in your foot when you originally stepped on the sharp pebble would have helped you detect the problem early and would have alerted you to deal with it before it became a serious injury.

Another example of the value of pain would be in the eyes, which involuntarily blink away dust particles all day long. Whenever you get a tiny fleck of dust in your eye, a pain signal immediately goes to your brain, which says to your eyelid, "flick it away". If that were not to happen, imagine how quickly in a day you would suffer from a serious eye infection.

Your body is constantly adjusting itself all day and night because of pain signals. Even while you are sleeping, as certain nerves go numb, your brain receives a signal to roll over. Standing in one position too long creates a strain on your back and legs, so your body adjusts its weight without any conscious thought. All this because of pain. In the same way, when there is pain in a relationship we make adjustments by apologizing, confronting or talking it through. If we were not sensitive to hurt, we would likely go blindly onward never growing through our failures.

In our American culture, we spend billions of dollars in an attempt to dull our headaches and to soothe our stomach aches. Maybe instead we should be thanking our pain for revealing a problem in our lives, and then dealing with the source of the pain. Doctors are in general agreement that a large percentage of the pain which we are trying to drug away is really a result of problems in our soul. The source of our pain has often very much to do with our fears, insecurities, unresolved anger, bitterness or unforgiveness. Pain is a gift from our creator which is trying to tell us that something is wrong.

Ignoring or trying to dull your pain with medication is like hitting your smoke alarm with a broom handle to try and stop the noise, rather than checking to see if there is a fire in your home. It's likely trying to tell you that there is a problem which needs to be addressed. Rather than curing our pain, we need to change our eating habits, exercise more or stop and take a rest at the quiet waters for a while. Pain that we experience in the valley of the shadow of death has something important to say to us.

Something is out of alignment

THE SECOND BENEFIT of our valley experiences is that they show me when my life is out of alignment. My life journey goes the smoothest and I am the most satisfied when I am aligned with my shepherd's plan. He had my best interests in mind when he prewired me to fulfill a certain destiny. His plan for my life is better than my plan for my life. When my ways match his ways and my days align with his days my life journey goes better.

In the letter that I wrote to you Kelly, about the Jewish concept of a day, I said that our days really begin at six o'clock the evening before. We rest in the evening and sleep at night to prepare for our days. While we are sleeping and resting, our shepherd has a twelve hour start on the day's journey. Rather than waking up to begin our day and asking God to go with us and bless our agenda, we should awake to join him in his plans which are already in process. That's what alignment is.

When you get into your valleys and the pain begins, understand that there's probably something wrong that is causing the pain in your soul. Whether it is self-induced or it is caused by God or evil, you need to run to your shepherd and make sure you're in alignment. It's like back pain. If I were to lift a heavy weight out of my car trunk using my back and not my legs, my back could easily go out of alignment. The resulting pain from a pinched nerve would tell me that it's time to see my chiropractor. He would do his thing and bring my spinal column back into alignment. The pain from my pinched nerve would stop when my back bones were back in place. A similar thing happens when my car wheels are out of alignment. At a certain speed my out-of-alignment car begins to shake; the vibrations and noise tell me that I'd better go see my mechanic. I'm not sure of all that he does, but he would bring my car wheels and frame into alignment again and all would be well.

Pain in my back, in my car or in my life tells me that something is likely out of alignment. When I go through pain in a dark valley along my journey, I know it's the right time to check and see if my personal agenda is aligned with the shepherd's plan for my life.

Going through valleys builds character

THERE IS A THIRD benefit to our going through valley experiences - it builds character in us. Going through difficult days and years builds perseverance, and perseverance builds character. The process of building character takes time.

When I graduated from college at twenty-three years of age, I, like most young adults, thought that I had life figured out. You could have asked me anything and I would have given you an answer. I thought that I knew it all and I was ready to conquer the world - that was until that same year when I was fired from my truck driving job and spent months trying to find another one. Even after I finally landed my first office job, I almost got fired from that one too! Every valley experience that I had humbled me, made me less self-centred and more willing to adapt my life to fit my shepherd's agenda rather than my own.

I've described several of those often embarrassing and fear filled episodes in other letters that I've written to you Kelly. They were sometimes caused by my own stupidity, sometimes by the failures of others, sometimes just by the way life is and sometimes purposefully by my shepherd; but each valley experience and my response to it has helped my character develop into maturity. Since those years in my early twenties, I've gone through at least another thirty winter seasons on my life journey. Even the ones which caused me the most fear have contributed to the formation of my character. Now, when I'm counselling and someone asks me why something bad has happened to them, my answer usually is, "I don't know why." I realize now that the older and wiser I get, the less I seem to really know. I may have less answers than I had at the age of twenty-three, but at least I have more character. It has been developed largely in the valley of the shadow of death.

Dark valleys purify our souls

THE APOSTLE PETER gives us the fourth reason for life's valleys. In a letter that he wrote to the first century Christians, who were being tortured for their faith by Emperor Nero, he said that dark and difficult days work to purify our souls. Nero, who tottered between genius and insanity, had likely started the great fire in Rome which destroyed half the city. The people of Rome thought that he had started the fire so that he could rebuild the city the way that he wanted. The heat was on him in his Emperor's seat and he needed a scapegoat, so by the time Peter wrote his letter, Nero had blamed the Christians for the fire and perpetrated an all out assault on them. He hunted Christians down and forced either submission to him or martyrdom. He stuffed them into wet leather bags which were then dried in the sun. The shrinking bags forced the breath out of the martyrs. He fed them to ravenous lions. He had them pulled limb from limb apart by four horses - all in front of cheering audiences. He even drenched them in pitch and made human torches of them to light up his palace gardens at night.

Peter, who himself was later crucified upside down, was writing to those who were hiding for their very lives from Nero's insane wrath. To these candidates of death, he wrote a letter which is still helpful for us today. He encouraged his flock to keep running the race. "Don't give up," he writes, "all this opposition will purify your soul like gold in the furnace". The smelting process is a good picture of how the fire of life purifies our souls. Like precious metals become purer as the flames burn hotter, so it is when the temperature of the evil around us increases, the dross in our character is burned away. The anger, self promoting ego-centric pride and rebellion melt in the flames. I've seen it happen over and over in men's and women's lives. The hotter the fire, the purer the gold that comes out on the other side.

For the ten years that you and Kristy were in elementary school Kelly, we lived back to back with another young family. During that decade my neighbor and I enjoyed many conversations over the back yard fence. Then we moved away and I didn't see the family for several years. I had heard that the husband had done well in business, but that was all I knew. A few months ago, Gary called me and set up an appointment for us to meet together. It was good to see him again, but it was obvious that he was in big trouble. Almost immediately after I closed my office door, his smile faded and he began to cry.

Everything that he and his wife had built over the past twenty-five years of their marriage was collapsing. His foundations were crumbling and his world was being ripped apart. He still had a strong marriage and family, but financially he was devastated. A couple of major business reversals had drained him of everything. He told me through his tears that if he could just hang on for three or four months, he may still be able to ride the storm.

Although he was not asking me for money and I had none to give him, I felt the pain he was going through, so I asked him how much he needed. He said that eight thousand dollars would get him to the other side. It would just be a loan and he would pay as much interest as was necessary. I phoned three friends who have money to loan and without pressing, asked if they could help my old friend. Their answers seemed hard, but I knew these were astute business men and I trusted them. All three men said basically the same thing, "The worst thing to throw a drowning man is money." They all agreed that he needed to completely fail before he could rebuild his life on a firm foundation. I met again with my friend and told him what the men had said. He thanked me even though it seemed like I had not helped him.

A couple of more months passed and he and his wife lost everything. Gary and Ruth are now being forced to move. Although they are starting over again in their late forties, they have never been happier. In their dark valley experience, they have come face to face with the shepherd of their souls, and for the first time in their lives they are getting clearly on the right track. During these past several months, the shepherd has done a miraculous work deep within their souls. Some of their life issues which had been cloudy and dirty have been purified. Money was not what they needed - crisis was. When the fire of their circumstances was turned up hot enough, their hidden pride and self-reliance came to the surface and was burned away. The crisis helped them see that their priorities had been twisted out of shape. Only in the pain of the valley could they clearly see the problem and make the changes necessary. As I sat at lunch with my friend last week, he recounted the lessons that he'd learned in the valley, how they had altered his entire perspective on life and how they as a family were doing better than ever. Although they were starting over financially, they all had made giant leaps forward in the success of their life journey. They are going to be just fine!

Faith grows in the valley

I WROTE EARLIER that the opposite of fear is faith. That's the fifth reason that our life journey often winds down into the valley of the shadow of death. Every time we see that our shepherd has successfully guided us through another valley, our faith in his wisdom and love grows. We become a little stronger in our spiritual centre. We may be growing weaker in our bodies with each passing winter, but we are getting stronger where it counts, as we walk through the valley of the shadow of death. Our souls and spirits after all are the real us.

Whenever we are pressed past our place of security Kelly, we have only two choices. We can either fall flat on our face or we can reach out to someone for help. Falling is not always as bad as it seems because most of us only learn through failure. How much better would it be if when we are being forced beyond our safety zone, we would reach out in faith and trust our shepherd to help us through the crisis. He is always there waiting for that moment. David reminds us, *Though I walk through the valley of the shadow of death, I fear no evil, for you are with me.*

To be honest Kelly, I have never enjoyed going through a valley where the shadow of death ominously lurked. Every valley experience along my life journey has been difficult and challenging. I have seen however, over and over again, how the benefits of the dark seasons in my life have far outweighed the pain that I have felt. You and Tom are young yet Honey, and I am delighted that the sun is shining so brightly on your pathway, but you can be sure that there will be some dark days ahead. The valley of the shadow of death is a part of our creator's design for every life journey.

During those fear-filled and challenging seasons ahead of you in your pathway Kelly, remember these three truths: Your shepherd loves you very much even when you are in deep pain. He has a wonderful plan of success and fulfillment uniquely designed for your life. And you do not need to be afraid because your shepherd is always there, walking ahead of you to prepare the way; walking beside you to lead you to wisdom and maturity; and walking behind you to protect you from evil and to cover your failures with grace.

In addition to those three life pillars, know that your mom and I also love you and your family more than words can say and that we pray for you daily. We pray that you and Tom and your children will not fear as you pass through valleys of the shadow of death along your life journeys even when you hear the howling of fierce and evil forces all around you. We pray instead that you will come through the other side not only unscarred, but also with increased character strength, healthy alignment to your shepherd, purity of soul, anointing for your destiny and an overflowing cup which will nourish those around you. I'll explain how all of these benefits can be your experience in the next few letters that I'm writing to you.

Love Dad

CHAPTER NINE

Spare the Rod, Spoil the Child

Your rod...it comforts me.

WHEN THE rod (which is used in the psalm as a metaphor for loving discipline) is diligently used by our shepherd, then we tend to walk more obediently and stay within the boundaries of our destined pathway, thus enjoying the comforting benefits of success and fulfillment.

Dear Kelly,

Awhile ago I was having breakfast with a forty year old man who shared the story of his life journey with me. It's fascinating to hear about the trials that people have had to go through to become who they are today. I benefit from these stories by learning about life through their experiences and failures so that I don't have to make the same mistakes myself. This man told me how he is finally in the process of getting his life on the right track. He described his adult years of emotional instability, failure in business, floundering marriage, drug and alcohol abuse and unhappiness. Wondering why his journey had been so troublesome, I asked him about his sovereign foundations and his early choices.

His mother had died when he was only a toddler and his dad literally gave him away to a stranger to raise. There had been a glaring lack of love and no order or discipline to his life at all. He was allowed to run free throughout all of his early years. He ate whatever he wanted, came and went whenever he pleased, hung around with whomever he felt like and did anything he chose. As he was speaking to me, two thoughts ran through my mind. One was that this was the kind of upbringing that every child dreams of - total freedom in all areas of life, no one telling him what to do and when to do it, no boundaries, no rules and no discipline! The other thought was of how opposite that his early life was to mine and how differently your mom and I raised you and Kristy.

We set clear guidelines for your behavior and insisted that you stay within those lines. We consistently, and even at times unfairly, taught you to live within the confines of our rules, hopefully in an atmosphere of love and respect. As my breakfast companion unburdened his anger toward his foster parents and his regret over hundreds of his own poor choices, I became increasingly thankful to my dad and mom for teaching me, by their example, how to use the rod of discipline. This man is just beginning to learn some of the disciplines that you and Kristy had mastered even before you began school.

This subject of discipline has been in hot debate over that past forty years. Our American society has bounced back and forth between using the rod and letting our children run free without correction. I'm grateful that your mom and I discovered early in our lives that true freedom really only comes in a world of love, order and discipline. I want to explain that healthy balance to you in this letter, and how our shepherd's rod of discipline brings comfort to us. In my next letter Kelly, I'll write about how he complements the use of the rod by using his staff to keep us on the right path.

The case of the stolen crayons

ALTHOUGH I WASN'T a bad child, I do remember a few occasions when your grandma and grandpa had to discipline me. More importantly, I remember the resulting life lessons which I learned. One was the time that I skipped kindergarten with my friend Gerry. Thank God that I was caught in my deception or I may have tried it at other times. The more we get away with things in life, the more relaxed we tend to become about rules.

When I was ten years of age, my dad began taking me on Saturday mornings with him to work at his lumber yard. I'm sure that I was more trouble than I was help, but dad was an excellent teacher of work habits, and felt that it was necessary for me to get an early start on learning about work ethics. Many of the lessons that he taught me through those experiences, I have never forgotten.

One morning when business was slack, as I was wandering through the hardware department, I eyed some hefty lumber-marking crayons. (I think they sold for nineteen cents a piece at the time.) Although I had no particular use for them, I stuffed four different colored crayons into my jacket pocket. Later as dad and I drove home together, I remember the feeling of the crayons burning in my pocket and my conscience nagging me. My treasures were worth less than eighty cents, but I felt terribly guilty because I had stolen them. Since the crayons didn't belong to me, I couldn't let anyone see them and had to hide them in one of my dresser drawers. They sat there for a couple of weeks until my mom found my stash when she was putting away my laundry. When she asked me where they had come from, I went with my first instinct and lied. I told her that Eric, the hardware manager, had given them to me. Now I was not only a thief, but I was also a liar and to make matters worse, your grandma somehow knew it! Since the crime was too serious for her to simply forget, she told my dad about what I had done.

I tried the crying thing and said that I was sorry, but it wasn't good enough. After considering what an appropriate discipline would be, my dad told me that I would have to go back to Eric, return the crayons and apologize. I still remember how humiliated and embarrassed I was paying my penance, but I have never stolen anything since that day. My mom and dad loved me enough to make sure that I learned the virtue of honesty early in my life.

Just a few months ago a similar thing happened at our church. One of the young moms caught her six year old boy and his friend in the kitchen, drinking out of the little creamers that were in the fridge. After they had drunk from a half dozen or so, they were stomping their feet on them, crunching the containers on the floor and splashing cream everywhere. The boys were giggling and having a wonderful time - until mom showed up.

I don't know what happened to the second boy, but I do know what happened to Ryan. Although the creamers were only worth a few cents, his mom made him take five dollars from his savings and had him put it in the church offering to cover expenses. Then he was made to write me, the pastor of his church, a note of apology. When I received his note in the mail I gave Ryan a call. I could hear him on the other end of the phone when his mom answered. She said, "Ryan, it's Pastor Barry."

I could only imagine his stunned look as he responded, "What does he want?"

"He wants to speak with you," his mom replied.

There was a long pause and then a very timid little voice said, "Hello, this is Ryan speaking."

I thanked him for his note and his offering and told him how proud I was of him for his behaviour. Ryan will never forget the incident with the creamers and the discipline that he received will serve him well for the remainder of his life.

My grandma's style of discipline

ANOTHER STORY that I remember happened at my grandparent's home when I was about eight. My grandpa and grandma had raised six kids and had been grim disciplinarians. However, by the time they were in their sixties, they were much more relaxed when it came to disciplining their grandchildren. I don't remember what I had done wrong that day at their home, but my dad was taking me into the back bedroom to give me a spanking. I overheard grandma saying to my dad , "Allan, it's my house so why don't you let me discipline Barry?"

She was only about ninety-five pounds and so I remember being relieved by her suggestion. Not wanting to make it a big deal, my dad agreed. I can still vividly recall the exchange between grandma and me.

"Are you sorry for what you did, Barry?"

"Yes, I am Grandma."

"Okay Honey, when I spank, you yell."

With that, she slapped her hands together loudly several times and I yelled in pretend pain. We both walked out of the bedroom smiling. I'm sure my dad knew exactly what had happened in the room.

As much as I loved my grandma and as much as I know that she loved me, I am very thankful that what happened on that memorable Sunday afternoon was not the way that I was raised. My mom and dad brought up six kids who understood the rules and who also understood the consequences that came when the rules were broken. We are now six adults, with well behaved children and grandchildren of our own. Everyone of you kids Kelly, justly deserves our pride in you.

The shepherd's rod of discipline

IT'S TRUE WHAT the Bible says; A father who disciplines his son loves him. The word discipline is related to the word disciple. A disciple is simply a follower or a learner. So to discipline our children is to train them to live according to the rules. We are disciplined in our work habits as part of our school curriculum; we are disciplined in our driving habits as part of our education; and we are disciplined in our health habits as part of our rearing through childhood. In the same way our parents, authorities and shepherd discipline us throughout our life journey to help us keep on the right path.

In the sheepfold, the shepherd's rod was his means of discipline, so the psalmist chose to use the word rod as a metaphor for the discipline of life. It does not mean that we should literally use a rod such as the shepherds carried to discipline our children, but rather that we should care for them enough to ensure that they are taught (disciplined) to live according to the rules. The lessons which our children learn about the disciplines of life in their early years will serve them well throughout their lives. Discipline will help them thrive in school, accelerate in business, maintain good health in their bodies and stay balanced in their spiritual lives. The rod in Psalm Twenty-three represents the many ways that our shepherd uses discipline to teach us how to be successful and fulfilled in our life journey. No wonder he says "your rod comforts me". The end result of a disciplined life is satisfaction and comfort.

Kelly, I titled this letter after a proverb which has been questioned by your generation; *Spare the rod and spoil the child.* Those who would spurn such advice, likely do not understand the meaning of the shepherd's rod.

Three thousand years ago, when David wrote Psalm Twenty-three, he knew the importance of the rod to a shepherd. In those days, a shepherd had very limited equipment. He no doubt had a sack for his meals, a water bottle and an oil bottle, but just as important were his rod and his staff. (I'll come back to the staff in my next letter to you). A shepherd in Palestine often carved his rod himself. It was likely cut from a young sapling and then shaped with care and precision. It had a rounded head, was well balanced and usually had his uniquely designed markings engraved in it. This was how each shepherd could recognize his own rod. The young trainee shepherds of that day would practice by the hour, learning how to throw their rods with speed and accuracy. The reason that they practised so diligently was that their rods were their main weapon of defence for both themselves and their sheep.

The rod was so vital to a shepherd that it was like an extension of his right arm. It was a symbol of his power and authority. It was his safeguard against danger, which protected him and his flock. It was also a means of disciplining a wayward sheep. The rod can be compared to a rifle or a handgun which is carried by a cattleman or shepherd on our ranches today. The connotation of power and authority is the same.

If a rebellious sheep were misbehaving by fighting, wandering away, approaching poisonous weeds or getting too close to danger, a shepherd would simply throw his rod through the air with just enough force to scare it back into its rightful place in the flock. Of course the shepherd would not hurt his beloved animals with his rod, but would aim it carefully at the sheep's thickly covered, well padded rumps. The impact of the flying rod was intended to startle him rather than injure him. That was usually all that was necessary to get the sheep back into order again.

I used to have a Social Studies teacher who used that tactic for disciplining his students. After a stern warning for us to keep quiet, if any one dared to talk out of turn, Mr. Tatroff would whirl around from the blackboard that he was writing on and hurl his chalk at the chatting student. His method of discipline was very severe and would be illegal these days, but it did serve to keep us very quiet. Of course, I'm not suggesting that we either hit or throw things at our children Kelly, but I am simply underlining the fact that the shepherd's rod was a tool of discipline for recalcitrant sheep.

The shepherd's rod of protection

IN ANCIENT PALESTINE, another use for the shepherd's rod was to use it to inspect the sheep's health. Maintaining his sheep's physical well being was a regular responsibility of every caring shepherd. As each animal would walk toward him, the shepherd would use his rod to part the sheep's wool to examine its skin condition. He would also use it when buying a new sheep. A shepherd would carefully examine the wool's cleanliness and the health of the hide by separating the fleece with his rod. The health of his flock was always on a good shepherd's mind.

Finally, the rod was used as a defensive weapon by the shepherd to protect himself or his sheep from danger. It was used as a club to kill a rattlesnake or as a projectile to scare away a preying coyote. The shepherd was skilled in aiming his rod and accurately striking his target. Protecting his sheep from danger of attack brought security and comfort to the defenseless sheep.

Spare the rod, spoil the child

KELLY, IT'S IMPORTANT to note in this short clause of the psalm; *Your rod comforts me*, that the rod belongs to the shepherd just as the sheep belong to the shepherd. Using his rod skilfully was a means of expressing his love toward his sheep. David doesn't use the term "his rod" in the third person.

He chooses to use the second person pronoun *your*; *your rod comforts me*. In times of discipline the shepherd and the sheep were in intimate relationship. Just like your mom and I disciplined you and Kristy because of our love for you, so the shepherd's rod was a symbol of his love and care.

In contrast to the undisciplined middle aged man whom I told you about earlier in this letter, I can remember several times when mom or I sat down with you girls and used the rod of discipline. Whether our rod was withholding a special treat until you finished all of your dinner, not allowing you to go outside before your room was cleaned or grounding you for an evening unless an assignment was completed, every time that we disciplined you it was because we loved you. We loved you and cared about you enough to not allow you to disobey. By using our rod of discipline, we taught you that obedience and order are right and good.

Sometimes it was a very serious issue which we had to talk about together. The process included sitting down to discuss the purpose and value of the discipline which you were about to receive, the application of the rod which was appropriate for the offense, (in your case Kelly, because you were so sensitive, the rod was often simply a warning or a stern reprimand. That would usually bring you to the place of contrition and right order) many hugs and "I love you's" added for good measure, and always forgiveness. There were times when you may have resisted our hugs and love because of the heat of the moment Kelly, but today I know that you and Kristy are both thankful that your mom and I loved you enough to correct your misbehavior.

We have been commanded by God to discipline our children by teaching them to do what is right. When he says that to spare the rod is to spoil the child, he means that if we do not discipline our children, they will not learn to walk on the right path. Wandering away from the right path, which has been prepared for every child by their loving shepherd, will lead them to hurt and ultimate failure. A parent who does not protect their children, as much as possible, from wandering into danger and destruction, does not really love them or is ignorant of the danger. When there is lack of discipline, they become spoiled children.

To spoil a child is to destroy them. This can be better understood by the example of a rotten apple. A spoiled apple is useless. It is not only ugly and unusable for its intended purpose, but because it will also expedite the rotting of other apples, it must be discarded quickly. Adapt that picture of a rotting apple to the spoiling of a child. A child who is never taught, through discipline, what is acceptable or unacceptable behavior will become an adult who will be inundated with difficulties throughout life. He not only will have difficulty fulfilling his own destiny, but will likely infect others along his path with his rottenness.

It is vital for us to always keep correction and love well balanced in the process of discipline. Love must always be our underlying motive and attitude as we apply the rod of discipline. We both know adults who have been severely damaged by either loveless discipline or undisciplined love. Either extreme can cause a lifetime of dysfunction and failure. The problem often comes when we react to our parents' system of discipline. If they were too strict or loveless in their discipline, we often tend to not be strict enough; or if they were too soft, we may be too severe. A healthy balance of love and correction are fundamental to good parenting, as well as to good shepherding. Our shepherd understands how to consistently love us, while at the same time diligently teach us how to walk in the right way.

The farmer, athlete and soldier

CONSIDER THREE CAREERS which underline this principle that discipline is necessary to the success of our life journey. Can you imagine a farmer who isn't disciplined and who doesn't work hard to remove the weeds from his soil, fertilize his crops, turn on the sprinkling system on a dry day or bring in the harvest when it is ready? He just doesn't feel like getting up at six o'clock in the morning when the alarm goes off. Even though the crops are ripe and ready for harvesting and the rains are coming, he decides to go fishing instead.

The idea is ludicrous. Of course the farmer knows his business. He knows the seasons, understands the cycle of his crops and he has learned by experience what to do and when to do it. Like a baby when ready to be born, ripe crops wait for no man. When they are ready, the farmer needs to be ready. If a farmer were not disciplined, he would fail in his chosen field.

Likewise, we cannot conceive of an athlete who does not consistently discipline himself to watch his daily food intake, diligently keep his body toned to precision or who does not practise his skills until he hurts. An athlete must always be ready to go when the starting signal sounds. He wouldn't be an athlete if he were not disciplined to the point of pain. Disciplined self-denial is the name of the athlete's game. It determines whether he will be a winner or a loser.

Think also of a soldier who is undisciplined, does not know his place in rank and who refuses to take orders. Since he hasn't practised with his rifle, he can't shoot straight and is undependable when it comes to being at the right place at the right time. You wouldn't want him driving a tank, dropping bombs from an airplane or standing face to face in combat with the enemy. An undisciplined soldier is an oxymoron. The very idea does not compute.

So it is with each of us. The rod of discipline is as necessary to a healthy balanced life as it is in the life of a farmer, athlete or soldier. Our good shepherd, parents, teachers, police force, superiors at work and our own willpower are all gifts to us for the purpose of keeping us within the perimeters of the right path as we walk through our life journey.

The good life is not always the best life

KELLY, FROM YOUR medical training, you know well that the most natural and enjoyable things in life are not always the best for us. For me, happiness may be eating a pile of chocolate covered peanuts, sleeping in late and sitting in my easy chair watching movies all day. Each may have its time and place, but these activities taken to extremes will do more harm to me than good.

Sheep are a lot like us, so we can learn many lessons from watching them. For example sheep, like we do, look for comfortable spots in their pasture to lie down and rest. But the soft comfortable places are not always what they appear to be. In a sheep's case, those soft grasses which they choose can at times hide ruts in the ground which can be disastrous for a resting sheep. As I mentioned before, because the sheep have such small legs and heavy bodies, they can easily roll over into one of these low spots in a pasture. While lying on its back, a sheep is totally helpless. They do not have the strength or the balance of weight to roll upright again. Without the shepherd's help she will likely die in her comfortable rut. And that sounds like me. I tend toward comfort and ease, but could before long easily destroy myself in those undisciplined positions.

Too much wool and too much fat are not good

WOOL IS A SHEPHERD'S bread and butter. One would think that the more wool that a sheep had, the better that it would be, but not so. Too much wool is unhealthy for a sheep. It can become matted with mud, manure and burrs and weigh the sheep down. Although sheep resist being sheered and it's hard work for the shepherd, it must be done for the sheep's own good.

People today, including you and me, tend to want to accumulate stuff, whether cars, toys, furniture or clothes, which tend to weigh us down and hold us back from realizing our prepared destiny. For my friend who lost everything in a house fire, it seemed like the worst day of her life when it happened; but in retrospect it was one of her best days because everything changed after that fire. She was pressed closer to her shepherd than ever before and she began to hear his voice clearly. That tragedy served as a discipline and became a pivotal point in her life, which ultimately led her down a different road - a road of new beginnings. Even we humans need to be sheered from time to time for our own good.

Besides tending to look for comfortable spots and accumulating too much wool, sheep also lean toward obesity. The fact is though, that a sheep which is too fat is neither healthy nor productive. They are easily cast down and are less agile when it comes to walking or running from danger. To prevent this, a shepherd's difficult challenge is to ration his sheep's food and to keep them on a more rigorous schedule. Although the discipline means more work for the shepherd and is unpleasant for the sheep, it is for the good of both of them.

Like the sheep Kelly, I tend to look for the easy, less stressful places in life; to want to accumulate stuff which I think will make me happier and to indulge in thoughts and activities which are not very healthy. And that is why I need a shepherd with a rod to teach me how to live a disciplined way of life. In the season of harvest, it's the disciplined farmer who brings in the most fruitful crop. In the final inning, it's the disciplined athlete who wins the game. At the end of the battle, it's the disciplined soldiers who conquer their enemies.

A disciplined life seems to be the hard way to live. If I didn't know better, I'd likely choose an undisciplined life over a disciplined one. At first glance, ease and self-gratification appear to be more desirable than the self-denial and discomfort that the rod of discipline offers. But I do know better and so do you! I know that the rod ultimately brings me comfort.

There are four principles that my shepherd has taught me over the course of my life that I'd like to share with you Kelly. These four principles have convinced me that the disciplined life is the right way to choose.

Laws and rules are good

THE FIRST PRINCIPLE is that laws and rules are given to us for our own good. Certain people find rules difficult. They resist all authority and rebel against anything that restricts them. They just want to be free to do their own thing. The fact is, however, that laws and rules promote freedom. Canada has always been known as a country where peace, order and good government prevail. Our history does not include the native rebellions, gold rush massacres, Boston tea party, civil war, or even the college riots which were highlights in the colorful history of the United States. Canadians value freedom, which is a positive, orderly, gentle word. In contrast Americans value liberty, which is a more aggressive word.

Canadians, who tend to be more passive and compliant, (perhaps apathetic) have never fought for liberty from mother England. We have submissively obeyed her rule. The Royal Canadian Mounted Police have been honored and respected throughout our history. Canadians value peace, order and good government and are generally liked by people in every country. I recognize that some of our apparent peacefulness has to do with our fear and apathy, but mostly it's a result of our desire to play by the rules that have been set by our authorities.

Can you imagine if we had no laws on the road and we could drive as fast as we wanted, anywhere we wanted, whenever we wanted? Can you imagine there being no red lights, no speed limits, no passing lanes and no police to give us tickets? - chaos and danger would reign!

Imagine if there were no laws for loggers, fishermen, doctors or businessmen and they could all do exactly what they wanted. At first thought it would seem wonderful, but then we would see the anarchy, confusion, chaos and devastation which would result. Without laws and rules we would not survive for very long.

Pain and suffering are not all bad

THE SECOND PRINCIPLE is that pain and suffering are not all bad. They serve a purpose. I talked with a farmer one time about his corn crop. It had been a good year with plenty of rain and so it surprised me when he said that his crops were especially vulnerable. He told me that even a short drought could have a devastating effect on his crops that year. When I asked him why, he explained that in times of frequent rains the plants are not required to push their roots down deeper in search of water. The roots remain shallow near the surface. If a short drought came after the rains, the plants would be unprepared for the lack of water because their roots didn't go down deep enough. The result would be that they would quickly die.

That crop of corn is a picture of you and me, Kelly. It's adversity which forces our roots to reach down deep in preparation for the inevitable droughts of life. A little bit of difficulty is heathy for us because it presses us into maturity.

One of the low times in my career at Canadian Forest Products came shortly after I was hired. I had always worked as a laborer or truck driver and I felt that I was in way over my head as I began my first white-collar office job. Almost everything I did brought out feelings of insecurity and inadequacy, but I was determined to do my best for the company and myself. I also desperately wanted to be liked by my co-workers and so I pushed past my timidity at every opportunity.

After three months of working at the new job, I felt like I was finally catching on to the routine and beginning to contribute to the team. I was not prepared for what I heard at my first job review. My boss began his appraisal of me with a few gracious words, but then he got straight to his point. He said, "Barry, this just isn't working out the way we had hoped." His words hit me like a brick. I knew the sound of a boss gently firing his employee - I had heard it before. I sat with my mouth open as he told me some of his concerns. One, which burned like a fiery dart in my heart, was that some of the guys had complained that I was withdrawn and unfriendly. They couldn't seem to get to know me. I was embarrassed and ashamed that the very thing I had tried to do had obviously not worked; but at the same time I knew my boss was right. I really did have a lot to learn about being winsome and congenial. I begged him to give me some more time to work on my social skills and thankfully he did.

Only one week later I got hit with another blow. I was standing at the sales counter having a conversation with a salesmen from one of our suppliers. The man was intimidating. He was tall, boisterous and had a loud authoritative voice. As I was listening to him and at the same time trying to hide my timidity, the man exploded, "For God's sake kid, look at me when you talk to me!" All of my co-workers were looking at the two of us.

I was mortified and felt like a little boy being attacked by the school bully. Even though this incident severely wounded my ego, it became one of the significant pivotal points on my life journey. From that day on I have consciously looked into the eyes of people with whom I am speaking. The pain of those two encounters with my gracious boss and the intimidating salesman has pressed me into changing my behavior. The marks on my soul left by those two blows of the rod of discipline were so severe that I have never been the same since. Beginning that week, I learned to stand tall, to confidently look at, listen to and care for the people to whom I am speaking .

We need to let others suffer

THE THIRD PRINCIPLE that I've learned about a disciplined life is that it is good and right at times to let other people suffer. To let others suffer, even when we know it's necessary for their own growth, is a very difficult thing to do. Especially when it's somebody whom we love that is suffering. The truth is Kelly, that if we don't learn to do this, we may be responsible for inhibiting the growth of the very person whom we want most to help. Practising this principle is very challenging for those of us who are strong in compassion.

One of the gifts that God gives to some people is the gift of mercy. Those gifted persons are often drawn to people helping careers, such as a social worker, nurse, pastor or counsellor. They can also be found volunteering at the cancer clinic, Red Cross and skid row mission. Although we thank God for these compassionate, mercy-motivated people, they do have a potential weakness. Their temptation is to help every person they see out of every mess that they get themselves into. Very often, the best help we can give to the person who has got himself in a difficult situation is to leave him alone. When we apply the rod of discipline, the shepherd teaches us to let him suffer and struggle his own way out. If we don't do this, we could ultimately be hurting the person more than helping him.

I'm reminded of a couple whom you and I both know Kelly, from one of our old neighborhoods. They are the nicest people and they wouldn't want anybody to suffer for any reason. Their sons, however, who are both in their early thirties are selfish and very inconsiderate. They have rarely, if ever, heard the word "no" from either parent and they avoid taking responsibility for anything in their lives. One of their sons has never held down a successful job in his life and his dad still slips him money whenever he asks. He is currently rebounding from a second failed live-in relationship and he has moved back home where his mom is looking after him and nursing his wounds. His brother, who still lives at home, attempted suicide last year after a long battle with drugs and alcohol.

While I was consoling the parents after their son's attempted suicide, they cried relentlessly. They have thoroughly loved their boys. What went wrong? Why have both of their sons' lives failed so miserably? The answer comes from the successful farmer, athlete and soldier. They needed discipline in their lives. As the old saying goes; no pain-no gain.

As I sat listening to them share their story, I understood their desire to rescue their children because I have been tempted to do the same thing with you and Kristy. I remember how your sister Kristy, all through school and university, would often put off doing her assignments until the night before they were due. Inevitably, she would come to me and say, with her big brown eyes batting irresistibly, "Daddy, can you please help me with this assignment? It's due tomorrow morning."

I'd respond, "Honey, when did you first learn that the assignment was due?" Usually, it was two or three weeks previously. You know how it goes. I'd often give in to her pleas. After all I didn't want her to fail her subject. The irony is that now she is a school teacher, who has the responsibility of teaching her students to discipline and pace themselves in order for them to hand their work in on time. Regardless of our tendencies to rescue those in need, if we want to truly help them, we are usually best to apply the rod of discipline along with a healthy dose of love and patience.

I mentioned in my last letter about a couple of friends who had got themselves into financial difficulty. I wanted to rescue them, but wasn't in a position to help so I telephoned a few of my wealthier friends to see what they could do. Each one of them refused to lend any money, even for my sake, because as they put it, financial help was not really what the destitute couple really needed. They had to learn some hard life lessons about handling money. They needed an application of the rod of discipline, which ultimately brought the comfort that comes from an orderly life. As I watched them emerge through their valley stronger than they'd ever been, I was once again reminded that sometimes, as hard as it is, the most helpful thing I can do is to let a person struggle through his own failure.

When you turned sixteen Kelly and I taught you to drive, I experienced one of those difficult times of learning to let go. I had helped you study the manual with all the rules in it. We had gone over the basics of how the car operates, but finally the time came for you to actually get behind the wheel of the car and drive us around. I was tempted more than once to grab the wheel from you, to slam my foot down on the imaginary brake on the passenger side of the car and even to ban you from driving for the rest of your days. There is however a time to back off, let go, keep quiet and let our children make their own mistakes and learn from their own failures. You eventually did learn to drive skilfully with only a few bumps and scratches along the way. Using the rod skilfully sometimes involves not saying or doing anything at all.

We each have our own natural weaknesses

THE SHEPHERD'S ROD of discipline is used in different ways as we move through the various life stages, which I wrote about earlier. In the first stage of life, *sovereign foundations*, our early years were largely predetermined. We held little control over what happened. We were born at a prescribed time, to pre-ordained parents into an already established set of circumstances. Gradually, as we travelled down our life pathways, we moved from predetermination to self-determination. More and more as we matured, our own choices have determined most of the consequences which we have experienced. The shepherd's rod became increasingly helpful to us as we made our first immature choices.

The second period of our lives, *experimental choices*, followed the sovereign foundations phase. In that stage our character was formed by the discipline we received from our parents and teachers, and by how we responded to that discipline. If I were to chart those two periods of my own life, they would cover about ten years each. Although technically they overlapped, generally speaking in the first ten years many choices were made for me, while in the second decade I was responsible for many of my own choices. What I had learned in my childhood years I tried out for myself in my teens. According to theory, after those ten years of experimentation, by age twenty, I was now a man.

From twenty to thirty is the *becoming an adult* stage, I grew into the man I presumed that I was at twenty. My character was formed, I began sensing my life direction and I tried out my new adult wings. The rod of discipline in my life was no longer administered by my parents and teachers; but was now in the hands of my employers, my government, myself and my shepherd. Some of the greatest lessons in my life were learned when I was in my twenties. In my case, your mom and I were married and had children during those years. I believe that we learned more important life lessons from each of those experiences than either attending university or getting our first job could have taught us.

My thirties held for me the *skill development* stage of life and were focussed on learning skills for my chosen profession. Built upon my sovereign foundations, my choices as a teenager and my lessons in manhood, I then had to grow into the role of pastor. The basic skills necessary for success in my career as a pastor took me about ten years to learn. By the time I reached forty years of age, I figured life was at last within my control. My character was formed, my skills were sharpened and I was ready to move forward.

That's when the fifth stage of my life cycle began; *the character honing* stage. My shepherd then took me aside and poked and probed at my soul with his rod. Areas which I had thought were securely under my control were now being exposed to the discipline of my shepherd. He loved me too much to let me get away with some of the infections that were festering inside of my soul. Diseases such as lust, fear and pride, which I figured had long been conquered, were revealed by his touch. The shepherd was preparing me for the productive years ahead, but there were some pretty severe disciplines necessary to endure before I was to arrive. Up to about fifty years of age my growth process looked like this:

STAGE 1	STAGE 2	STAGE 3	STAGE 4	STAGE 5
Sovereign Foundations	Experimental Choices	Becoming a Man	Skill Development	Character Honing
years 1 - 10	years 10 - 20	years 20 - 30	years 30 - 40	years 40 - 50

I learned in my fifth decade that every person has natural character weaknesses. Just as we have physical weaknesses, we also have vulnerable areas in our souls. They fall into three categories: lust of the flesh, lust of the eyes and the pride of life.

The lust of the flesh is glandular. My drives to eat, to drink, and for sexual gratification fall into this category. Within healthy boundaries each of those desires were placed in me by God, but when I stretch past those boundaries, my lust will lead me into failure. The lust of the eyes has to do with my wanting things that I see; material possessions, clothes, houses and cars. Although all those things may be right and good, the problems come when I move past propriety into jealousy, envy, anger, insecurity, criticism and hate. The pride of life is probably the most sinister of all and I found that this was my own most vulnerable area. This category deals with self-centredness, self-righteousness, self-consciousness, fear, anger and pride. It often follows on the heels of success and is even found in the pursuit of godliness. Of all the hundreds of people to whom Jesus preached and spoke in his days on earth, he was the hardest on the religious leaders who were rancid with spiritual pride. He described the self-righteous Pharisees as white-washed tombs who were clean on the outside, but as rotten as a dead man's bones on the inside.

This *character-honing* stage of life was very challenging for me. My shepherd and I had a lot of work to do. Both his rod and his staff were in constant use, but I noticed over the decade that an obvious growth was taking place in my life. As the years passed he began using his staff more than his rod. The staff was still for the purpose of disciplining and was ultimately aimed at bringing comfort and peace, but it didn't seem to hurt quite so much as the rod.

Thankfully, I've come through most of the challenging character honing stage and I am moving into the sixth and most pleasurable phase of my life journey - the years of *convergence*. So far, I've loved the ride. But, according to your grandma, the seventh stage of *afterglow* is even better. That's getting ahead of us though. We are still in our walk through the valley of the shadow of death, thinking about our shepherd's rod and staff - his two instruments of discipline and teaching.

Kelly, I hated disciplining you as a child. Like many parents say, it hurt your mom and me more than it hurt you, but I'm grateful that we consistently corrected misbehavior in your early years. I look at you now as a young woman, wife and `mother and see such maturity, emotional health and balance. I'm very proud of you! I know that long before your mom and I stopped disciplining you with our loving rod, you began disciplining yourself. Both you and your shepherd are doing a great job and the good news is that it gets easier as you grow older. You'll find as you continue to move through each of the life stages ahead, that your shepherd will use his staff more often than he uses his rod. In my next letter, I'll explain how the shepherd's staff is designed to bring reassurance and comfort to your life journey. I love you, Honey.

Love Dad

CHAPTER TEN

The Shepherd Speaks

Your rod and your staff, they comfort me.

THE GOOD SHEPHERD guides us down the right path by speaking to us in many ways. His communication to us is metaphorically referred to as his staff that comforts us. Successfully hearing and obediently responding to his words are our daily responsibility.

Dear Kelly,

A golden anniversary party was given for an elderly couple. The husband was moved by the occasion and so he wanted to tell his wife just how he felt about her. She was very hard of hearing however, and often misunderstood what he said. With many of their family members and friends gathered around, he toasted her. "My dear wife, after fifty years, I've found you tried and true!"

Everyone smiled in approval, but his wife said, "Eh?"

He repeated himself, but much louder this time, "After fifty years, I've found you tried and true!"

His wife shot back, "Well let me tell you something - after fifty years, I'm tired of you too!"

Good communication is vital to any healthy marriage and that means good listening as well as good talking! Kelly, I've watched you and Tom communicate with each other over these last several years and I honestly feel that your ability to hear accurately and respond wisely are two of your greatest strengths. You have always amazed me, even when you were a child, how perceptively you have listened. You seem to have developed the skill early of not reacting to negative comments immediately, but carefully considering what was behind the words and then responding with grace. You carefully pay attention to body language and tone of voice, as well as the words being spoken. When you do speak, you have already considered what you are going to say and how you are going to say it. That's one of the many reasons that you are doing well in the medical field. You have a thoughtful and wise way of communicating with emotionally charged people.

The other evening, you surprised me again by your listening perception. At a noisy family function, where we were all talking and laughing, you suddenly perked up your maternal ears. I don't know how you did it, but you heard your son's voice from another room above all the other noise. I hadn't heard a peep from him!

Kelly, there is another voice that's even more important to hear clearly than all the others. It's more important than your parents', husband's or friends' voices. I'm referring to the voice of your shepherd. When he speaks, you're wise to have your ears tuned carefully to his words. It's the shepherd, after all, who guides you throughout your life journey. He is the only one who knows the way into tomorrow's experiences. In this letter, I will tell you one of the most valuable lessons of life - how the good shepherd uses his voice to direct our paths each day. In Psalm Twenty-three, David calls the shepherd's voice, his staff that comforts me.

The shepherd and his staff

THERE IS AN OLD story about a man and his wife sitting watching television together. On the show that they were watching, the man leaned toward his girl, with flowers in hand and told her how beautiful she was and how much he loved her. The wife, watching the romance, wistfully turned toward her aloof husband and asked him, "Ernie, why don't you ever tell me that you love me?"

He didn't even make a gesture as he responded, "I told you that I loved you thirty years ago when I married you and if I ever change my mind, I'll let you know!"

As sad as that humour is, that thoughtless husband is what most people think that our good shepherd is like. "I told you that I loved you two thousand years ago and if I ever change my mind I'll let you know!" But our shepherd is not mute. The character of our Lord is that he desires to talk with his people. In Psalm Twenty-three, the shepherd's staff is a picture of his desire to communicate with his sheep. There are at least four ways a shepherd uses his long staff to guide his sheep: he uses it to keep them from straying, to draw them near for personal care, to guide them down the right path and to snatch them from danger.

The first way is with newborn lambs. Sometimes, in the excitement of birthing season, lambs will become separated from their mothers. The shepherd is always watching for stray lambs so that he can pick them up with the crook of his staff and gently place them next to their mothers.

Just last week, your grandma and grandpa watched a deer give birth to two fawns in their back yard. When the mother deer seemed to desert her babies by leaving them for over twenty-four hours, your grandpa went to their rescue. He and grandma bought a baby bottle and began to nurse the young fawns until they had enough strength to find their mom. After doing what they could, grandpa called the local vet to get some advice: When asked if they had touched the young deer, grandpa said he had held them while grandma gave them the milk. The vet reprimanded him and suggested that the mother would likely never claim her fawns because of the smell of a human on them. The good news is that the mother deer did return and care for her babies. It all turned out well, but the reason the shepherd uses his crook is to carry the lambs to their mothers and prevent his human scent from causing rejection by the ewe.

Secondly, his staff is used to reach out and catch individual sheep for examination. He draws the timid sheep close to himself so he can better care for their needs. The long staff is like an extension of the shepherd's arm.

Thirdly, the staff is used to guide the sheep. As shepherd and sheep are walking along a new or difficult pathway, a shepherd will lovingly reach over and press the staff against the side of his sheep to guide it where he wants it to walk. The sheep actually like this personal attention. In our world, it would be like you reaching out and taking Alexander's hand as you both cross a busy street. The shepherd's touch to his sheep is as vital as a mother's touch is to her child.

The fourth use of the staff is evident in the parable about the shepherd who is counting his sheep when he notices that one out of a hundred is missing, and so he goes and searches for the one that is lost. When he finds it, whether it has fallen deep into a rock crevice, been caught between two trees or stuck in a thorn bush, he deftly takes his staff and reaches out to save his lost lamb from danger. The staff is a symbol of the shepherd's love, care, guidance and protection. We, like the sheep, have the promise of our shepherd that he is always near to lovingly keep us from straying, draw us near for personal care, guide us down the right path and snatch us from danger. To do these four things, he uses his staff.

The shepherd's "how to" manual

THE STAFF, TO ME, is an unmistakable metaphor of our shepherd's words. The Lord loves, cares for, guides and protects us with his skillful use of communication - both written and verbal. I've heard many people complain, "If God would just talk to me, I'd know what to do!", but I believe that our shepherd has clearly spoken and does speak to us more than we realize.

Kelly, you and Tom, like most of us, have at least a couple of Bibles in your home. The Bible is our shepherd's "how to" manual. It explains to us in detail and illustrates with hundreds of gripping stories how life is supposed to work. Your Bible is like the instruction manuals that always comes with the things that we buy.

When your mom and I recently purchased a new video recorder, which was much more complicated than our older one, the first thing I did was read the new owner's manual from cover to cover. I sat in my big easy chair and tried everything the book suggested, until I was comfortable with the remote and the video recorder. Imagine buying a new computer or video game and not learning how it works. In our pride and ignorance, (especially us guys) we sometimes take weeks to figure out what we could have picked up in an hour of study.

I actually learned that lesson the hard way. When you and Kristy were very young, we bought you girls a new swing set. Thinking that I knew what I was doing, I put the swing set together without even a glance at the instructions. I got it together all right, but discovered I had a few extra parts left over. I had neglected to add a couple of important safety features, so I finally turned to the "how to" manual. It took another two hours to take it apart and then put it together right.

Although most people have at least one Bible in their homes, I honestly doubt that many of us have read God's instruction manual from cover to cover. It is amazing how many concepts and principles, which are vital to a successful life journey, are thoroughly and clearly explained in the Shepherd's Instruction Manual. Every one of us could save years of struggle in our journey if we were to not only read the manual, but also practice what its author prescribes for healthy living.

I've recommended to hundreds of people to first of all purchase a modern translation of the Bible. (The King James Bible was translated in a vernacular used four hundred years ago. It's very poetic but difficult for most of us to really understand. There are many up-to-date translations which can make our Bible reading not only palatable, but fun.) Secondly, I tell people that reading their Bible for about fifteen minutes a day, will get them through the entire book in one year. I can't think of a better investment of our time.

Our shepherd is not mute

KELLY, MY DESIRE in this letter is to unveil a secret, which has been hidden throughout the ages. The secret is that our shepherd is not mute. He speaks to us regularly and clearly as he guides us through our life journey. David refers to the shepherd's words as his staff which comforts us.

The word *comforts* in the Bible is worthy of note. It comes from two Greek words which mean to come alongside. The one who comes alongside us when we are walking through the valley of the shadow of death is our comforter. As he walks beside us, he comforts us by showing us the way to walk. Both his written words and his spoken words are his staff, which comforts us.

Remember the story of the Jewish rabbi, Catholic priest and Baptist pastor, who went fishing together. They were in the boat not too far from land when the rabbi said to his friends, "I forgot to bring the thermos of coffee. It's back on the beach."

The pastor suggested that they row back to shore and get it, but the rabbi said, "It's okay. I'll walk." With that, he stepped out of the boat and walked across the water, got his thermos, returned and climbed back in to the boat.

Just as the rabbi got back in the boat, the priest stepped out onto the water, saying, "I forgot to bring the bait." He then walked across the water, got his bait and came back to the boat. The Baptist pastor sat stunned, with his mouth wide open, but he figured that if a Jew and a Catholic had that much faith, then surely a Baptist should be able to walk on water too. With a sudden burst of bravado, he stepped out of the boat, onto the water and promptly sank. As the other two leaned over to rescue their naive friend from the waves, they smiled at each other and said, "I guess we should have told him where the rocks were!"

Our shepherd comforts us as he guides us through our life journey, by showing us where the rocks are for us to step on.

How is your hearing?

JESUS TOLD A STORY to his disciples, which underscores the value of cultivating good listening skills. His point was that there is no lack of clear guidance from our shepherd, but there is a serious deficiency in our hearing. Learning to listen well is fundamental to enjoying a successful journey down any life pathway. Here's the story: *Listen! A farmer went out to plant some seed. As he scattered it across his field, some seed fell on a footpath, and the birds came and ate it. Other seed fell on shallow soil and underlying rock. The plant sprang up quickly, but it soon wilted beneath the hot sun, and died because the roots had no nourishment in the shallow soil. Other seed fell among thorns that shot up and choked out the tender blades so that it produced no grain. Still other seed fell on fertile soil and produced a crop that was thirty, sixty, and even a hundred times as much as he had planted.*

Today, we might use a city metaphor such as tuning into a desired radio station by turning the dial to the correct band. The reception ranges from being incomprehensible to a clear pure sound as we adjust the knob. Music will even be received better by moving the treble, bass, equalizer or balance sliders. Our listening and hearing equipment in our heads and hearts needs to be tuned in the same way, in order for us to hear the shepherd's voice clearly.

To Jesus' audience however, his story about the four different soils should have made perfect sense. They understood farming because most of them lived an agrarian life, but as closely as his disciples were listening to him, they still did not understand. Jesus gently chided them by clearly emphasizing his main point, "Anyone who is willing to hear should listen and understand!" He even repeated himself a minute later, "Anyone who is willing to hear should listen and understand!"

Because of the primary importance of this parable, Jesus explained it in detail, to his followers, later on, He taught: *The farmer I talked about is a picture of those who bring God's message to others. The seed that fell on the hard path represents those who hear the message, but then satan comes at once and takes it away from them. The rocky soil represents those who hear the message and receive it with joy. But like young plants in such soil, their roots don't go very deep. At first they get along fine, but as soon as they have problems or are persecuted because they believe the word, they wilt. The thorny ground represents those who hear and accept the Good News, but all too quickly the message is crowded out by the cares of this life, the lure of wealth and the desire for nice things, so no crop is produced. But the good soil represents those who hear and accept God's message and produce a huge harvest - thirty, sixty or even a hundred times as much as had been planted.*

(A couple of simple words of interpretation may help Kelly. For my purposes, when the concept of God's Good News is introduced here, I am referring to the shepherd's instructions for staying on the predetermined right path for our life journey. When some people read the word, satan, although you and I personally believe in a real evil being called satan, they may safely insert the word adversary. I don't want anyone to miss the main point simply because they do not believe in either a personal God or devil.)

Back to Jesus' explanation of his story about the four different types of soil. He is saying that the four soils represent four different degrees of listening. Because you are so much like me Kelly, you will see yourself at different times in each of the four pictures. I can relate at every level. At times my heart is hard; at times it's shallow or weedy; and still at other times it's soft. Let's look at each of the four soils more closely.

Hard soil - a hardened heart

THE HARD SOIL is pictured as a beaten down pathway that the farmer's seeds merely bounce off. It would be like the dirt path near your house Kelly, that you and Tom take when walking Alex to the park. Birds eat the seeds on the hard soil as fast as they are scattered. A person may have a hardened heart because he has been stepped on and beaten down so often in the past that he has lost his ability to hear.

An example might be Lee Harvey Oswald, the fellow who reportedly shot President John Kennedy on November 22, 1963. Oswald was born to a mother who had already been married three times. She gave him no love or discipline in his early years. A school counsellor wrote about young Lee that he probably didn't know the meaning of the word love. He was rejected by his peers, failed academically and received an undesirable discharge from the marines. As an adult, he was small, scrawny, not talented or skilled and had no sense of worthiness. His own wife viciously belittled him for failing as a provider and for sexual impotency. She even locked him in the bathroom as a punishment and finally forced him to leave their home.

Lee Harvey Oswald's heart had been stepped on so many times, it was not only hard, but was bruised and crushed almost beyond hope of repair. It's no wonder that he got so far off the right path that he shot and killed the one man who embodied success, beauty, wealth and power more than any other man on earth.

You or I Kelly, have never been hardened to such an extent, but there have no doubt been times when we have been hurt by someone so much that when that person did say something encouraging, we didn't even hear it. In addition to hurt, disappointment can also make our hearts hard. It often happens in marriages. One brick at a time is laid between husband and wife, one disappointment after another, until there is a wall built so thick that it is impenetrable. Hardness of heart is at the root of most marriage breakdowns because communication can't take place when our hearts are hard.

Rocky soil - a shallow heart

ROCKY SOIL IS a picture of a shallow listener. Most of us husbands can relate. A couple of days ago, your mom and I were sitting on the front porch reading and drinking our morning coffee. As your mom would read something from the newspaper that she thought was interesting, she would interrupt my reading to tell me about it. I responded with the obligatory, "Uh huh" or "really!". At one of those times, she was talking about something and I was agreeing, when the phone rang. Your mom went to answer it and returned in several seconds. As she sat down she asked, "Now what was I telling you?" I didn't have the faintest idea, but the funny thing was that she couldn't remember either. That's a perfect picture of either rocky soil or old age - I'm not sure which.

Rocky soil is when we hear words, but we really don't get the message being sent. The seeds of communication do not get well rooted because of the rocks.

Thorny soil - an overcrowded heart

THORNY SOIL DESCRIBES an overcrowded life. We are so busy with other things, that when our shepherd does speak to us with instructions for the day, his voice is choked out. Three areas where we get overcrowded in life are as follows: First, is being too overly concerned or worried about our health, jobs, families, marriages or debts. Our anxiety filters out the shepherd's comforting words. Second, is being preoccupied with the pursuit of wealth. Those who are poor are as susceptible to these thorns every bit as much as those who are wealthy. Third, is being dissatisfied in our souls or our spirits. Dissatisfaction comes from not enjoying the green pastures, which the shepherd has provided for feeding our empty souls, or not stopping long enough to drink from the quiet refreshing waters intended to quench the thirst of our spirits. Dissatisfied people are always looking for something else. "Maybe a new car, a boat, golf clubs, a condo in Hawaii or a new wife will fill my emptiness." These three groups of people - the overly anxious, the preoccupied or the dissatisfied are not going to clearly hear their shepherd's guiding instructions. His voice will be choked out by the distractions around them.

Good soil - a healthy heart

FINALLY, THE GOOD soil represents our hearts when we are listening well. The shepherd speaks to us from the Bible, through our kids or a friend, in the quiet of the night, while we're half asleep, in our conscience or through our four year old neighbor, and we can actually hear his voice. We not only hear his voice through our ears, but deep in our heart we know it is the shepherd's voice that we are hearing.

These times of hearing his voice will always be turning points in our life journey. Sometimes the turn will be around a slight corner, while at other times it may mean an entire shift of career or priority. Good soil is a soft heart that receives the seed of the shepherd's word, which ultimately bursts into new life. The seeds that are planted in the good soil are the shepherd's instructions, affirmations, warnings or life principles. Sometimes, a seed will have in it all the DNA of an entire life destiny. I'll describe such a seed that changed my life forever in another letter to you Kelly.

A living seed in soft soil has enough latent power in it to alter the entire course of your life. Consider an apple seed. Cut it open and it appears so small and impotent, but place it in fertile soil and it can grow into a huge apple tree. But that is not the end of the story. Each apple on the tree has a half dozen seeds in it and the potential in one tree's annual crop of apples is to produce an entire orchard of apple trees. Do you get the picture? These seeds that the shepherd is scattering over our heart's soil when he speaks to us are charged with life changing energy. The fruitfulness of our lives is entirely dependant upon the condition of our heart ears. How good is the soil of your heart? How well do you hear his voice speaking to you?

Two vital life lessons

IN JESUS' STORY of the soils, we learn many lessons. A major lesson is that you and I cannot live even one day, much less an entire life, successfully and fruitfully without hearing the guiding words of our shepherd. We're lost without his voice. (I'll return to the subject of success later, but for now know that success is simply fulfilling our life purpose and destiny. We could therefore be rich, famous and powerful and still not be truly successful.) Even Jesus himself said that he only did and said what his father, the shepherd, instructed him to do and say. He modelled in his own life the type of listening heart which he taught us to have.

Let's listen further to the important life lesson that he taught to his disciples. Following his story about listening hearts, Jesus made his second major point; there are two types of people in this world; those who are useful to the shepherd's purposes and those who are useless. We are divided into the two groups by how well we listen with our hearts.

We tend to base our feelings of usefulness or uselessness, in this world on an entirely different value system. Our American culture judges our worth according to our intelligence quotient, emotional quotient, looks, weight, skin colour, wealth, influence or age. The shepherd, who prepared our destinies before we were born, lays out the right pathways and guides us through our life journey, says it has nothing to do with any of those false standards. Our usefulness relates entirely to our ability to listen to his voice and obey it.

Life is a mystery

REMEMBER THE KEY to this story of the four soils that Jesus repeated, "Anyone who is willing to hear, should listen and understand." After making that statement about listening and understanding, he said a strange thing to his followers: "To you has been given the mystery of the kingdom of God, but I am using these stories to conceal everything about it from outsiders."

The word mystery used in this passage refers to a secret that is revealed by the shepherd, only to those who are listening. It is an open secret revealed only to the initiated. For example, if I were to read an Agatha Christie mystery novel, by the time I finished the last page, I would know that the butler did it. I could then go to a friend and tell him, "You have got to read this book. It's a great mystery novel!" All the while, it would be a mystery to which I knew the secret. I would be one of the initiated who had read the end of the story.

This is similar to our lives in that the shepherd has already seen the end of my life journey. He has already written my biography. As I listen to him day by day, he guides me down his pre-destined plan for my life by unveiling mysteries, as necessary along the way, which help me fulfill my destiny.

The second definition we need to understand is the phrase the kingdom of God. The kingdom of God includes everything within the king's domain. The ultimate King, who reigns in authority over every human king, is the same shepherd who guides me down the right path for my life. If I choose to live my days under his guidance, then I am part of his dominion which he calls the kingdom of God.

Our privilege to unlock the mysteries

WHAT I AM SAYING Kelly, is that the shepherd uses mysteries to hide his life principles, to separate those with listening hearts from those who have hard, rocky or thorny hearts. God loves to conceal truth, especially in nature, which is only revealed to those who listen to his voice. Consider what Solomon says; "It is God's privilege to conceal things and the king's privilege to discover them." The king here could very well be anyone who chooses to rule with God in his kingdom. We then, as kings in our own circles of influence, have daily opportunities to see mysteries unlocked.

You can no doubt remember moments in your life Honey, when it seemed like a veil was suddenly lifted from your eyes. Some call it an "Ah ha!" moment. One that occurs to me was when my dad, brothers, sisters and I saw the lifeless body of my mom after she had been prepared for burial. As an eighteen year old boy, it was the first time that I had ever touched a lifeless body. As soon as I touched my mom's hand, I instantly understood that our bodies are simply temporary living places for the real us. Your grandma's spirit and soul were with her shepherd and it was okay for us to bury her body. She was finished with it. That was an, "Ah ha!" moment for me, which has since helped me give comfort to hundreds of people, who have lost loved ones.

Truth is hidden in nature

BACK TO THE STORY that Jesus was telling. He says; *For whatever is hidden is meant to be disclosed, and whatever is concealed is meant to be brought out into the open. If anyone has ears to hear, let him hear.* God especially loves to hide truth in nature. Walk a day with the good shepherd and listen to him teach, "Watch the birds of the sky; look at the guy over there sowing grain; see that fig tree, or that mustard seed or that lily."

When I woke up this morning, the sun was streaming through our front door window. Because the window is made from cut glass, there were several vividly coloured rainbows painted across the hardwood floor of our entry hall. They were a delightful reminder of the faithfulness of my shepherd. One of the mysteries of life that God has revealed only to the initiated, is that in every rainbow there is a reminder of a promise of his faithfulness.

If we think of life as a giant jigsaw puzzle, the life as a mystery concept becomes more clear. In this life puzzle there are many people co-operating to make sense of it, each putting their corner of the puzzle together. Your mom's and my marriage is a simple example of how our sections of the jigsaw puzzle come together. Before we were married, your mom grew up only twenty-five miles from me, but in a totally different environment from mine. She and her family were working on their corner of life's jigsaw puzzle, while I and my birth family were working on ours. When we were married, our two sections of the puzzle were connected. Since that day in 1969, everything I've done in my circle of influence, has affected your mom and her world and what she has done has affected me and my world. We are connected. Don't you love it when life comes together! It's just like you and I putting a puzzle together on one of our family vacations - I worked on the clouds and sky while you worked on the trees and lake. Suddenly one of us found a connecting piece and the whole picture began to make sense.

The physicist, chemist, biologist, geologist, theologian and psychologist are all helping us understand the mysteries of life, but all of them included will never get it together without the help of the great shepherd. Only he can explain mysteries of the kingdom, and he explains them only to those who have ears to hear. Any of us with listening ears, who are initiated, has the unique privilege of being in an intimate communicative relationship with the great shepherd himself.

What you seek is what you get

JESUS GOES ON to say; *Consider carefully how you listen. With the measure you use, it will be measured to you - and even more.* In other words, if we listen a little bit, we will hear a little bit. If we listen more, we will hear more; and there will even be a bonus for those of us who have soft attentive hearts.

Like mining for gold or silver, the precious metals do not pop out of the earth by themselves. The miner has to search and dig them out. King Solomon reminds us; *My child, listen to me and treasure my instruction. Tune your ears to wisdom, and concentrate on understanding. Cry out for insight and understanding. Search for them as you would for lost money or hidden treasure.* Jesus said it again here in his story that if you listen attentively, you will discover the mysteries of life that the Lord has hidden. The more we seek, the more we will find - plus a bonus amount.

How to hear more clearly

FINALLY, JESUS GIVES us further insight into the hearing and growing process; *To those who are open to my teaching, more understanding will be given. But to those who are not listening, even what they have will be taken away from them.* As hard as this concept is for us to grasp Kelly, it is true in all of life. In medical terms, it's called atrophy. If I were to not use my arm for a long time, I would ultimately lose the capacity for its use. Use it or lose it! Doctors tell us that older people do not lose their ability to remember as much as we may think. They simply do not continue learning. Even in a healthy eighty year old person, the more he uses his brain, the more capacity he will have to learn and remember. We see it in your grandma, Kelly. Even at eighty-three years of age, your grandma still is taking courses, reading and listening attentively. Her mind is still as sharp as the mind of a forty year old.

And so it is with us in our intimate relationship with our shepherd (and with our spouse), the more we nurture our listening hearts, the more our relationships will be enriched. The less we hear, because of hardness, shallowness or overcrowding, the less and less healthy our relationships will become.

The final exam

GOD CAN ALWAYS be counted on, as a teacher, to test us on what we have just been taught. As sure as each lesson comes, an exam will follow. In the story I've just told, about the farmer sowing his seed on various types of soil, Jesus has clearly taught his disciples that listening with their hearts is fundamental to unlocking all the other mysteries of the kingdom. He says to them, "If you can't understand this story, how will you understand all the others I am going to tell?" Watch Jesus and his followers, as they move from these lessons on listening, to the final exam. We have to run the tape forward to the next day when Jesus is spending time with the huge crowd who has been following him and listening to his teaching.

Remember what we have just learned that the key to unlocking the mysteries, which explain our life journeys, is in our ability to hear the shepherd's voice. In all the stories we read in the instruction manual, we should be asking, "What's my shepherd saying personally to me in this section?"

Here, as Jesus is spending time with the thousands who have been with him for the past few days, he is very sensitive to their physical needs as well as their spiritual needs. Listen to his conversation with his disciples:

They came to him and said, "We're in a desolate place out here and it's getting dark. Why don't you send the crowds away, so they can find a bakery in town to buy some bread from?"

He responded, (now listen for the test!) "They don't need to go away. Why don't you give them something to eat?"

Judas complained, "Are you kidding? It would cost a fortune to feed this many people!" (There were several thousand.)

Then Andrew came tentatively up to Jesus with a young boy in tow. "This boy has five rolls and a couple of little fish."

Jesus smiled, "Bring them to me."

"Now," he said, "have all the people sit down in groups of about a hundred each." After they did what he asked, he looked up to heaven, gave thanks and blessed the food.

Mouths were gaping in wonder as he began, and kept on, breaking the rolls and fish into small pieces. As fast as Jesus broke the few morsels, the twelve disciples distributed the pieces to the crowd, until everyone was full. When the miracle moment was over, they gathered up the left-overs into twelve full baskets! What an unforgettable day!

As you read about Jesus feeding the five thousand men with the little boy's lunch, look past his feeding the hungry and ask this question, "What is this story saying to me? What mystery is unveiled here?"

Actually, the question above is answered if we read on because Jesus clearly revealed his concealed message to his followers. After everyone except his close friends had gone home, he told them that in the feeding of the hungry men with the fish and bread, was a hidden message. The message was that he is the Bread of life. As men and women assimilate the shepherd's words into their own lives, they will find him sufficient to meet the deep spiritual needs of their lives. He taught them that as bread satisfied the bodies of those five thousand men, so the good shepherd can satisfy every need of our souls and spirits. He'll meet us at the point of our need.

How is your listening?

DID YOU HEAR what he was teaching in his story? Do you think that his followers heard him? Were their hearts' soils hard, rocky, thorny or soft? To find out what his followers were hearing, Jesus immediately gave them another test. Now watch closely Kelly, because our shepherd does exactly the same thing to us. He teaches us something and then gives us an exam to see if we were really listening and understanding it.

Following the story about the loaves and fish, we read of this next incident; *Immediately after this, Jesus made his disciples get back into the boat and head out across the lake to Bethesda, while he sent the people home. Afterward, he went up into the hills by himself to pray. During the night, the disciples were in their boat out in the middle of the lake and Jesus was alone on land. As often happens on the sea of Galilee, a fierce storm suddenly raged. Jesus saw that they were in serious trouble, rowing hard and struggling against the wind and waves. About three o'clock in the morning he came to them, walking on the water. Then he started to go past them.*

Now let's stop to see what was happening in this drama. He made them get into the boat without him and gave them the assignment to row across the twelve mile lake to the other side. Some of these men were fishermen so this was not too difficult, but Jesus didn't go with them. The fact that he sent them out alone is significant. Whenever we go through a testing time, we feel alone. You know from your many years of schooling Kelly, that when you wrote exams the teacher did not sit with you. The very nature of a test is that we are pressed beyond our comfort zone. But even though the men were alone on the lake, in the dark, notice that Jesus was watching them from land during the whole time. The meaning behind the shepherd's staff is that it brings comfort to us. His staff comforts me. Remember that the word comforter literally means one who comes alongside - Jesus has literally had his eyes on his disciples throughout the test even though they could not see him.

The story within the story

THIS STORY, although it really happened, is also a parable. The boat is a picture of what he had just been teaching them. It was their security in the middle of the sea; a metaphor depicting their safety in the shepherd's care. The followers of Jesus were secure in the boat. The sea is a picture of the uncertainty of life and the storm is a picture of the conflicts, persecution, difficulties and challenges of life, which blow at us with fury and try to drown us.

Although they were actually very safe in the boat, when the storm began to blow furiously at them, they felt alone and scared. You and I can identify with them Kelly. We have all been in uncomfortable places in life where the challenges of life seemed like they were going to topple our security and drown us.

Only hours before, the lesson that Jesus had been trying to teach his disciples was that he was their provider, he would meet them at the point of their need and that they were safe in his love, protection and care. Now, he had providentially sent the storm as a test, to see if they had been listening to what he had been teaching them. Can you relate to the test

Kelly? I've been there and you likely have also!

All the while, he had been watching his disciples in the moonlight, from the shore and had seen them straining at their oars. That's when he decided to add another dimension to the test. He walked on the water right past their boat! Can you imagine what those seasick men thought when they saw their teacher walking past them?

Now, don't think that his walking by them was a sign of his disinterest in their plight. He was intently interested in them. You remember Kelly, when you were in high school writing exams, and your teacher would walk up and down the aisles to see how you were doing - that's what Jesus was doing to his students. He wanted a response from them and he got it! They were petrified, thinking they were seeing a ghost walking by!

You'll remember this story from your days in Sunday School, how Peter, Jesus' most precocious disciple, finally recognized him. With a burst of faith, Peter jumped out of the boat and started walking toward Jesus. It looked for a moment that Peter was going to get a passing grade. He was proving his trust in Jesus' care by walking on the giant waves toward him. Then as quickly as he had taken a couple of steps, his eyes were diverted from his shepherd to his situation. He was again overwhelmed by the winds and waves, and he fell into the water. Eventually, Peter and Jesus both climbed into the boat. The teacher immediately spoke to the wind and stopped the storm. The disciples sat there stunned in the quieted waters.

When the test is over

IT SEEMED APPARENT that Jesus had sent the storm as a test. As soon as the storm had accomplished his purposes, he stopped the wind and rain. The applications to life are many, but here are six simple principles. First, God conceals his Kingdom truths in mysteries. Second, those who have listening ears are able to easily understand those truths. Third, he expects us to remember and practice the life principles, which he teaches. Fourth, he tests us to reveal to us what we have understood and what we have yet to learn. Fifth, the failures and crises that follow act as plows to prepare our hardened soil for the next season of planting. And finally, these tests are continuously repeated in our maturing process.

At the end of the story, the disciples got their final grade; *They still didn't understand the significance of the miracle of the multiplied loaves, for their hearts were hard and they did not believe*. Their hearts were hard. They had failed the listening test because they had missed the central truth that their security, care and protection were in their shepherd. The jigsaw puzzle wasn't fitting together yet.

Of course life goes on. We have all failed more times than we can remember, but we can be assured that our shepherd never gives up on us. We actually learn and grow more from our failures than from our successes. Just as we are continually given more tests to learn more lessons, the disciples also were given many more over the next couple of years that they spent with Jesus. The good news is that they finally did get it together. They ultimately understood what the meaning was behind the feeding of the five thousand men. As the bread and fish satisfied the bodies of those men, so our shepherd who is the bread of life can satisfy every need of our soul and spirit. His words are breath and nourishment for our life journey. When the disciples finally did get it together, they influenced the entire world with their message of hope.

Do we learn from our mistakes?

WE ALL FAIL at times, Kelly. Both you and I have hard soil, rocky soil, thorny soil and good soil during various seasons in our life journey. Failure is not the problem; that is, if we learn from our failure. When we fail a hearing test like Jesus' followers did, it's not the end of the world. I'll give a few illustrations of my own failures in the next letter. What often happens in times of personal failure is that we are humbled and broken, and it's at those times that we begin to grow.

I was working in our flower garden last week and because we have soil with a lot of clay in it, the sunshine had hardened it substantially. So I took my rake and forcefully broke up the soil around my plants. As I was doing that, the weeds were loosened and I was able to pull them out, roots and all. The violence of my picking at the soil broke and softened it, so I could remove the rocks and weeds. It also allowed the water to penetrate and nurture the flowers.

That's what failure does. It exacerbates the crisis which we are going through, and that process breaks up the hard soil of our hearts so that they are prepared to receive more seeds. Of course it's much better to learn from somebody else's failures, and not have to go through the same valley experience. But just like our children rarely learn from our mistakes, so we adults often have to fail ourselves and reap the consequences, so that we learn the lessons of life.

Follow the light

OUR SHEPHERD KEEPS speaking to us regardless of our responsiveness. He keeps clearly giving directions for each day's journey. He signals us when to turn, slow down or go faster. Begin today, to practice tuning your radio receiver to hear his voice. The more we hear and obey, the more clear his instructions become and the more insights with which he will trust us.

Our shepherd's staff is an incredible gift to mankind. It's exciting to think that the Lord, who controls the universe, has a personal plan for our life journey. He has created us with eternal destinies, and not only that, he willingly communicates with us on how we can move into that destiny. His staff is his communication in both, the written word and his spoken words.

Last Sunday afternoon, your Uncle Dave and Auntie Carol invited your mom and me out for a leisurely cruise on their boat. It was a beautiful warm day, but as we were returning to the marina, the sun had set and it was getting dark. When we were about a mile from our destination in Burrard Inlet, Uncle Dave pointed up ahead to two bright lights shining from the shore of Port Moody. The lights, he explained, were strategically placed to guide boaters into their docks when it was dark outside. If the captain could see two separate lights, he would know that he was off course, but when the two lights blended into one, he would be assured that he was right on target.

What a fascinating metaphor for the way our shepherd guides us with his staff. The two lights are the owners instruction manual and his spoken word. There have been times when I have felt like I had clear direction for my life, but either the written word or what I heard with my heart ears did not line up with the other. Only when both line up together do I know that I'm on the right path in my life. In the next letter, we'll look at the strange truth that we hear better when we are surrounded by our enemies than we do when everything seems to be going great.

Kelly, I can't overemphasize how important the lessons of this letter have been in my life lately. They have taken me half a century to really grasp, but I know that if you can learn these principles at your young age, and better yet, instill them in your children even earlier, you will far surpass any success that I have known. You will also save yourself and your family from many of the wrong turns that most of us make in our life journeys. Keep on listening and obeying as your shepherd guides you down the path of life. I love you, Honey!

Love Dad

CHAPTER ELEVEN

Surrounded By My Enemies

You prepare a table before me in the presence of my enemies.

IN THOSE SEASONS when we feel harassed and obstructed by the howling and growling of enemies all around us, our shepherd is not only there to protect us from evil, but is setting a bountiful table before us. His feast is intended to nourish and prepare us for the destiny just ahead.

Dear Kelly,

I just returned a couple weeks ago from a trip to Seoul, Korea where I had a memorable experience. I, like you, Kelly, have never seen war first-hand. I've heard your grandpa tell many stories of the years that he spent overseas in the RCAF, during World War II and I've seen a few movies about the Vietnam war and the World Wars, but thankfully Canada has not been wholly involved in any serious fighting since I was born in 1947.

I had occasion, during my time in Seoul, to climb a mountain where some of the Korean War was fought. From the mountain top where I stood, I could see North Korea and could even hear where they were testing bombs miles away. The reason that it was so memorable to me was that as I was looking north toward the communist held territory, I was standing on top of a concrete bunker. It was fairly easy for me, with *Saving Private Ryan* images in my memory, to imagine eighteen and nineteen year old boys hiding in the fox holes and bunkers around me, with enemy fire charging up the hill toward them. I went inside the cramped concrete structures, with slits for windows, and saw in my mind's eye three or four young men sitting at the little table that was there, trying to eat their rations while the sounds of grenades and AK47's exploded around them. It was the closest that I have ever felt to both the realities of war and eating at a table while surrounded by my enemies. Neither are experiences that I desire to have.

Although I have never experienced the horrors of an enemy shooting guns and exploding bombs around me, I have had a fair amount of experience with seeing and feeling the pain of emotional and spiritual enemy fire. As a pastor, I see people every week who are caught in the crosshairs of an enemy's weapon. Enemies such as divorce, loneliness, unemployment, cancer, rebellious children, suicide and depression abound in our neighbourhood.

But I have also seen something else; something that gives me great hope amidst the minefield of the devastating war around us. I have seen time and time again, the shepherd of our souls preparing a feast and setting it on a table right in front of a person while he is surrounded by his worst enemies! I'm not talking about turkey and its trimmings when I speak about a feast, rather I'm talking about an emotional and spiritual banquet fit for a king.

I'll give you a fresh example. Two days after I returned from Seoul, Korea, I sat in my office with a lady whom I had only met one time before. She is living a life so difficult that if I were on a battlefield under siege by an enemy troop I would not want to trade places with her. The whole story is too personal and involved to unveil, but in summary this mid-life woman is suffering from a debilitating illness, because of which she is unable to work; her income is far below comfort; her estranged husband has just undergone an operation to change himself into a woman; her two teenaged children are suffering from their dad's choice and acting out in unhealthy ways; her best friend is going through a devastating loss and is pulling back from their relationship. On and on the saga goes. "Bang, bang, kapow," explodes the enemy arsenal on every side.

Now Kelly, I don't in any way want to sound insensitive to this dear lady, but I want to share my response that I gave to her that day. Although my heart breaks for her and I pray for relief in every difficult battle that she is facing, all the while she was talking to me I felt a very deep sense of optimism inside me. Naturally, I was hesitant to share my positive feelings with her. I was afraid that she'd slug me if I told her glibly that, "Everything is going to be just fine!" And I wouldn't have blamed her!

I did however, sensitively tell her about my intuitions. I felt like her shepherd was beginning to set a bountiful feast on a table before her while she was still surrounded by her enemies. Although he was not the cause of her troubles, the shepherd was very much aware of them and was going to use them to lift her into a destiny beyond that which she had ever dreamed. You see this woman has some very important gifts for a reason. She is amazingly objective, considering what she is presently experiencing. She is wonderfully articulate and wise beyond her years. She seems to understand the spiritual principles that her shepherd is teaching her. As we talked at length about the process of her life journey, especially through the valley of the shadow of death and I explained that the Lord does his best work in the dark valleys, she began to reveal a vision that she felt her shepherd had recently given her.

A ray of hope on the horizon

SHE TOLD ME, and I heartily concurred, that she was thinking about writing a book about her and her husband's experiences with trans-sexuality. Both he and she, as well as their children, have insights which could touch and help thousands of people going through similar secret valleys. She has amazing insight into this difficult issue which could encourage and help heal countless women like herself. As we talked together, she and I both felt like she is going through a life changing shift in this very dark season of her journey. Her shepherd is preparing a succulent table before her right in the presence of her enemies.

Her enemies are not backing down. Guns are figuratively being fired at her on a daily basis, but in the midst of it all there is the fragrance of a feast! That Kelly, is what this letter is all about.

If this book had accompanying music, there would be a victorious crescendo beginning to build about now - like in the *Rocky* movies when he's been whipped and humbled by his opponent, but begins to train like there is no tomorrow. The music gives away the coming victory. Everybody watches, sits up straight and leans forward to cheer the final knock out. The loser becomes a winner!

In our life journey so far we have rested and prepared ourselves in the green pastures; refreshed our spirits beside the quiet waters; we've been restored in our soul and we're happily walking down the right path, when out of nowhere appears the valley of the shadow of death. We've moved into a season of darkness and insecurity. We've sensed the discipline of our shepherd, while at the same time he has been nudging us closer with his staff. Now although we're surrounded by our enemies, there's a feeling deep down inside that we're going to make it!

There's a light slowly dawning; life is beginning to make sense. We dare to hope that maybe there is a bigger plan after all. David, the shepherd, wrote about it when he said; *Your eyes have seen my unformed substances, and in your book they were all written, the days that were ordained for me, when as yet there was not one of them.* We're still in the valley, pressed in by our enemies, but we see a light at the end of this long tunnel.

You prepare a table before me

WHAT THE PSALMIST is referring to by the word table is a mesa. Mesa is a Spanish word for table. Kelly, we've been to the well-known mesa just south of Grant's Pass in Oregon. You'll remember it as an amazingly flat land high up in the hills. In Israel mesas make ideal summer feeding grounds for sheep. Early in spring after the snow thaws, the shepherd will scout out these mountain fields to prepare for the sheep's journey. He lays out blocks of salt and other minerals for summer nourishment and checks the growth of the grass in different areas. Often, hidden among the healthy plants, are poisonous weeds which can paralyze a young lamb with only one bite. The shepherd will either keep his sheep far away from the weeds or pull them out to avoid any possible danger.

Although wild animals are smart enough to stay out of the way of the shepherd's gaze, he is constantly aware of their presence. Wise sheep know that they had better stay close to their shepherd's love and protection. The shepherd also takes care to clear the water supplies of accumulated twigs and leaves which have fallen throughout the winter. After the shepherd has thoroughly prepared the tablelands for his sheep, he returns to lead them up the long trail for their summer feeding. The sheep follow closely as they anticipate the tasty grasses which have been made ready for them.

I've wrestled with this sentence for a few weeks now. *You prepare a table before me in the presence of my enemies.* I had no problem with the picture that David had painted for us of the shepherd preparing the tablelands for his sheep, but I knew there was deeper mystery hidden in the story. Then, as I was mowing the lawn a couple of days ago, an understanding of this concept was instantly made crystal clear to me. I had an "Ah ha!" moment. It was like the unveiling of a work of art. The cover was removed and there it was.

There are several paradoxes in the shepherd's handbook which are uncovered for us as we go through difficult times in life. Consider; *the first shall be last* and *the last shall be first; or give and it shall be given to you*; or *I must die before I can live*; or *blessed are the poor in spirit for theirs is the Kingdom of God.* In each of these paradoxes is a life changing revelation for those of us with soft listening hearts.

Remember the story from the last letter that I wrote to you, Kelly? When the farmer sows his seed on hard soil nothing happens, but when he sows his seed on good soft soil new life sprouts up. That's the way it is with the mysteries of life hidden in the pages of your Bible - when your heart is soft, seeds of truth begin to sprout. As I was mowing the lawn thinking about this statement, *you prepare a table before me in the presence of my enemies*, a tender green blade of revelation shot up in my mind. This concept is synonymous with the Apostle Paul's statement, *when I'm weak then I'm strong.* Let's fast forward from David's psalm, about a thousand years to the New Testament and think about Paul's life journey. By unwrapping his story maybe we can get a hold on the truth concealed in this picture of the sheep and their shepherd on the tablelands of Israel.

The Apostle Paul was as religious as any good Jew, so zealous about what he believed that he viciously persecuted anyone who controverted Jewish traditions, including Christians. During one of his rampages to arrest Christians, Paul was apprehended by a miraculous appearance of Jesus himself. Everything changed for him from that day forward. He became as zealous for the Christian faith as he had been for his Jewish religion. Because of the Lord's preordained destiny for him, this young zealot began walking down an intense pathway of preparation to become the greatest preacher this world has ever known. In addition to persecutions like few of us have experienced, (or perhaps because of his persecutions), he also enjoyed intimacy with God beyond our imagination. He was even taken up to heaven and saw things which were so far beyond his comprehension that he could not even write about them. If anybody had reason to boast about an exciting life journey, the apostle Paul did.

A thorn in the flesh

BUT HE ALSO had a problem. He was given by God what he called a thorn in the flesh. We don't know what this thorn was, but some have speculated that he had an infectious eye problem and was going blind. Some think it was a type of malaria which gave him blinding headaches. Others see it as a person who constantly harassed Paul making life extremely difficult for him.

Whatever his thorn in the flesh was, he saw it as evil and believed that God should heal him of it or at least protect him from it. That's why he earnestly prayed for relief. Three times he begged God to take it away. And three times God said, "No." Kelly, I'm sure you've asked for something from your shepherd and thought that he hadn't heard you, when actually he did hear you and he did answer you. The answer was, "No." Paul didn't like that answer any better than we do.

The third time that the Apostle was told "No" it came with an explanation. His shepherd told him *that power is perfected in weakness*. Just the other evening when you and Tom were over to our home, Alexander and his cousin Jacob were wrestling over a toy. Because Jacob had it first, you said to Alex, "No." You explained to your son why Jacob would be allowed to play with it and why he wouldn't be allowed. Alex's sad face and real tears reminded me of times when my shepherd has said, "No" to me. I could feel his pain. Thankfully, Paul went on to explain what he came to understand from that answer. In his letter to the church in Corinth, Greece, he unveils one of the great mysteries of life when he says, "I've discovered that when I'm weak, then I'm strong."

Kelly, I know that you've already experienced this truth, but if you're anything like me, you'll have to learn it several times before you really grasp it. Remember the ferris wheel metaphor from my fourth letter to you? Life is like a ferris wheel; up, up, up to the top of the ride, and then when we finally reach the top, it's down, down, down. On the way up we feel secure and happy. Life is as sweet and fragrant as a bouquet of spring roses. But as soon as we get to the top we suddenly feel like our security has been knocked out from under us. While coming down the back side of the ferris wheel we become fearful and insecure. Then as sure as we reach the bottom, the ferris wheel heads back around again.

That's the way our shepherd has designed our life journey. The bottom line reason for the downswing is to keep us from thinking too highly of ourselves. Every one of us has the same basic problem. It's called pride and it's reflected in self-centeredness, criticism, bragging, timidity, anger, jealousy, fear, control and dozens of other ugly ways. As sure as we rise to profit, popularity or power, pride rears its subtly insidious head and sets us up for a fall. Pride always precedes destruction.

To protect us from the devastation which pride precedes, our shepherd kindly arranges for something to knock us off our pedestals. He knows that the higher we climb the greater the potential crash that we will experience. As I wrote to you before Kelly, there are several sources of opposition which our shepherd allows to harass us. Most opposition comes as a natural consequence of our own choices, but there are also the general effects of life, the choices of others around us, the rod of our shepherd and our evil enemies. Each of these thorns in the flesh is allowed by our shepherd, while under his protective eye, for the purpose of building our character.

When our character is finally strong enough, then we are better able to handle profit, popularity and power. Each of these blessings are wonderful gifts in themselves, but can be devastating to the man or woman who does not have the character strength to handle them.

A word about the enemy

BEFORE WE GET to the steps of character formation that our shepherd has planned for our life journey I want to unmask our evil enemy. Sometimes when we take the mask off an adversary, he is not so threatening. It's funny now Kelly, but when you were a toddler I remember well the absolute terror that you had of clowns. Our first family trip to the big Labour Day Parade in Vancouver, ended abruptly when a tall red headed clown came too close to you. Unable to stop you from trembling, we finally had to go home. Your mom and I carefully tried to explain that he was just a man wearing a mask, but we discovered that we had failed to convince you a couple of months later.

It was Halloween night and one of our first guests was a friend of ours and his little daughter. The girl was dressed up as a princess and her dad was in a full gorilla suit. That gorilla was enough to scare you to tears again. As quickly as you began to cry, our friend whipped off his mask and showed you who he really was. I saw the light dawn on your face as you saw the man whom you thought was a gorilla was actually our friend. He wasn't as scary as you had thought once the mask came off. The same is true of the enemies which are surrounding us here on the tablelands.

The personification of evil is the devil or satan. Both are the same being who opposes us as we work at walking on the right path. The devil always uses one of two disguises. He comes as an angel of light or as a roaring lion. He has only two means of getting us off track into darkness- one is through deception when he appears as our friend. That's how he tricked Eve in the garden of Eden. The other way is through fear and intimidation. He tries to scare the wits out of us so that we will lose faith in our shepherd and wander from his care and protection. When we remove his masks, we come to realize that in comparison to our shepherd, he is really very weak. So for us sheep, the only thing that protects us from our evil adversary is to stick close to our shepherd. The shepherd's staff will keep us from the enemy's deception and his rod will protect us from ultimate harm.

There's a table set

NOW BACK TO the metaphor of the tableland. We're still on the downswing of this psalm. We've entered the valley of the shadow of death where his rod of discipline and the staff of his word are keeping us on track. We're surrounded by enemies and because of their presence we are pressed into close proximity to our shepherd.

That's the benefit of weakness. It keeps us dependent on our shepherd. Rather than, "I'll do it my way," it's "I'll do it his way." That's why when we're weak, we're strong - because doing it his way always leads us to success!

Here in the presence of our enemies, the shepherd has prepared a bountiful table for us. This is the place where we can be nourished in our souls more than any other place on our journey. Although it may feel like the worst, it is the best place in life to be. The enemy, whoever he is or whatever it is, is forcing us to stay close to our shepherd. Only when we're close beside him, can he most clearly guide us down the right paths and best restore our souls.

When I wrote to you Kelly, about how our shepherd uses his rod, I introduced to you the concept of life stages. My life looks something like this:

STAGE 1	STAGE 2	STAGE 3	STAGE 4	STAGE 5	STAGE 6
Sovereign Foundations	Experimental Choices	Becoming a Man	Skill Development	Character Honing	Convergence
years 1 - 10	years 10 - 20	years 20 - 30	years 30 - 40	years 40 - 50	years 50 - on

I made the statement that by the time I reached forty, I figured life was in my control at last. I was now a man, and my skills were developed and I was ready to go. And so began the fifth stage of my life which is often called mid-life. I've chosen to call this stage of my life journey *character honing*.

During these years (at fifty-three I may not be through the process yet) my character has been probed by my shepherd in at least five ways. All five points of my failure fall somewhere under the three main categories of human weakness: lust of the flesh, lust of the eyes, and pride of life. Every one of us is vulnerable in all three points but we are each especially weak in one of them. For me, my primary weakness was pride of life.

As you are very aware, my sovereign foundations were very stable. I have like you have Kelly, a loving family, including parents, brothers, sisters, wife, you children and grandchildren who are all healthy in body, soul and spirit. I didn't choose to be born into this family or into our suburban Canadian life. I didn't choose what I was to look like, my IQ (Intelligence Quotient) or my EQ (Emotional Quotient). They were assigned to me and I am thankful for what I have been given.

My experimental choices were quite mild compared to most boys who were my peers. I never smoked, did drugs or drank alcohol and was mostly a pretty good boy growing up. Some things I learned from the mistakes of others and some I had to learn for myself.

Becoming a man was as slow for me as for anyone, but because of my first good twenty years, it was not overly difficult. I was married at twenty-two and we had you and Kristy when I was twenty-four and twenty-five. You girls have been part of what contributed to my maturing process.

I love my career and so my skill development stage, although challenging, was a thoroughly happy decade. I was breezing through life so easily that some would look at me or my family and accuse the shepherd of being unfair or at least biased. A few years ago, I completed my forties and I now feel like my shepherd has prepared a table before me in the presence of my enemies. Although your mom has endured cancer and a few difficult treatments, causing us all some serious stress, my greatest enemies during the decade were my own weaknesses.

I needed a check up for my soul

WHEN I GO for a physical checkup at my doctor's office, he does a lot of probing. He checks my lungs carefully because my mother died of lung cancer at forty-two. He checks my heart because my lifestyle is fairly sedentary and my dad suffered symptoms of a heart attack when he was about my age. He does the dreaded prostate probe and presses in dozens of other vulnerable points. Wherever I tell him that I feel pain, he looks much more closely. As I leave my doctor's office, he invariably tells me to eat better and exercise more, but everything else seems to be holding up all right.

My shepherd also gives me a regular checkup in my soul. In the areas of my character which I presume are strong and healthy, he has a way of touching with his probing finger and I experience pain. My yelp gives away my weakness and that's where he does his work. During this last decade, the Lord has been pressing me in at least five weak spots. He knows that, like on a rubber dinghy, even one weak spot can cause the entire boat to sink.

Last summer a neighbour and I were trying to pull a large root out of our front yard. After several unsuccessful minutes of effort, I hooked a chain around the stump and through the bumper of my car. When I slowly pulled the car forward and stretched the chain, it snapped with such a kick that it almost hit my neighbour across his chest. One weak link in the chain caused the break and just about wounded my friend very severely. It would only take one unhealthy link in my soul to cause a disaster in my life and ministry, so my shepherd takes every weakness in me very seriously.

Your checkup may look entirely different from mine Kelly because your weaknesses will be your own. Your shepherd is very aware of the enemies which surround you and is working on protecting you even as you read this letter. He has prepared a bountiful table for you to enjoy as you come through each test.

The five weaknesses that I am about to reveal are certainly not my only ones. They are simply illustrations of how the character building process works. Remember also we're not comparing degrees of badness. Because of the sovereign foundations that I enjoyed and because of my career choice as a pastor, my appraisal and requirements are different than yours will be. Each of us is judged according to our particular assignments and gifts.

A lesson on humility

ALTHOUGH ALL OF the following weaknesses deal with pride in one way or another, I'll begin with a very simple example of how my shepherd put his big finger on a destructive root of pride deep inside me. First, we need to understand that pride has many faces. Because, like you Kelly, I am wired as an introvert, I tend to make excuses for my timidity or aloofness, but they are both simply different expressions of self-consciousness, which is pride. A couple of years ago I was flying by myself on a business trip. I am always less secure without your mom beside me, so it was with a false bravado that I approached the ticket counter. The airline representative in front of me said that I needed to put ID tags on my suitcase and my briefcase, so I took the first two tags which I saw in front of me. They were stickers. I filled them out on the counter while she processed my ticket, but I felt the impatient stares of the long line of passengers waiting behind me. As I went to stick the name tag on my new leather brief case, I suddenly realized that the sticky glue on the back side would tear the leather when I would remove it later. As quick as the mind thinks, I knew I should throw the sticker that I had written on away and take one of the tie on name tags instead. But the ticket lady was finished and the guy behind me was watching over my shoulder. I didn't want to embarrass myself by looking like I didn't know what I was doing, so I confidently stuck the sticker on my briefcase and walked away. As sure as I knew it would happen, when I removed it later, the sticker ripped the leather surface off my briefcase.

The noticeable scar on the top of my expensive case is a daily reminder of my foolish stinking pride. The good part of that story is that as I am reminded of my weakness every day that I open my briefcase, I become stronger in my humility. Remember the paradox, when I'm weak, then I'm strong.

A lesson on integrity

INTEGRITY IS HONESTY on the inside where nobody can see it. It's being honest with myself. It was several years ago that I learned a lesson on integrity that I cannot forget. It may seem simple and trite to you, Honey, but to me it was a foundational character builder.

It was a Sunday morning and I was almost ready to begin the church service when one of our elders came up to me. In our conversation, he casually mentioned to me that he had driven by my office at 6:30 a.m. on the preceding Tuesday morning. He noted that the light was on and was commending me on the early start that I must be getting at my job. The truth was that I had simply left my office light on the evening before. I actually hadn't started work before nine that particular Tuesday morning. But I was flattered by his commendation and in my pride wanted him to believe that I really was a hard-working pastor.

What I told him was the truth, (I really do work fairly diligently), but the problem was in my lack of integrity. I responded to him, "Yah, I do get a pretty early start some days!" He walked away from the quick exchange with a smile and so did I. Just before the beginning of the service, I was in the prayer room getting myself ready on the inside when my shepherd spoke to me. "What you said to Lance was not the truth." I responded, "Yes it was. I do get up early for work quite often." He didn't need to say more but he did, "Before you stand before your congregation and preach this morning I want you to confess your sin to Lance and apologize for your lack of integrity."

I knew that I had no choice and so with my head low I found Lance and set the record straight. I sincerely apologized and I was deeply humiliated, but that was okay. When I lower myself my shepherd raises me up. He sets a table before me right in the midst of my enemy of pride.

A lesson on trust and patience

TWO OF MY weaknesses that my shepherd directly addressed a few years ago are my thinking that I know what I'm doing and my wanting to charge ahead on my own schedule. The lessons that he taught me were expensive and humiliating. Those two factors make this experience unforgettable.

It was 1984, and our church had been meeting in a rented elementary school for about five years. It had been a difficult season for us in the school. Each week we had to bring in our own chairs, sound system, signs and church furniture to set up. Our children had to meet in hallways and storage rooms. The heat in the gym where we met often didn't work and we were always under threat of losing our contract if we touched anything that belonged to the school. I, along with our other leaders, was anxious to get our own place, but with less than a hundred people, buying property was more of a dream than a possibility.

Then a miracle happened! Or so we thought. A contractor offered us a free building. All we had to do was move it about twenty-four miles! I and a couple of other guys looked at the forty-four hundred square foot building and got excited about the possibilities. If we could just get some property and if we could hire a house moving company to haul the building to our town, we could have a church building of our own in a couple of months! We were young and full of enthusiasm at the time.

I checked with a couple of house moving experts and got a price of thirty thousand dollars to cut the building into three pieces, haul it away and set it on a new foundation. Wow, this plan really could come together! Of course we prayed for guidance from our shepherd during this time. We asked him repeatedly to bless our plans.

To shorten the story considerably, we were able to borrow some money to buy an acre and a half of property, but couldn't arrange the rezoning on time. After some exhaustive research, I found a place to park the three sixty-foot sections of building for a few weeks, half way to the final destination - just until we worked out a few details. Eighteen thousand dollars got the buildings moved to a large trucking firm's property. There they sat while we wrestled with our City Councillors to get rezoning for our new church property.

The bottom line was, we never did get the rezoning that we were asking for and so our plan had to be scrapped. The problem was that we had those three albatrosses to deal with. It took our guys about three months, working every Saturday, to rip those three buildings apart, piece by piece and haul them away. I remember well the humorous comment of one of our church leaders. We were just about finished our demolition project and he said, "The next time someone offers us free buildings, let's remember to move them closer to the dump!"

We lost another twenty-five thousand dollars when we sold our new property in a time of falling house prices. Altogether our small group of young families lost a total of forty-five thousand dollars which we couldn't afford to lose. Like I said Kelly, it was an expensive lesson which I'll never forget. All through the few month process of fluctuating between hope and hopelessness, I kept asking my shepherd, "What's going on here? What are you trying to teach me? Where are you leading us? Please talk to me!" It's a funny story to tell people now Honey, but it was very difficult living through it as it was unfolding.

All the time while I was scurrying about trying to make something happen on my schedule, the Lord had a bigger and better plan. He let me learn the hard way by watching me exhaust myself and our bank account. Then when I was on empty, my shepherd spoke. We seem to hear best when we are on empty! I should have waited for him to lead me, but instead I tried to lead him where I wanted to go. I should have known that my shepherd had a better plan all along, but instead I tried to make my plans fit. The lessons of patience and trust that I learned that year have been well worth the forty-five thousand dollars we spent.

A lesson on submission

SUBMISSION IS A military word Kelly. It means to get into line; to come under authority, and we usually learn it the hard way! My schooling in submission came on the heels of the lessons that I had learned about trust and patience. Shortly after the fiasco that I have just described, we were informed about the five and a half acre site which we ultimately developed and built on. I told you that story in my letter about the valley of the shadow of death.

I wrote how the price miraculously fell significantly in only one year and how our shepherd guided us through the entire two year process. The lessons I learned of the faithfulness, trustworthiness and goodness of our shepherd during that time are more valuable to me than the beautiful church facility that sits on that property today. But lessons do not come easy to me.

When the church authorities who are over me said "No" to our original proposal to purchase the property, I was deeply hurt. Actually it was my pride that was damaged. I had a good plan. I knew what I was doing. I was doing God a favour. Don't these men understand? As you remember Kelly, in the end they were right and I was wrong. The plan was right, but my timing was wrong. By waiting only one year (a reminder of my earlier lessons on trust and patience), we were able to see the property developed and the church built for a quarter of a million dollars less than we had originally proposed.

During that dark week when I received the word that those eight board members had said, "No" to our plan, I seriously thought about breaking away from our denomination. I figured that if we didn't have those negative thinkers over us, we would be free to fly. We could accomplish great things for our shepherd. If we were to become an independent congregation, everything would go ahead without opposition.

I am reminded of a story that I read to you when you were just a little girl, Kelly. It was about the kite that wanted to be free. The kite was happily flying in the blue sky, attached to a string held by a little boy, until he saw a bird fly by him. The bird flew up and down and around, free to go wherever it chose. The kite, noticing that the bird had no string attached to it, said to the bird, "If only I had no string tied to me; if only that little boy was not holding onto me and controlling me, then I would be free to fly like you! Would you cut my string with your beak so that I can be free of its hold?"

When the bird did as the little kite asked, you can guess what happened. The kite fell to the ground. Broken and humiliated, the kite lay on the dirt realizing that freedom came only in submission to the string that seemed to be holding him back.

And so it was with me. I learned through that difficult process that the Lord puts authority in place and that true freedom only comes through order and submission to those who are over us. Whether they are our parents, teachers, church authorities, police or government leaders, they have been given to us as gifts by our shepherd. They should be honoured, heard and submitted to. Ultimately the Lord is my shepherd and he retains the final say, but meanwhile his favor flows through those who are in healthy alignment to authority.

A lesson on self-discipline

ALTHOUGH I AM still in process, my forties were years when my shepherd pointed out several vulnerable spots in my self-discipline.

Self-discipline can be compared to the emergency brakes on our cars. I know by experience what happens when we do not use the brakes which we have been given with every car we purchase. Many years ago when your mom and I were still dating, I owned a shiny new Chevrolet Malibu SS. It was the pride of my life. One day while shopping in Vancouver, to keep from getting the doors dinged I parked my car carefully on a sloped side road. It was pointing downwards on the hill which was about six blocks long and had six roads crossing it. The hill ultimately ended at the Burrard Inlet. You can guess what happened as soon as I got out of my car and locked the doors. It started to roll down the hill. As I desperately and vainly tried to chase my beautiful car to unlock the doors, it continued to roll faster and faster toward the water below. Certain tragedy would have resulted if after two blocks it didn't, all on its own, turn left, jump over the curb and glide gently into a tree. Sheer panic would hardly describe the depth of my emotions that I felt as I helplessly watched the Malibu roll away from me that day.

The emergency brakes on my car which I almost lost to the ocean that day are a pretty good picture of self-discipline. The brakes were in working order, but were only effective when I applied them. Because I failed to use my brakes, especially when parked on a hill without my wheels turned toward the curb, I could well have expected my car to crash or drown. I was responsible for my car's failure because I neglected to apply my brakes when I should have.

I need to apply my brakes when it comes to diet, exercise, sexual attraction, diligence at work or controlling anger - I am the owner of my own soul. Each of the areas I've illustrated from my life: pride, integrity, trust, patience, submission and self-discipline were entirely within my own control. Add to the list anger, fear, lust, envy, abusive talk or a hundred other weaknesses we may have. Unless we take responsibility for our own failures and move past blaming our parents, our teachers, our spouse, the government or the system, we will never enjoy the bounteous table which is set before us in the presence of these enemies. Blame, anger and excuses will keep us far from the right path.

How to get back on track

IF YOU WANT to find out what liquid is inside a sponge, you simply need to squeeze it. Like the sponge, when our shepherd wants us to find out what's inside our souls, he simply gives us a squeeze. As painful as the squeeze is, our knowing what's inside of us is part of the process of restoring our souls; and rather than excusing ourselves or blaming others for what's inside, we can take the three steps necessary to bring us back to the right path. They are confession, repentance and self-discipline. I'll illustrate the process from my own life.

Many years ago, when your mom and I were young marrieds, I had a problem with speeding in my car. As I reflect back on the story, I am grateful that the police kept giving me speeding tickets because the tickets were my shepherd's rod disciplining me for my failure to obey the law. By the time the following incident took place, because of the multiple infractions, I had already lost my licence for a one-month and a three-month suspension. I knew that one more ticket would result in a six-month suspension. I also knew that your mom would be very upset with me if that were to happen again - but it did. I was charged with speeding once again.

The situation had become serious. For me to lose my driver's license for six months would severely handicap me in my work as a truck driver, so I made two decisions: one was that I would go to court and fight the ticket, and two, that I wouldn't tell your mom about the charge. After all, it would only worry her!

When the day scheduled for my court appearance came, I carefully hid my suit and tie in the trunk of our car, drove your mom to her job at Safeway and then went to a gas station washroom to change into my good clothes. I successfully appealed my case before the judge and got out with a fifty-dollar fine and no suspension. Then I changed back into my work clothes and headed back to my job. I had pulled off my deceptive plan without a hitch and your mom was none the wiser.

After work, on the way home, your mom told me an interesting story. A man had come through her till at Safeway and had seen her name tag, Susan Buzza. "Buzza," he said, "that's not a common name, but I was just at the Provincial Court and there was a young man there who was fighting a speeding ticket!" Your mom turned to me in the car, looked at me directly in the eye and asked, "What do you think of that?" I was caught!

Confession, repentance and self-discipline

OF COURSE I was forced into a confession and it would have been much better for me to have been honest from the beginning. But now was the time to go through the three step process: confession, repentance and self-discipline. Only then could I silence my enemy (which was my own failure to obey the law) and enjoy the benefits of obeying my shepherd. Applying his rod of discipline was an act of his love for me. The shepherd wanted me to move forward toward my destiny, but saw that I was being held back by my own lack of self-discipline. The feast that he set before me was the forceful kick into maturity that I experienced on that dark day.

I confessed my failure. I had been wrong in repeatedly speeding in my car. I had been wrong in ignoring the many warnings I'd had. I had been wrong in deceiving my wife. I said I was sorry and asked your mom to forgive me. But step one, confession, is hollow without step two, repentance. To repent means to turn the other way. If you've been going one way and discover that it's the wrong way, then turn around and go the other way. I was doing wrong by speeding, so I stopped speeding. I was doing wrong by deceiving, so I stopped deceiving. That's repentance. It gives meaning to confession when we repent.

But the sincerest repentance is empty without step three, self-discipline. Self-discipline is the ongoing practising of the lesson learned. For me, it meant using the emergency brake on my Malibu, especially when it was parked on a hill. It meant watching my speedometer carefully and keeping to the speed limit. It meant sitting down with your mom every day and telling her the whole truth!

This three step process of confession, repentance and self-discipline are ongoing parts of my life. Practising each of them every time I hear the howling of my enemies around me prepares me to enjoy the feast that comes from obedience to my shepherd.

Listen to your enemies

KELLY, DON'T RUN from your enemies, listen to them. Your shepherd has allowed them to harass you for a purpose. That purpose is ultimately to press you into maturity. The howling of your enemies is intended to drive you closer to your shepherd and reveal your own weaknesses. You can learn something from every experience of opposition, and that lesson is the feast that your shepherd wants you to enjoy!

We think that the days surrounded by our enemies were our worst days, and the days when there are no wolves or lions in the bushes were our best days. But it is not necessarily so! We learn our most memorable life lessons when we are surrounded by our enemies.

And the best news is yet to come! In the next letter that I am writing to you Kelly, I am going to tell you the most important insight that King David gives us in the Shepherd's Psalm. For now though Honey, don't fear the sound or the sight of opposition around you; when you hear or see an enemy nearby, start looking for the bountiful table that your shepherd is setting right in front of you! I love you!

Love Dad

CHAPTER TWELVE

Ready For My Destiny

You anoint my head with oil; my cup overflows.

OUR DESTINY IS usually revealed to us when we are deep in the valley of the shadow of death surrounded by our enemies. During this time, we often turn a corner into what may become the most fruitful season of our life journey.

Dear Kelly,

One of the greatest moments in your mom's and my life was when you gave birth to our first grandson, Alexander Josiah William Brown on August 16, 1998. Because it was on a Sunday morning I had to be at church, but I can still feel the emotion that I experienced as I drove to the hospital after the service to meet your son for the first time. What a wonderful gift to our family he is!

Your sister Kristy was not to be beat though! At eight o'clock the following Sunday morning, she gave birth to Jacob MacKenzie Low. It was almost too much blessing for your mom and me to endure. I was ready to burst with pride as I announced at each of our morning services on August 23, "We did it again!" The church clapped and cheered for both of you.

In early December, when the boys were just over three months old, we celebrated their dedication at a Sunday morning service. There's no way that I can adequately describe to you, Honey what it's like to be both your dad and your pastor. As I held our two perfect grandsons on the platform of the church, I prayed a prayer of dedication over them and over you four parents. I felt a sense of joy, thankfulness, privilege and pride. I was holding in my arms the fruit of your mom's and my love and labor. A new generation was budding on our family tree.

Twenty-six years before, we had dedicated you to the Lord's care and protection at the church where I grew up and where I had also been dedicated. There is no greater joy for a parent than seeing the circle of life turning successfully. I am so very thankful to my shepherd for leading our family down the right path.

As I've held Alexander, and now your new son Maxwell, over these past few months, I have often wondered what future destiny has been prepared for them. I can't tell you how many times I've prayed over them that they will be protected and make wise choices as they mature. It is with your and your sons' life journeys in mind that I write this letter to you. This subject of our destiny is the climax of David's psalm. Everything else that he has written leads to this point in our lives; *You anoint my head with oil; my cup overflows*. Let me begin with a couple of stories.

The car accident that changed Candy's world forever

ON MAY 3, 1980 at 1:30 in the afternoon, Cari Lightner, age thirteen, was killed while walking in a bicycle lane near her home in Fair Oaks, California. A car suddenly swerved off the roadway and struck her from behind. Cari died and the driver of the car did not stop. Four days later, the California Highway Patrol arrested the hit and run driver and determined that he had been drunk at the time of the crash. In fact, he had just been released from jail on bail two days before, where he had been serving time for another hit and run drunk driving accident. There were three other drunk driving arrests on his record.

On November 2, with the court considering his alcoholism a mitigating factor, he was sentenced to two years, which he served at a work camp and halfway house. He was released ten months later and was eligible to have his driver's licence re-instated. As any of us parents would do, Candy Lightner, Cari's mom, questioned the system that would allow a person with such an extensive record to continue driving.

As a result of her daughter's death and Candy's difficult walk through the valley of the shadow of death, she formed Mothers Against Drunk Drivers, MADD, in May, 1981. Today MADD has four hundred and seventy-six chapters in forty-seven states, Canada, England and New Zealand.

From the mountain top to the valley bottom

ANOTHER STORY IS of Jim and Tammy Faye Bakker, who reached the pinnacle of success before they were fifty years old. They had built the largest Christian broadcasting station in the world; had almost completed a world class theme park, called Heritage USA; and had all the visible accouterments of success. They had expensive clothes, cars and homes and were able to jet anywhere at anytime. They were loved by millions of viewers who watched their popular PTL program. They rubbed shoulders with dignitaries from famous actors to presidents. Seemingly, nothing stood between Jim and Tammy and their standing on the pinnacle of the American dream. It was all wrapped in the mantle of Christianity and respectability.

In the third letter that I wrote to you Kelly, we saw life as a ferris wheel. The upside is fun and exciting, but inevitably we all come to the top of the ride and all visible means of support are seemingly kicked out from beneath us. The ride down stretches and frightens us. The Bakkers were at the top of the ferris wheel of life because of a flow of God's grace, naive followers and skilful use of their charismatic leadership gifts. As they were quickly climbing from their humble beginnings toward international fame, power and wealth, Jim and Tammy were tempted, like any of us would be, by personal pride. What goes up always comes down. The upward swing of life presses those of us who do not have healthy souls toward pride; and pride always goes before destruction. And so it happened. As a combination of cracks appeared in the PTL foundation, it began to crumble and soon the entire conglomerate lay shattered on the ground. Jim and Tammy, being on top of the heap, fell the hardest of all.

Their already weak marriage collapsed shortly after their fall. Their son slowly declined into his own hell. Their personal fortune was totally wiped out. Jim was unfairly sentenced to forty-five years in a federal penitentiary and their reputations were destroyed. From the top to the bottom in a very few days; from the mountain top to the lowest valley they tumbled. Most of their friends turned away from them and the rest of the world mocked them.

Having read Jim Bakker's book, *I Was Wrong*, my respect for him is greater now than it was, even when he was at his best. Jim followed the only road which leads back to the path of righteousness. That road is called humility. In contrast to the high road of pride and self-centeredness, which ultimately leads to death, humility is the low road. The word humble comes from a Latin root humus, which means ground. It's the same root that the word human is derived from. A well centered, healthy person doesn't lose sight of his beginnings or his end. We're reminded of our humanness at every funeral service when the pastor says, "from dust to dust." So walking the pathway of humility is always keeping our feet on the ground, knowing who we are and who we are not.

As I wrote earlier Kelly, in my last letter, there are three steps to get back on the path of righteousness. They are confession, which realistically admits when we are wrong; repentance, which turns us back onto the right path again; and self-discipline, which keeps us on that pathway. Walking down the way of confession, repentance and self-discipline, Jim Bakker is moving into the greatest success he has ever known. It was in the depths of prison where his character, which had been forced out of shape by fame, wealth and power, began to be reshaped. His loving shepherd, after severely using his rod of discipline to force Jim off his throne, used his staff of love to lead him back to health again.

Both Candy Lightner and Jim Bakker have experienced in their own personal ways the truth of this difficult and exciting concept, which is that growth occurs when we least expect it - in the dark valleys where we often feel discouraged, insecure and defeated. When we think that our future is on a downhill slide into oblivion and that our hope is gone, this is often the time in which our shepherd reveals the next step in our life journey. We are forced to trust him because there is nothing or nobody else to lean on.

We must die before we can live

THERE IS A LIFE principle which most of us experience, but few of us understand - death must precede life. A grain of wheat, for example, will always remain a single seed until it is placed in the ground and dies. Only after it is seemingly dead is it transformed into a stalk and multiplied a hundred times over. All great leaders will testify that they grew into their positions through lessons learned in the furnace of failure. A bank president was once asked by his young protegee how he had attained such great success. His answer was, "Through wise decisions." When asked how he had learned to make wise decisions, he responded, "Through experience." Finally the young man pinned him down, "But how did you get the experience?" His answer, "Through failure."

While still in the presence of my enemies, you prepare a bountiful table before me and reveal my unique destiny. In this verse the enemies metaphorically referred to are sometimes feelings of hopelessness, fear and inadequacy. These subjective feelings pull us back from success because they frighten us into personal insecurity. Thoughts such as; I'm a failure; I always knew I was stupid; My life is one big mistake, are enemies which howl at us in our lowest moments.

But it's in those dark and lonely moments that our shepherd's voice is often heard the most clearly. The verse above says: *You prepare a bountiful table before me, in the midst of my enemies.* The table represents our shepherd's provision, which appears only when we have nothing of ourselves left on which to rely. Those feelings of hopelessness, fear and inadequacy are not healthy in themselves, but they are often the doorways to the place of humility where the bountiful table is set.

It's like you coming home as a young girl Kelly, after a tough day at school, and your mom having a savory batch of double chocolate chip cookies and milk waiting for you on the kitchen table. Right in the middle of your dry, stressful day, there is a refreshing oasis in front of you. That's the scene we have before us. As difficult as it first seemed this is turning out to be a very memorable day.

Back to the sheepfold for the anointing

YOU PREPARE A *table before me in the presence of my enemies. You anoint my head with oil; my cup overflows.* To understand the heart of this key metaphor in Psalm Twenty-three we need to see the context in which David, the author, uses the four important words: anointing, oil, cup and overflow. Each picture represents a profound life principle.

The oil of anointing

ANOINTING REFERS TO the intimate connection between the shepherd and his sheep. A caring shepherd in the Middle East would rub a compound of oil, sulphur and spices on the sheep's noses to protect them from pesky insects, as well as to heal them from scratches or infected bites. Sheep love to be pampered by their shepherd's touch. Once the solution had been applied, the sheep would happily graze again and soon lie down in peaceful contentment.

The word anoint simply means to smear oil over someone. You've seen it in church Kelly, when we pray for a person and carefully place a drop of oil on his forehead so that his clothes or hair do not get greasy. But the picture here is of a shepherd pouring a flask of oil over his sheep and smearing it all over its head. It would be more akin to our covering ourselves with suntan lotion before going out into the summer sun. We rub it in thoroughly from the top of our head to the bottom of our feet.

In the time of King David about three thousand years ago, a mixture of olive oil and spices was used to anoint people for three different reasons: The high priest would use it to anoint a king or queen, a prophet or priest for service. The oil was a symbol of the sufficiency and authority of the Lord, who was there with the person being anointed, to prepare and empower them for their destined assignment. The idea was that as the high priest rubbed oil all over the head of the chosen person in the physical realm, the Spirit of God was entering and filling the king's soul in the spiritual realm.

For example, when David was chosen as king of Israel, Samuel was the spiritual leader among the priests, prophets and king. Samuel, the judge and priest, heard from the Lord that it was time to appoint another king. The Lord had told him that the new monarch would be one of the sons of Jesse so he went to Jesse's home to look over the boys. When he saw Jesse's eldest son, Eliab, Samuel thought that this had to be the next king because Eliab had that regal look. He was tall, handsome and authoritative, but the Lord was teaching Samuel and us an important lesson. He said, "Do not look at his appearance or height...for God sees not as man sees, for a man looks at the outward appearance, but the Lord looks at the heart."

Finally, after Samuel had seen all of Jesse's sons except one, David came in from attending the sheep. Samuel was surprised when he saw young David. He was shorter than his brothers with a ruddy complexion and very beautiful eyes, but was not particularly majestic looking. Nevertheless, the Lord told him that this was the right man for the job so Samuel took out his flask of anointing oil and poured it all over David's head. The story records that something miraculous happened to David when the oil ran over him. Even though David didn't fully realize what was going on, his destiny as the greatest king Israel has ever known was being revealed.

This anointing as the future king was prophetic in nature. It came at a time when David least expected it, anticipating a day many years in the future when David would be in a deep, dark and difficult place in his life. The Lord was saying to the teenaged shepherd something like this, "One day David when you're in a valley season of your life journey, and the enemies are howling all around you, and you feel like you are worthless and purposeless, I am going to lift you to a place of unimaginable prestige and power. I am going to crown you as the king of Israel!"

The oil, representing the authority and sufficiency of the Lord coming upon the young royal candidate is a graphic picture to all of us that the anointing process empowers the recipient to move forward into his or her assigned destiny. David still had many years of training and preparation to go through before he would be ready. There would be much shelf life and long periods in many red hot furnaces before he was finally ready to become one of the most renown kings in all history.

The potter and his clay pot

KEEP IN MIND KELLY, where we are at this point in our life journey. We are still surrounded by our enemies and are coming through the valley of the shadow of death. We are deep in the winter season and there are virtually no signs of life around. It appears like all is lost and hope is nowhere to be found. We can't see that the light is going to shine just around the next corner, but it is. Everything that we go through in the preparation stage has an ultimate purpose.

I have in my office, sitting on one of my library shelves, a beautiful gift that you made for me more than twenty years ago. I think you were in grade two when you crafted the little candy dish, painted it red, scratched your signature, "to Daddy, with love from Kelly" inside a heart and baked it in a kiln. You presented it to me on Father's Day and it remains one of the treasures of my life. Because you've been the creator of such a valuable piece of pottery, you'll understand when I compare your life journey with the production cycle of a clay vase. I want you to note that the time that it takes to craft something of value often takes longer than we think it should.

The potter begins the long process by selecting out of a slimy clay pit a lump of raw material just the right size and texture. He then takes the clay and carefully places it in the exact center of his wheel. Round and round it turns, while the master deftly forms the clay into a shapely vase. After the vase has been formed out of the mass of clay, it still is not ready for use. The potter sets it on the shelf to harden for a long period of time before the painting process begins. He then meticulously applies the colour and design, lets it dry and later covers it with a glaze. As good as it looks at this stage, the vase is still not ready for use. Into a very hot furnace it goes for the hardening process.

If we were clay pots Kelly, there would be many times during that long preparation process when we would think that we were ready for use. Maybe after we were specially chosen by the master potter out of the murky clay pit; or perhaps after he had artistically shaped us into a slender vase; but we would still not be ready yet. Onto the shelf we would be placed for an unknown length of time. There are always long waiting periods when nothing appears to be happening in the destiny forming process. We hate these seemingly wasted seasons of sitting on the shelf.

Even when the shelf time had been completed, we would still not be ready for use. Off to be painted and glazed we'd have to go, our personalities and characters having to be readjusted. After the designing stage, we would sneak a quick look at ourselves in the mirror and say, "Surely someone will pay a pretty price for me now." We would glow with pride thinking that we were finally ready for use. But before that happened, we would have to endure the most difficult time of all - the fire. Into the furnace we would have to be placed, hotter and hotter, until we think we were being burned to a crisp. Then when we think we could not possibly wait any longer, after a long cooling off period, we head for our destiny.

King David received his anointing as a king when he was only a teenager. Although his ultimate destiny had been revealed, he did not see it fulfilled until many years later. There were several years of character honing for him to endure to prepare him for his future as the king of Israel. Three thousand years later, we have the advantage of a wider perspective and can see why the shepherd put young David through such a rigorous preparation period. In the end, David's prominent place in the family line of Jesus Christ helps us see the purpose to his repeated seasons in the furnace of opposition. I'm not sure whether David wrote Psalm Twenty-three as a young man before he went through the fire or as an older king reflecting back on his journey, but his psalm certainly gives an accurate picture of what each of us can expect in the maturing process.

The making of a clay vase is a pretty clear metaphor describing the process of life. Don't be surprised by the length of the journey Kelly. Before any of us are really ready to handle our destinies, there will be the long periods on the shelf and then ultimately there will be the fire. And it will be hot!

The world's most famous con-artist

WHEN YOU SEE the ceremony of anointing alluded to in Psalm Twenty-three, understand that this is a picture of the time when our destiny is being unveiled. Just as the prophets, priests and kings of ancient times were ushered into their callings and destinies through the process of anointing, the psalm tells us that this will happen to us also. Remember though that the anointing often happens when we least expect it and usually when we are surrounded by our enemies. It will often take place in the valley rather than on the mountain top. Candy Lightner and Jim Bakker are only two of those whose destinies were revealed in the valleys. Kelly, I have in my library literally hundreds of biographies of some of the greatest men and women in history, almost all of whom were forged for their destinies in the midst of the fires of life. Following are three more examples.

A boy named Phineas Taylor

PAUL AURANDT WRITES in *More of Paul Harvey's - The Rest of the Story*, that back in the early eighteen hundreds there was a boy named Phineas Taylor. When Phineas was christened as a baby, his grandfather presented him with a deed to a sizable piece of property. He referred to it as Ivy Island. The deed changed Phineas' life. After that day he was always referred to with a little awe, because even as a boy he was a land owner. He continued to play with his friends, just as if he were a common poor boy like the others, but his dreams were of his inheritance. One day he would be the lord of Ivy Island.

When Phineas was ten, because of his incessant pleadings, his father agreed to take him to see the island which his grandfather had described as the most valuable farm in all Connecticut. He could hardly wait to see his fortune. Finally Phineas, his father and a hired hand arrived and the young boy ran with vigour over the last hill to see his island for the first time. He could hardly believe what his eyes fell on. It was five acres of barren, snake-infested, worthless swampland. There were a few struggling trees with ivy vines clinging for their lives. It was a swamp and nothing more.

As Phineas stood staring at his land, while his dream of future fortune lay shattered before him, his father and the hired hand roared with laughter. The gift of Ivy Island was the most protracted practical joke that old grandpa had ever played on anyone. That one devastating day in Phineas Taylor's life shaped the rest of his life journey forever. Because he had been made a fool of, he decided at that moment to become the biggest con-artist the world had ever known. He was deceived by his own grandfather and was therefore inspired to make a life long career of deception. The man, who boldly declared, "There is a sucker born every minute," spent his life proving it.

As a boy I grew up in awe of the clowns, acrobats, lion tamers and magicians in the circuses I saw. The man who made it all happen was Phineas Taylor...P.T. Barnum of Barnum and Bailey circus fame. At the lowest point in Phineas' life, in his greatest humiliation, his destiny as a sideshow con-artist and ultimately a circus entertainer was unveiled. Like David, the waiting period between the revelation and the ultimate fulfillment covered many years.

An owl, a boy and his destiny

THE SECOND STORY, which also took place in a boy's very formative years is about Walter Elias. When Walter, a city boy, was not quite five, his parents moved from Chicago to a farm in Missouri. At seven years of age, when Walter was out in the apple orchard exploring one day, he saw the most amazing sight he had ever seen. It was a real owl, apparently asleep, perched on an apple tree. His father had taught him that owls sleep in the day and hunt at night. In a brave but boyish moment Walter decided to catch the owl and make it his pet. He cautiously crept up to the bird so that he wouldn't awaken it; then he suddenly reached up and grabbed it by its legs. Of course the owl awoke with a start and began to fight for his freedom. Walter was frightened so badly that he didn't know what to do and without a thought, he flung it to the ground and stomped it to death. Realizing what had happened as he stared down at the pile of feathers and blood, Walter cried and ran home. Later he returned, buried the owl and gave it a proper funeral, but for months after he couldn't sleep. Walter never killed a living creature again. Instead that year, as if to make peace with his past, he began to give life to animals by drawing them and allowing them to run free. The boy is now gone, but his animals still bring laughter and awe to millions. His full name was Walter Elias Disney and he received the first anointing for his destiny at seven years of age in the midst of tragedy.

An experience that changed your life forever

I'M SURE, AS YOU reflect back over the years of your life Kelly, that you can pinpoint a dozen or so experiences which have altered the course of your life forever. More often than not, those memorable experiences likely seemed very negative as you were going through them. Some of them you would rather forget. But parents often view life from a higher perspective than their children do and see what their child thought was a nightmare was actually one of the most pivotal points in their life. I'll give you an example.

You may not thoroughly remember the years before you were eight years old, but you were about as shy as any little girl could be. As beautiful and bright as you were, you would hardly speak to anyone outside of our immediate family. The name your mom and I had chosen for you, Kelly which means bold and confident, hardly seemed to fit your timid personality. During the first couple of days of school in grade four you were sick and had to stay home. That was unfortunate because it made it all the more difficult for you to go to school and fit in with your new class who were already getting to know each other. And to make it even harder, this was the first year that you had a male teacher rather than a woman.

Because you had been absent, you missed the day when the teacher read out the class rules, one of which was; *do not chew gum, if you do, you'll be made to put it on your nose!* On about the third week you'll remember that you were caught chewing gum by the teacher. For some reason he decided to make an example of you and so he followed through on his threat by making you stick your gum on the bridge of your nose. I guess you could only take the humiliation for a few seconds because you finally burst into tears and fled from your class. You ran through the halls, out the front door and straight home, intending to never to return again.

I was off work that day and so was home when your teacher hurriedly called us to apologize and explain what had happened. You came into the house a couple of minutes later and I remember that we all cried together. Of course the teacher was simply following through on his warning. Maybe his punishment was unwise, but he had stated it up front. Unfortunately he hadn't remembered earlier that you were away on the day that the rules were read. Nevertheless the crisis had already happened. But that was not the end of the story. Up until that horrible day in September 1980, just before your ninth birthday, you had been so quiet and shy that you had never entered into class discussions. You had hardly ever opened your mouth. Most of your teachers knew that you were smart, but your report cards reflected your quietness. They were good, but not exceptional. After the gum incident, your teacher felt so bad about what he had done that he spent the rest of the school year trying to make it up to you - maybe even favoring you a bit over the others.

However it played out, you responded exceptionally well to his teaching and began to blossom. From that year, all the way through several years of university and beyond, you never got less than an "A" in any subject again. Your confidence in yourself, as well as your sense of calling and purpose has delighted everyone around you. You have grown into your name - bold and confident. It all began with a little piece of peppermint gum and a teacher whom your shepherd placed in your path for a purpose. I remember well when you graduated from grade seven, talking to that same man who had been your teacher in grades four, five and seven and watching him beam with pride because of his successful student. I wrote him a letter that year to thank him for being one of the major influences in your life. I saw him just a few months ago and the first question that he asked me after all these years was, "How's Kelly?"

Almost every one of our heroes has a story to tell of how the revelation of their destinies came out of the fire or in the depths of the valley. It's often here in the valley or in the fire where the shepherd anoints our heads with oil. You may have picked up from my three stories of king David, P.T. Barnum and Walt Disney, and even from your own experiences, that the anointing for our destinies often takes place repeatedly. It may be in your childhood, like Barnum or Disney, that you first sense your life direction. That unveiling process may become clearer when you are a teenager or a young adult, and then be finally revealed many years later.

For me, I first felt an inner sense of destiny (some might use the term "a call") when I was eighteen years of age. At thirty I knew the time had arrived for me to step thoroughly into my God-ordained profession. It wasn't until five years after that, that I was literally anointed with oil by the president of our denomination, and even as recently as a couple of years ago that I felt a fresh anointing by my shepherd. You can see from my experiences how the process of anointing is often progressive rather than at one defined moment.

Years ago in our Vancouver newspaper, the Sun, there was a contest in which a mystery picture was slowly unveiled a little more each day. On the first day no one could interpret what the picture was, on the second, third and fourth days there were hundreds of guesses, but nobody was right. By about the seventh picture, someone finally saw it for what it was - a kitchen blender! And she won a prize. I think that this is what often happens in life - maybe even in king David's life - that for a long time after the anointing process begins, we don't fully realize what's happening until finally certain pieces of the puzzle come together. But when we do understand what our destiny is, then our cups fill up and begin running over. Let me explain.

Our cups run over

THE PSALM READS, *you anoint my head with oil; my cup overflows.* While the oil represents the sufficiency and authority that the shepherd gives us to move forward in the gifting which he has given us, the cup symbolizes the realm of our experiences and the circumstances into which we have been sovereignly placed. These are situations that life hands to us. They may produce either negative or positive reactions, but they are challenges given to us which we must face. We don't have any control over many of our life circumstances such as if we are born with no right hand; our parents give us up for adoption; an uncle sexually abuses us; a drunk driver strikes our car; our home is struck by a tornado. On and on the list could go of challenges that life seemingly whimsically hands us. Our only choices are the attitudes with which we receive them.

Remember Jesus, before he died on the cross prayed; "My father, if it is possible, may this cup be taken from me. Yet not as I will, but as you will." The cup that Jesus was handed by the shepherd was bitter opposition and ultimately execution on the cross. He didn't want to die such a violent death any more than you or I would, but he willingly accepted the cup, symbolically drank it and changed the world as a result. Two billion people today claim to be followers of Jesus Christ. No person in history has affected humanity so profoundly.

The cup then, is the realm of circumstances into which we are sovereignly placed or that we experience as a consequence of our own choices; and the oil is the shepherd's empowerment to move fully into the destiny that he has purposed for us. The circumstances are designed by the shepherd to help prepare us for the destiny ahead.

My cup overflows

DAVID WRITES IN Psalm Twenty-three that when we are in the deep valleys and our destinies are unveiled, our cups become so full that the oil literally runs over the edge. *You prepare a table before me in the presence of my enemies. You anoint my head with oil; my cup overflows.* There is not only enough oil, but it's running over our cup. The overflowing cup is the effect that our lives have on those around us.

Here's the picture. Every one of us is born with a predestined purpose in the shepherd's mind. At just the right time, usually in the valley of the shadow of death, he gives us a glimpse of that unique destiny. Then comes the long, difficult preparation period. We make choices which bring a variety of circumstances into our story; or the shepherd sovereignly allows obstacles to be placed in our pathway. He then provides all the necessary strength and resources for us to overcome the opposition. In the process of overcoming, we gain wisdom, experience and strength which prepare us for our predestined futures.

The gifting, wisdom and strength that he gives to us are always more than enough. His expectation is that they will not only fill our cup, but they will run over the cup to stimulate and encourage the people whom we touch each day. The principle illustrated by the overflowing cup is; *give and it shall be given unto you.* The shepherd gifts us with wisdom, wealth, talents, power or notoriety; and our responsibility is to share what we've been given with those inside our circle of influence. It's important to keep in mind that if we are resistant to sharing, the flow of blessing will either dry up or begin to rot. If we respond to his blessings with generous overflow then he will keep on refilling our cups.

By way of summary, our shepherd's promises are that: We do have a personal destiny; it will likely be unveiled in the midst of a valley experience; even though life seems to be handing us an unfair cup, there will be an ultimate fulfillment that comes with our receiving it; our shepherd will give us more than enough strength and wisdom to overcome; and to the degree that we allow the overflow of our lives to touch others, the blessings that accompany our destinies will keep on flowing. While we stop for a moment at this climactic stage of our life journey, let's look around and make some observations. At least seven questions are important to ask ourselves.

What is my vision of my future?

IN THE SIXTH letter that I wrote to you, Kelly, I described the dream that I had in October, 1997. In the picture I saw a narrow trail in an uncharted forest with the words; *Stick close! I've been this way before*, written below it. It was during this dream that I experienced a flowing of this anointing oil being poured over me. I didn't literally feel the oil and I wasn't aware of it at the time, but in retrospect that's what was happening. The shepherd was giving me a veiled picture of my future destiny and he was preparing me with the sufficiency of his power to accomplish what lay before me.

We used to put a lot of jigsaw puzzles together when you and Kristy were young. They were a good vacation activity to keep your minds alert and fill your days. When we would go to the store to buy the jigsaw puzzles, two criteria would be in our minds; the difficulty of the puzzle and the picture on the box cover. If we were to buy a puzzle for your son, Alexander next Christmas, we'd probably look for a Barney picture with six or seven pieces to it. If we were buying one for your mom, it would have a picture she'd like with maybe a couple of thousand pieces to it.

Each of those two criteria for buying a jig saw puzzle relates to our life destiny. First, there is a picture of the completed puzzle on the box. The picture represents your ultimate purpose; what you'll look like when your journey has been completed. The difficulty, unlike working on a jigsaw puzzle, is that we rarely get to see the fulfilled picture before it begins to come together. Only our shepherd who has already seen the future knows what picture is on the box. We may get quick glimpses of it once in a while, but seldom do we see more than a shadow of the real thing.

Secondly, the difficulty of the puzzle is adapted by its designer to our age, experiences and abilities. The Barney puzzle would be appropriate for Alexander and the two thousand piece puzzle would be just right for your mom. Our shepherd never allows more than we can handle to come our way each day. Corresponding to each challenge, the shepherd makes available to us the needed spiritual power to successfully live out the day.

Jigsaw puzzles that we buy at the store do not come to us already put together and neither do our destinies, but we do have all the necessary pieces within our reach. These pieces are the resources, both sovereign and learned, which fit perfectly together when they are in their right places. By starting in the corners and at the side to set parameters, we begin to see our purpose take shape. These are the givens; such as our gifts, temperaments, passions and past experiences. Then we put the puzzle together day by day, bit by bit, often blindly trying pieces, sometimes finding out that they don't fit together at all. Finally there is such satisfaction as the picture comes to life. We begin to experience the joy, which comes from discovering and accurately placing a piece of the puzzle which connects two previously unrelated sections. This deep satisfaction comes not because life is easy or even profitable, but because we are fulfilling our destinies.

That's what was happening to me on that dark October night when I had my dream. Although I couldn't see the entire picture on the box cover and still haven't to this day, I was given a very brief glimpse of where I was headed. What the experience gave me was the assurance that the shepherd was with me in this mid-life transition time and also the motivation necessary to move forward into the next phase of my destiny. Since that night, I have seen the pieces of the jigsaw puzzle begin to fit together. Although I cannot see the final picture that will yet be formed, there are discernable sections of the puzzle coming to life.

The process often begins with a vision, a sometimes faint picture of where we are headed. It then slowly unfolds as we move along the path already prepared for us. It may come from a book which we are reading, a dream, a conversation with a friend or in a quiet moment of meditation.

Who am I?

IT TAKES MANY years to work this second question through and to be content with the answer, but if we are ever to fulfill our destinies, we must be realistic about who we are. What were my sovereign foundations? For example Kelly, you were born into our family on October 13, 1971. You really had nothing to do with the fact that we are your parents, that we are white, middle class Canadians or that you are blonde with big beautiful brown eyes. You were sovereignly placed in this world and were given a certain temperament, personality and intelligence. You are expected to use what you have been given for a worthy purpose. That purpose may be to change the world or it may be to be one very small, but vital cog in a larger mechanism which will ultimately change the world.

Esther, back around 465 BC, was an example of being a person sovereignly set in the right place at the right time and making a difference in her world. She was a Jewess, who won a beauty contest to become the wife of a powerful Persian king. The story took place at an all time low point in Jewish history. Because of repeated failure in obeying their shepherd, the Jewish people had been dominated by Persian (modern day Iranian) power. The Biblical story of Esther gives us an intimate glimpse into a period of time which saw the Jews almost entirely snuffed out. Of course if that had happened, the human family line of Jesus would not have existed five centuries later and history would have been written entirely different than it is today.

According to the account, there had been an evil plot devised by the wicked, anti-Semitic Haman to obliterate the Jews. Although the king had ultimate authority, he was ignorant of the hellish scheme. The shepherd however was very aware of everything that was happening and so he predestined that Esther would be in the right place at the right time. That's when the shepherd arranged for her to win a beauty contest and thus become the Persian king's favored queen.

At the perfect time, while Esther was enjoying all the privileges of Persian pomp and power, she was asked by the shepherd to approach her husband, the king, as a mediator to save the Jews from evil Haman's plot of annihilation. Her uncle Mordecai, who was her personal counsellor and mentor said to her, "Esther, who knows, but that you were born and placed into this position, for such a time as this?" Queen Esther risked her life and her reputation by approaching the king in order to save the Jews. She succeeded in her mission, saw Haman humiliated and executed, and changed world history forever. To honour Esther's world-shaping heroism, the Jews to this day annually celebrate the Feast of Purim. That one day when she saved her race from total annihilation was Esther's destiny. What she did twenty-five hundred years ago still affects you and me today.

As we live each day to its fullest, seizing opportunities as they are presented to us, we really have no idea how a conversation, encouraging word, chance meeting or act of kindness may alter our life or the life of another person. One day at the end of our journey, each of us will stand before the shepherd for a review of our entire lives. Each of us will be held accountable for the way that we have used the gifts, abilities, temperament, wisdom and influence which we have been given. The criteria will be how faithfully we have used the gifts that we have been allotted and how we have completed the assignment that has been handed to us. We cannot compare ourselves with any other person and their combination of gifts and assignments. Each of us has a unique purpose in our life journey and each of us will be accountable for our own piece in the giant jigsaw puzzle of humanity.

One of the ways that you can discover who you are is to make a note of your passions. What are you passionate about Kelly? What do you enjoy doing the most? What satisfies you? Knowing what makes you jump out of bed with enthusiasm in the morning will give you a strong indication of who you were made to be.

You and your sister Kristy were both raised the same by your mom and me. You both came from the same parents and lived in the same environment, with the same disciplines and values. Yet you are obviously two very unique women, with different passions and different purposes. Kristy is an excellent teacher, who loves little children and music and is somewhat disorganized and excitable. You are a medical technician, who loves the human body systems and are extremely orderly, disciplined and level headed.

Both of you are gifted teachers, but Kristy's passions are fun, music and small children. Your passions are kinesiology and order. Your different passions have led you into separate fields. Even though you love each other dearly, your discovery of who each of you is has been related directly to your own unique passions.

Fulfilling our passions will just feel right. It will satisfy us. Knowing our gifts and what we are passionate about will help us to understand who we are and why we are here on earth. As we walk on that right path before us and seize opportunities as they come, we will fulfill our unique destinies.

How can I use my past to help me in the future?

RATHER THAN REGRETTING or cursing our past or gloating in its superiority, we should ask: Why was I given these sovereign foundations? Why was I born to these parents in this country? Some of your friends will have to ask: How can my abusive, alcoholic or sickly parents' failures or weaknesses help me? Those of us who have overcome obstacles as children or youths will be much stronger than those of us who haven't. It wasn't by accident that you were born into the family that you were - it was by design. The shepherd gave you the privilege of learning vital life lessons through personal experiences that are preparing you for your future destiny.

A few years ago, when you and Tom had to move into a small apartment in downtown New York because of a job that he had taken, you struggled with the change. It was the first time that you both had lived a long way from family and friends. The culture and climate of the eastern United States were radically different from ours in western Canada. The area where you lived was noisy, crowded and seemed somewhat dangerous. But as lonely and challenging as the two years that you spent there were, they were also pivotal points in both your and Tom's character and career growth.

Every negative experience is a potential stepping stone to a healthy, purposeful destiny. An eagle in flight encounters opposing winds, but he uses them to help him soar to greater heights. A tree that is forced by drought to push its roots down deep is braced for powerful storm winds in its future. Thank God, the shepherd, that he had enough confidence in you to give you your past and to prepare you for your future.

How can I step out of my comfort zone?

IF THE AVERAGE person watches television, plays computer games or surfs the net for two hours a night, he is using over seven hundred hours a year. I'm not saying that any of those leisure activities are bad in themselves, but if we find ourselves regularly perched in our favorite easy chair, drinking coffee and munching potato chips, perhaps we have grown lax within the safety of our comfort zone. The fact is that we can never grow strong in our inner person, while sitting in an easy chair. Growth happens when we dare to step outside of our comfort zones.

Kelly, you and I are similar in many of our ways. We both like peace and order in our lives and therefore our temptation is to maintain the status quo. Change shakes things up too much for our comfort. The following story will challenge you like it did me.

A couple of years ago, four friends were climbing Mount Lyell, the highest peak in Yosemite National Park. Two were experienced climbers and two were not. The most difficult part of the two thousand foot climb was the crossing of the glacier. Earlier in the afternoon one of the inexperienced climbers, wanting to take a short-cut to beat the others, was separated. He soon found himself trapped in a cul-de-sac of rock looking down several hundred feet of sheer ice at a forty-five degree angle. Only ten feet away was a rock on which he would be safe, but one false slip would inevitably cause him to slide down to the valley floor miles below. He was scared stiff.

After being stuck on the rock for an exhausting hour, believing that he was going to die, he heard the voices of his friends. Within minutes they responded to his cries for help and were standing on a rock only ten feet away, but separated by the seemingly impassable ten foot slope of ice. One of them carefully chiselled two little footsteps in the ice between them and gave these instructions to his friend, "Buddy, you must step out from where you are and put your toe in the first foothold. As soon as your toe touches it, without a moment's hesitation swing your other foot across and step into the second foothold. When you do that, reach out and I'll take your hand and pull you to safety."

What his friend said next struck fear into the stranded climber, "Make sure though, that as you step across the ice you do not lean into the mountain. If anything, lean out a little so that your feet will not slip out from under you." Of course any of us would want to hug the mountainside for security, but the safest thing for him to do was to lean out over the icy precipice.

The climber quickly made his decision to trust his friend. In two frightening seconds he took the double step over the icy slope and was caught safely on the other side. As much as we are inclined to stay in our comfort zones and lean against the mountain Kelly, we have to push out in faith and take the next difficult step toward our destiny so that we can successfully complete the journey we've been assigned.

Not long ago, I was in the pet store buying food for our kitty. As I wandered up and down the aisles, I came to a row of aquariums. There were all kinds of fascinating fish, but the one that caught my eye was a six inch shark. I'd never seen one so small and so I asked the pet store owner, "Why would anyone want to buy a shark?" He told me that sharks were growing in popularity as pets. As surprised as I was by that, I was fascinated when he answered my second question, "Will it keep growing?" He said that if you place a small baby shark in an indoor aquarium, it will only grow in proportion to the tank it is kept in. The shark in a small aquarium will be full grown at a few inches. That same shark in the ocean may grow to twelve feet long.

The lesson was not lost on me. When we stay in our small worlds afraid to take a step outside, we limit our growth in a similar way. Maybe we were destined to be ten or twenty times more influential or successful than we can be where we are. We need to step into our destinies, Kelly. What do we really have to lose?

What is my particular assignment?

LIKE ESTHER, we may not know the answer to this question until our assignment is complete, but we need to understand the idea that each of us has a purpose in the overall life of our planet. Just as every piece of the jigsaw puzzle is important to the full picture so is every person vital to the eternal plan of our shepherd.

Consider your body, which is composed of thousands of parts. Which is the most important part? Your eyes, kidneys, thumbs, teeth, blood cells or hair? The fact is that they are all important. Each part has its own purpose and is necessary to the health of your whole body. Two of the significant parts of my body which I seldom give the credit that's due them are my big toes. Without my big toes I could not stand in front of our church and speak. It's those toes that keep me from falling flat on my face.

Kelly, your grandma almost lost her hearing as a child, because of one malfunctioning unseen bone in her inner ear. She got an infection when she was a young girl, which destroyed one tiny bone so that it could not carry out its assigned purpose. Just as that seemingly insignificant bone limited your grandma's hearing throughout her life, so we who do not live up to our responsibilities, limit the influence which we were intended to have in our life journey.

If I were to lose my thumb, my fingers would compensate; or if I were to lose my sight, a seeing eye dog could help me; but nothing is quite as efficient as the unique part which was originally created to do the job. Each of us has a distinct purpose and each of us, doing our own part, is necessary to the work of the whole circle of life.

Do what is set before you and do it with enthusiasm. The word enthusiasm is made of two words *en* which means in, and *thus*, which means

God. Enthusiasm is doing something in God's strength, Kelly. Whether you are helping your son Alexander learn to tie his shoes, running an errand for your boss, cleaning your home, teaching a Sunday School lesson or doing an ultra sound on a patient's abdomen, do what you have been assigned to do in the power of the shepherd's anointing!

What if I don't fulfill my destiny?

WE ARE NOT alone on this planet. Everything that we do or don't do affects someone else. When I do not obey the traffic laws, others as well as I pay the price. If I were to say to myself, "I don't want to stop just because that light is red," or "These speed limits do not apply to me," or "What does it matter if I have a few drinks before I drive?", others would suffer the consequences of my choices.

If your mom and I had not disciplined you and Kristy when you were young and taught you the consequences of making poor choices; or if we had not assured you of our love regardless of your behaviors or achievements, you could have been scarred or warped for life. If we don't pull our weight at work, someone is going to have to pick up the slack or our production and profits will go down proportionately. It does matter what we think and what we do.

Our words carry life or death. We can destroy someone with careless gossip, criticism or accusations, or we can save a life from self-destructing by speaking an encouraging word. As a pastor, I have more opportunities than most people to give people courage and hope. Sometimes I have no idea how my words affect people and encourage them to keep going. A man told me a while ago that his forty-five minute visit to my office a year earlier had kept him from putting a gun to his head. I only vaguely remember the conversation, but that didn't stop the power of my words from taking effect. Every word that we say does matter.

Rather than dwelling on missed opportunities or even years that we've wasted in the past, remember that there is forgiveness and restoration. The shepherd of our soul was not surprised when we failed in that particular assignment last year. He is not watching over us with a big stick just waiting for us to slip up. He loves us and wants the best for us. Upon request, he instantly forgives failure and sets us back on track again.

It's like the Lionel trains that Uncle Dave and I used to play with as boys. If we were careless as engineers, the engine would skip off the track and roll over. When that happened, although it would affect all the other cars behind it, we would simply stop the electric motor for a couple of seconds and place the entire train back on the tracks. We did that quite often, but we never got frustrated and threw the entire train away. It was still valuable even though it got derailed from time to time. We, as the engineers, just had to figure out why it was failing to stay on track and correct the problem. That's the way it is with the shepherd of our souls. He helps us determine why we keep getting derailed, so that he can help us stay on the right track.

If you feel at this point in your life that you have not even discovered your destiny, much less fulfilled it, all is not lost. Your shepherd is right beside you to forgive you for your past and to set you on the right path. Let him deal with your past as well as your future. You will be amazed by how much he wants to not only guide you from this day forward, but also to use your past, positive and negative experiences, to help you on your journey.

What is success?

THIS IS THE LAST question to ask on the road to our destiny, but it is no less important than the others. In the tenth letter that I wrote to you Kelly, I said that success is defined as fulfilling the life purpose and destiny assigned to each of us. We could therefore be rich, famous, beautiful and powerful, and still not be truly successful. None of those qualities is a prerequisite to ultimate success.

Consider the pen in my hand. It is successful if it writes, under my power, the words on this page. The flower pot in front of me is successful if it looks good, holds the flowers and does not leak. The rose food that is sitting beside me is successful if it nourishes our roses and contributes to their fragrance and beauty. The concept is simple, but somehow we often miss it. Success for me is different than success for you Kelly. Success for you may be to be the best mom that your children could have. It may be to diagnose a patient's cancer before it spreads too far to stop. It may be to teach a thirteen year old girl how to relate to boys her own age. It may be to encourage that guy you meet tomorrow at the airport. Successfully fulfilling your life purpose is both a one time event and an ongoing daily adventure. Sometimes it's a word, a gesture or a thing that you do on a specific occasion; but it is also living each day on the right path, listening and responding to the guiding voice of your shepherd.

I'll never forget the story that a person told me several years ago. She was shopping at Safeway, standing in line when she heard a voice in her soul say, "I want you to talk to that young boy packing groceries and tell him that God loves him. He needs you to encourage him right now." She dismissed the voice as her overly compassionate nature and even though it persisted, she refused to obey it. She felt it would have been too embarrassing to tell him that God loves him right then. After all, there were several people in line behind her. Maybe another time, she thought.

She went out to her car, put the groceries away, went to the shoe repair and came back to her car, but the voice would not give up. She had to go tell him. When she entered the store, there was a confused, frightened atmosphere apparent. She saw that the boy was not at the checkout stand where he had been before and so she asked the clerk where he had gone. The clerk, with wide eyes and obvious emotion said, "He just went to the lunch room and put a bullet through his head!" Success for my friend simply would have been to say "God loves you. You're going to make it." Thank God that he forgives us and puts us back on the track when we fall off.

On a more positive note, the following story goes back to before the nineteenth century. William Wilberforce had pushed in the British parliament for the abolition of slavery. Because of repeated failure, Wilberforce was about to give up the fight. The great preacher John Wesley, while on his deathbed heard about his friend's discouragement and wrote this note: "Unless God has raised you up for this very thing, you will be worn out by the opposition of men and devils. But if God be for you, who can be against you? Are all of them stronger than God? Oh be not weary of well-doing! Go on, in the name of God and in the power of His might, till even American slavery shall vanish away before it."

Six days later John Wesley died, but the encouraging letter was enough to spur his friend on for the next forty-five years. In 1833, three days before his own death, William Wilberforce saw slavery abolished in Britain. John Wesley's life journey was an ongoing success made up of hundreds of small steps such as this one along the way. He never did find out during his lifetime how much that one short note affected the course of our world today. You too may never know Kelly, this side of heaven, how successful you have been in your life journey, or how a certain word or action affected another person's life forever. But whether you know the final results or not, the effect will still be the same. When you walk on the right path, which has been prepared for you, and complete the assignments which you are given each day, you will fulfill your purpose and destiny.

Kelly, you are a young woman with your most productive years still before you. Your mom and I are very proud of you and Tom. You have far exceeded our hopes and dreams already, but your answers to these seven questions will help you to discover the path that you are to take from this day forward. I know from experience that every step of the road ahead will not be easy. You wouldn't want it to be. But I also have confidence in your maturity and wisdom, that you will live every day to its fullest, seize challenging opportunities as they cross your path and stay very close to your shepherd as you travel each phase of your life journey.

I love you, Honey. I pray for your health, safety and success as he anoints you with oil for your destiny and as your cup overflows with success.

Love Dad

PART IV

Home At Last

CHAPTER THIRTEEN

A Promise From God

Surely goodness and lovingkindness will follow me all the days of my life and I will dwell in the house of the Lord forever.

THE PSALM ENDS with this promise: As we follow our shepherd down the path that he has designed for each of us there will be a bounty of benefits to bless both ourselves and those who come after us.

Dear Kelly,

One of the hardest things that a dad or mom has to do in life is to release their children. Whether it's the first time we leave our children with a babysitter, we say goodbye to them on their first day of school, we drop them off to spend a week at summer camp or ultimately when they move away from home, our thoughts are mixed with both pride and pain. It's wonderful to see our children grow and mature, but it's difficult to let them go. As I come to the last of my thirteen letters to you Kelly, I'm feeling that same mix of emotions again. I've passed on to you many of the lessons that I've learned about our life journeys and now it's time for me to commit you to your shepherd's care and guidance. But first let's take a look at the last section of King David's inspired description of our life journey.

So far it has been both a wonderful, fun, exhilarating ride, and at the same time a discomforting, challenging and faith-producing adventure. This path that we are on has been designed by our shepherd to keep us trusting him for each day, to bring us to health and wholeness and to ultimately lead us to successfully completing our destined assignment. The end of Psalm Twenty-three assumes that we have been following our shepherd's lead so far through the hills and the valleys of life. We've been anointed by the shepherd for our destiny and are on the path headed toward the finish line. His promise now is that goodness and lovingkindness will follow us for the remainder of our journey.

My weeping willow cries no more

WHEN YOU WERE fifteen Kelly, we built a home on a one acre lot on the outside edge of the city. During the six years in which we lived in that house, I spent hundreds of hours landscaping our property. As a matter of fact, it was because it took so much of my time that we finally decided to sell it and buy a home with a smaller yard. The reason that it took so much time was that every garden and section of lawn had to be put in and maintained by hand. At the time, trees were very expensive to buy, so we were able to plant only a few each year.

On about the second year that we lived there, I got a real deal on some trees. While browsing around the garden shop, after pricing trees at fifty to one hundred dollars each, I found a section of dismal looking, half dead trees off to one side. I figured the owner of the nursery was going to discard them and so I asked him if he would sell them to me at a bargain price. I happily bought all eight of the sad trees for a total of twenty-five dollars.

There was a certain amount of pride that I took in watching each of the trees return to health after two or three years of love and care. A couple did eventually die, but I loved taking mom and you girls on a spring tour every year to show you the new buds on the trees that lived. One of those trees that I nurtured was a scrawny six foot tall willow tree. I had visions of it growing to be like the huge willow tree that stood in the backyard of my childhood home. There was a certain stately bearing about the majestic weeping willow that I wanted to replicate for you girls to enjoy. So I found the perfect place to plant it which would allow plenty of room for its future growth. My new willow was going to be a beauty, if only it could survive that first year.

I guess the shock of transplanting the willow was too much for it. Even though I pampered the tree with fresh manure, fertilizer, good soil and plenty of water, one by one it dropped its tiny green leaves. Going into the cold winter season my willow wasn't showing much promise, but I'd seen miracles in springtime before so I held out in hope for a healthy growing season.

In the early spring I went out to check on the condition of my weeping willow, but there were simply no signs of life. It had flatlined. April came and went and still there was no promise of leaves. By all rights I should have pulled the four foot barren stick from the ground and written it off as a good try. After all, most of the other trees had made it through the winter and I should have been thankful for them. Every week when I mowed the lawn nearby I carefully checked my willow, but throughout the entire year there was no growth.

One day in March of the next year, I was walking through my garden and casually glanced toward my unfruitful willow. There before my eyes was the most wonderful surprise. At the root of the tree were a couple of two inch green sprouts. It was alive! My willow that I had thought was dead was alive again! I ran and got your mom and you girls to come and see the little miracle. You were all polite enough, but somehow you didn't feel the same joy that I was experiencing.

That year, seven tender willow sprouts sprung up from the roots of their mother to heights of eighteen to thirty inches. Over the winter I left them all in their place, but in the early spring I snipped them all off the old root and transplanted them each to a new spot. Throughout that fourth year, five out of the seven babies took root and grew into healthy four foot weeping willows. Today, six years later, the willow trees are strong, healthy and beautiful. Every summer my young willows proudly wave at me as I drive by our old property. When we moved to our present home, I brought a twig from one of those trees and transplanted it into our new yard. That majestic little willow tree constantly reminds me of the resurrection hope that our shepherd has promised us. He loves to bring new life out of what we once thought was dead.

Easter comes every springtime

THE STORY OF my willow may be the story of any life. All of us at times may feel like we have failed at marriage, money, friendship, family or careers and we may even think it's too late to turn it around. We only see ourselves as failures, but there is hope and a future for everyone of us. Our shepherd (or our gardener, depending on the analogy we choose) loves each of us a million times more than I loved my dead-looking willow tree. He still has a destiny and a plan for every life and it is never too late to get back on to the predestined pathway prepared especially for you or me.

This fourth part of the shepherd's psalm brings us around the circle of life to springtime again. We have made it through the valley of the shadow of death and new life is beginning to bud. Springtime always reminds me of the shepherd's miracle power for our lives. Resurrection life is illustrated in all the new life around us. The grass gets greener, blossoms appear on the trees, animals give birth to their babies, butterflies color the skies, weddings abound, people begin to spend more time outside, the days are longer and the air is warmer. Our shepherd's Easter touch is evident everywhere.

A final lesson from the sheep

SURELY GOODNESS AND lovingkindness shall follow me all the days of my life. What an expression of utter confidence in the shepherd! No matter what we have come through or will yet face, David assures us that when we are following the good shepherd, he will never lead us anywhere that will not ultimately make us better people. He has the ability and the goodness to use even the poor choices that we have made or that others have made for us to propel us further down the right path towards maturity.

The word lovingkindness in the Hebrew language is a very powerful word. It refers to the promise that one person makes to another to love him regardless of how they respond. It's the love that we hold for our children even when we are appalled by their behavior. There may be times Kelly when you feel absolutely no emotional love for your children; you may be gravely disappointed in a choice they make, but they are still bound to you by blood. They are your children and you will always want what's best for them. You have made a decision to love them no matter what they do. That's the word David used in this last section of Psalm Twenty-three - lovingkindness.

Kelly, in all honesty, I cannot think of a day in your or Kristy's life when you were difficult to love. You made parenting very easy for your mom and me, but I have seen a few children whom I would find difficult to love. Whether it is their self-serving attitude, insulant tone of voice or rebellious body language, there are those among us who beg to be rejected. But the fact is that our shepherd loves us all regardless of our response to him. We cannot do anything to cause him not to love us. No matter how far we stray from his intended plan or his prescribed path for us, he will always love us and respond to us in kindness. Understanding his constant lovingkindness makes us want to follow him all the more. The sheep that David is describing in this psalm recognize that they are a privileged flock under wise, caring, capable ownership. They know that no matter what happens, their shepherd will always be good to them and have their welfare as his top priority.

There have been times in my fifty years of following my shepherd that I have thought that I would be better off on my own doing my own thing. I have thought that I could take better care of myself and would then be free of his rigid oversight. It's taken me many years to figure it out, but I think I've got it now. True freedom comes only when I am under his care. With him leading me, I'm safe and feel assured that my soul and spirit will continue to be well nurtured. I am free within the perimeters of his laws. Freedom is found only on the inside of the path, not on the outside. Outside of his care and love are anarchy, chaos, purposelessness and ultimately death.

Goodness and lovingkindness follow me

THE PSALMIST WRITES that goodness and lovingkindness follow me. That says two things to me: one is that they are not to be sought after as goals, but are rather the results of walking down the right path. If we were to pursue our shepherd's favor we would be missing the point. As we pursue him and his plan for us, regardless of what they look like, then goodness and lovingkindness will follow us. It's a promise!

The second thing that I see here is that there is a legacy that is left on the trail of the man or woman who follows the shepherd. It is a rather coarse picture, but the manure left behind healthy, well cared for sheep is the best balanced fertilizer that is produced by any domestic stock. When scattered efficiently over the pasture, sheep manure adds enormous benefit to the soil. In some ancient literature, sheep are referred to as those of the golden hooves simply because they are esteemed so highly for their positive effect on the soil.

What am I leaving as a legacy?

THIS OBSERVATION BEGS the questions: What am I leaving behind me on my trail? Do goodness and mercy follow me? Do I leave in my wake peace, forgiveness, joy and love; or do I leave behind confusion, discord, bitterness and conflict? The seeds that I sow behind me have enough power to either make or break the next generation. Kelly, do you remember the story of Johnny Appleseed? As he traversed the nation preaching the Gospel, he planted apple seeds by the thousands. The pioneers that followed his trail years later were often sustained by the bountiful crops of apples which he had planted.

If we follow the shepherd as he guides us down the right paths, by green pastures and quiet refreshing waters; if we stay very close to him as we wind downward through the dark valleys of the shadow of death, and enjoy the bounty of the table that he sets for us even while our enemies are growling in the distance around us; then we will rise to our destinies as he anoints our heads with oil and there will be a legacy of goodness and lovingkindness, which will follow us as we walk through our life journey. That is the circle of life as our Lord intended it to be.

Finishing well

There is one more life stage that I didn't mention in the chart that I drew earlier Kelly.

STAGE 1	STAGE 2	STAGE 3	STAGE 4	STAGE 5	STAGE 6	STAGE 7
Sovereign Foundations	Experimental Choices	Becoming a Man	Skill Development	Character Honing	Convergence	Afterglow
years 1 - 10	years 10 - 20	years 20 - 30	years 30 - 40	years 40 - 50	years 50 - on	

You can see that *convergence* follows *character honing*. We covered that stage in a previous letter that I wrote to you. Now following convergence comes the *afterglow* stage of life, which could also be called *finishing well*. Our most productive years may be in our convergence years, but much of our lasting legacy may well be left behind during our afterglow life stage. These are the years when we as elders, like your grandparents

Kelly, quietly model the goodness and lovingkindness of our shepherd. In our golden years we will pass on to the next generation the peace, wisdom, gratitude, goodness, courage and kindness that we have learned and developed through our many winter seasons in the valleys of life.

In a football game, what really matters is how the game ends. At half-time a team may be down fourteen points, wounded, discouraged and hopeless, but the game is not over yet. Often times, it's those last seconds of the game that determine the winner.

In conclusion Kelly, I want to tell you two stories about finishing well. The way that we choose to spend the last years of our life journey is almost entirely up to us. In a survey by Cornell University researchers, they inquired of employees, nursing home residents, former students and retired professors about their biggest regrets in life. By nearly two to one, what people failed to do nagged them more than anything they had actually done. Most cited missed educational opportunities and failure to seize the moment as their worst regrets. They missed what may have been their destinies by doing nothing.

Don't let fog discourage you

THIS FIRST STORY took place on July 4, 1952. Florence Chadic was attempting to swim from Catalina Island to the California coast. It wasn't that she was unprepared for the challenge. Florence had already crossed the English Channel successfully both ways.

The water was numbing cold as she waded into the Pacific that day and the fog was so thick that Florence could hardly see the boats in her party. Several times sharks had to be scared away with rifle blasts. Despite the adversity, Florence Chadic swam fifteen hours before finally asking to be taken out of the water. Although her trainer tried to encourage her to continue she insisted on quitting. When she looked ahead, all she could see was the fog. She quit only one half mile short of her goal. Florence gave up not because of the cold, fear, exhaustion or even the sharks. She quit because of the fog.

As you walk down the path set before you on your life journey, you are bound to hit foggy patches from time to time. It may seem like staying on track is nearly impossible. You may feel like you are never going to reach your destiny, but don't quit. Hang in there. The other shore is in reach and you will make it!

Hang on for dear life

THE SECOND STORY will inspire the kind of tenacity we need to finish well. On a commuter flight from Portland, Maine to Boston, Massachuset, Henry Dempsey heard a noise near the rear of his small plane. Turning the controls over to his co-pilot, he went back to check out its source.

As he neared the tail section, the plane hit an air pocket and he was thrown against the rear door. It was then that he discovered the source of the noise. The rear exit had not been properly latched before take off and it flew open. Henry was instantly sucked out of the jet. The co-pilot noticed the red light indicating that the door was open and promptly radioed the nearest airport requesting permission for an emergency landing. He reported that the pilot was missing and requested a helicopter to search the ocean.

After the plane landed, they found Henry Dempsey. He was holding on to the outdoor ladder of the airplane. Somehow he had caught the ladder on his way out and had held on for ten minutes as the plane flew two hundred miles per hour at an altitude of four thousand feet. Then as they were landing, he managed to keep his head from hitting the runway only twelve inches below him. Not surprisingly, it took the airport personnel several minutes to pry Henry's fingers from the ladder.

As you walk down the prescribed pathway of your life journey Kelly, there are going to be foggy patches where you will want to just give up. There are going to be difficult days when it would seem much easier to simply let go. On those days, remind yourself of Henry Dempsey and hang in there. Ultimately goodness and lovingkindness will follow you all the days of your life.

Dwelling in the house of the Lord

THIS PICTURESQUE PSALM opened with two words, which unlock its hidden secrets - *The Lord*, and now closes with the same two words - *The Lord.* Those words are the key to a successful life journey. The Lord truly is at the beginning and end of our life journey.

In one of David's other psalms, as he describes a particularly difficult phase of his journey, he gives a graphic picture of the Lord's presence; *You have enclosed me behind and before, and laid your hand upon me. Such knowledge is too wonderful for me. It's too high. I cannot attain to it.*

A couple of months ago, I was teaching this lesson to a group of primary children. To enact the truth of the Lord's watchful care, I invited three children up onto the platform. I placed one of the boys, David, in front of the audience of children. I then put Mark in front of David, Jonathan behind David, and then placed my hand over David's head. As I did this and the boys stood in their places, I explained to the children that our shepherd is always in front of us leading the way, always standing behind us protecting us and always has his loving and guiding hand over our heads. I emphasized that we are never alone as we walk down the road of life.

Teachers are never quite sure what impact their lessons ultimately have on students, but we are always delighted to hear when something actually sinks in. Two weeks later David's mom, Sue, told me that he and his friend were camping overnight in a tent out in the back yard. As it got darker that evening, David's friend was getting a little scared. They came in for a flashlight and Sue overheard her son comforting his young buddy. "You don't have to be afraid Ryan. The Lord is not only right behind you and in front of you, but he has his hand on top of your head. You are safe even when it's dark outside."

Right on, David! The Lord is my shepherd...I will dwell in the house of the Lord forever. Coming home to the house of the shepherd completes the year long journey of the sheep. They have been made to lie down in the green pastures. They have been refreshed beside the quiet waters. Their souls have been restored and they have been guided down the right paths. They have walked through the valley of the shadow of death and felt the comfort of their shepherd's rod and staff. They have eaten from the bountiful table, even while their enemies looked on. They have been anointed for their destinies so fully that their cups have run over. And now, they are coming home.

Home represents familiarity, security, family, protection and nourishment. The barns are full and the fence surrounds them. Early in the next spring they will be leaving on another circuitous journey, but for now they rest contentedly at home.

An important reminder

IN CLOSING, KELLY, let me remind you of the most important principle that David taught us. It has to do with our shepherd who is the Lord. The story is told of a captain of a ship who looked into the dark night and saw faint lights in the distance. Believing that another boat was headed straight toward them, he immediately told his signal man to send a message to the other ship. "Alter your course ten degrees to the South."

Promptly a return message was received, "Alter your course ten degrees to the North." The captain was angered because his command had been ignored and so he sent a second message, "Alter your course ten degrees to the South. I am the captain!"

Soon another message was received, "Alter your course ten degrees to the North. I am seaman third class, Jones."

Immediately the captain sent a third message, knowing the fear it would evoke, "Alter your course ten degrees to the South. I am a battleship."

Then the reply came, "Alter your course ten degrees to the North. I am a lighthouse!"

Every one of us is walking (or sailing) on a uniquely designed pathway. Sometimes it's dark and foggy and sometimes it's bright and clear, but regardless of the surrounding circumstances, don't ever forget that our shepherd is always right. There is a real tension between his sovereign plan and our freedom of choice, but the right choices for our life journey will always be his way. He is the lighthouse!

Kelly, I have thoroughly enjoyed this process of writing these letters. It has been as good for me to remind myself of these important life lessons as it has been for you to read them. Thank you for listening to me as I bared my father's heart to you. As your children grow through childhood and into adulthood, you will understand more fully the love that your mom and I have for you and the desire that we have to see our shepherd's plans fulfilled in your lives. Your mom and I pray for you, Kristy and your families every day that you will continue to walk in the paths that you have been destined for and that you would daily enjoy the goodness and lovingkindness of the Lord on your life journeys.

May you always remember that the Lord is your Shepherd, so that you will never be in need. May you benefit from lying down in green pastures and be nourished beside the quiet waters. May your soul be wholly restored as he guides you down the right paths for his name's sake. And Kelly, even when you walk through the valley of the shadow of death, may you fear no evil and know that the Lord is with you, comforting you with his rod and his staff. May you always see the bountiful table that he prepares for you in the midst of your enemies and may your life overflow with blessing as your shepherd anoints your head with oil. I pray that goodness and lovingkindness will follow you all the days of your life and that you will dwell in the house of the Lord forever. Amen.

Love Dad

The Lord is my shepherd, I shall not want.
He makes me lie down in green pastures;
He leads me beside quiet waters.
He restores my soul;
He guides me in the paths of righteousness
For His name's sake.
Even though I walk through the valley of the shadow of death,
I fear no evil; for You are with me;
Your rod and Your staff, they comfort me.
You prepare a table before me in the presence of my enemies;
You have anointed my head with oil;
My cup overflows.
Surely goodness and lovingkindness will follow me
All the days of my life,
And I will dwell in the house of the Lord forever.

The author may be contacted at:

LIFE PATHWAYS
1477 Lougheed
Port Coquitlam, BC
Canada V3B 7M6
email: nsbarry@attcanada.net